IRELAND'S SPECIAL BRANCH

First published 2022 by Eastwood Books

Dublin, Ireland
www.eastwoodbooks.com
www.wordwellbooks.com

2

Eastwood Books is an imprint of the Wordwell Group

Eastwood Books
The Wordwell Group
Unit 9, 78 Furze Road
Sandyford
Dublin, Ireland

ISBN: 978-1-913934-42-2 (Paperback POD)
ISBN: 978-1-913934-29-3 (Trade Paperback)
ISBN: 978-1-913934-36-1 (Ebook)

British Library Cataloguing in Publication Data.
A catalogue record for this book is available from the National Library of Ireland and the British Library.

Front cover image: Special Branch detectives at the scene of an arms find at Killakee in the Dublin Mountains on 13 June 1931. Courtesy of the National Photographic Archive.

Copyediting by Conor Reidy
Layout and design by Wordwell
Published in Ireland. Trade edition printed in the EU.

IRELAND'S SPECIAL BRANCH

Defending the State, 1922–1947

Gerard Lovett

EASTWOOD BOOKS

CONTENTS

ACKNOWLEDGEMENTS

I wish to thank the many people without whose assistance this book would not have been written.

I owe a great debt of gratitude to the wonderfully kind and helpful staff of the National Archives in Bishop St, Dublin, under the (now deceased) Higher Archivist Gregory O'Connor. God rest his noble and generous soul. My thanks also to author and historian Dr Ann Matthews for her invaluable advice and assistance, and to Mr Ronan Colgan, Ms Courtney Fitzmaurice and the team at Eastwood Books and Wordwell for their assistance in completing this book.

I also wish to acknowledge all those, particularly the relatives of murdered Special Branch men, who generously gave me permission to use the photos published in the book and who kindly shared their recollections with me. In particular, Marie Hyland; Orla Murphy; Elaine Warren; Orla McKeown; Patrick Brocklebank; Michael Dalton; Maurice Kavanagh and his son Brian Kavanagh; Noel Hynes; Helen Coakley; Michael Lernihan, General Secretary of the Garda Síochána Retired Members' Association; Garda Commissioner Drew Harris; Detective Chief Superintendent Justin Kelly, head of the Special Branch; Inspector Aidan Hannon; Tony Hearty; Commander Daniel Ayiotis of the

Military Archives; the National Archives; the National Photographic Archive; the Garda Review; and my good friend and ace photographer, Patrick Hugh Lynch.

However, I owe the greatest debt of gratitude to Vanessa Fox O'Loughlin, literary agent and founder of the writing resources websites www.writing.ie, and www.inkwellwriters.ie, a fantastic resources for debut writers. She is also a bestselling author of crime fiction under the pseudonym Sam Blake. Her advice and guidance was truly invaluable and without her assistance this book would not have seen the light of day. I cannot thank her enough.

INTRODUCTION

People sleep peaceably in their beds at night only because rough men stand ready to do violence on their behalf.

George Orwell

The origins of Ireland's Special Branch can be traced back to the Fenian Rising in 1867 when the Royal Irish Constabulary (RIC) set up *ad hoc* units to deal with the rise of militant republicanism. Two of these RIC men were killed during encounters with Fenians, prompting the setting up of a full-time unit known as Crime Branch Special in 1882. It consisted of some forty men (mainly sergeants) scattered throughout the country who gathered intelligence on local activists and forwarded monthly reports to Dublin Castle. In 1890 they had forty-two men working on subversion and had 105 spies on their books. The spies were paid from £3 for a specific piece of information, up to £100 per annum – a substantial sum for the time.[1]

In Dublin city the Dublin Metropolitan Police (DMP) already had a full-time detective branch set up since March 1843. It was known as the 'G' Division, or more informally, 'G-Men.' Dublin was then divided into six police divisions denoted by the letters, 'A' to 'F' so the detective division was simply given the next letter in the alphabet – 'G'. They investigated murders and other serious crime throughout the city and also supervised pawnbrokers' offices. From the 1860s they were heavily involved in investigating militant republican organisations such as the Fenian Brotherhood during which four DMP men (two G-Men included) were killed.[2]

In the 1880s G-Men led by Inspector John Mallon successfully investigated the murders of chief secretary Frederick Cavendish and under-secretary Thomas Burke, who were stabbed to death in May 1882 in the Phoenix Park by a militant republican organisation called the Invincibles. Their investigation resulted in five men going to the gallows.[3] In the weeks prior to the 1916 rebellion, Detective Superintendent Owen Brien had two informants inside the Irish Volunteers nicknamed *Granite* and *Chalk* who were feeding him valuable information. He was given chapter and verse on what the Volunteers were planning, including the date of the Rising but, despite the accuracy of the information, it was not taken seriously by the Dublin Castle authorities.[4]

The Anglo-Irish Treaty of December 1921 led to the creation of the Irish Free State in December 1922. It consisted of twenty-six counties with a parliament in Dublin. Six north-eastern counties with a pro-British unionist majority remained under British jurisdiction with a parliament in Belfast. Despite the treaty being approved by Dáil Éireann on 6 January 1922, civil war broke out the following June. The anti-Treaty IRA insisted that all thirty-two counties should form the new state while the pro-Treaty IRA, now the National Army, accepted the treaty. By May 1923 the anti-Treatyites (officially referred to as Irregulars) had been defeated and anti-Treaty leader Eamon de Valera called on them to 'dump arms' until a more appropriate opportunity arose.

Though soundly defeated militarily, the IRA continued in existence and from time to time presented a serious challenge to the new state. They not only refused to accept defeat but even saw themselves as the true inheritors of the (thirty-two-county) Irish Republic proclaimed during the Easter Rising. They even considered themselves to be the lawful government of that Ireland, with a right to bear arms and declare war. Uniquely among terrorist organisations worldwide, their primary target was not their native country but Britain, whom they saw as a colonial power still occupying six Irish counties. They viewed the government of the new Irish state as British stooges and traitors to whom they owed no loyalty.

To confront this challenge, the government set up a cadre of armed policemen as a more acceptable alternative to leaving the army on the streets. The first unit, set up in 1922, was based in Oriel House. Most of them had service with Michael Collins' Squad, who had carried out at least twenty-five killings of police, military and civilians, during the War of Independence.[5] The unit had a fearsome reputation for carrying out beatings and unofficial executions which led to its subsequent disbandment. After Oriel House was disbanded, a number of hand-picked men were amalgamated with the G Division of the Dublin Metropolitan Police. The DMP was in turn amalgamated with An Garda Síochána in 1925 and the G-Men formed the nucleus of a national unit that became known as the Special Branch. After Eamon de Valera's Fianna Fáil party returned to power in 1933, the unit was beefed up by several hundred of his supporters (all anti-Treaty IRA men) who became known as the Broy Harriers after then-Commissioner Eamon (Ned) Broy. Officially called the Special Detective Unit (SDU) it is still widely known as the Special Branch, even by members of that unit. Monikers have a habit of lasting long after the organisation has changed and, even in recent years, Special Branch members have heard militant republicans refer to them as Harriers.

Since its foundation the Special Branch has been the subject of much vilification by its opponents such as anti-Treaty IRA man C.S. (Todd) Andrews, who referred to them as 'a gang of police thugs'.[6] As will be seen in these pages, much of the criticism was justified given the hardball tactics and summary beatings handed down by the early anti-subversive unit. An IRA news-sheet described them as, 'these unfortunate renegades and perverted types are in the category of the bailiff, the bum, and the emergency man'.[7] But the prize for the most colourful depiction must surely go to playwright Brendan Behan who described them as 'fugh-faced bastards intent on nothing less than grievous bodily harm'.[8]

This book traces the non-stop battle against the IRA between 1922 and 1947. It includes investigations into the shooting of unarmed British soldiers on shore leave in Cobh, coordinated attacks on garda stations, and the assassination of Justice Minister Kevin O'Higgins. It describes the fraught relationship with the newly elected Fianna Fáil government in 1932 who, on taking office carried out a major purge of the Special Branch, though the realities of office and an increasing IRA threat would, in time, lead to a change of direction. In the 1930s they faced down not just the IRA, but the quasi-Fascist and short-lived Blueshirt organisation. The war years from 1939 to 1945 led to a merciless clampdown on the IRA resulting in the execution of several of its members and the deaths of six Special Branch detectives.

Despite long hours and modest wages, this tough squad of detectives fearlessly confronted the ruthless gunmen of the IRA who did not hesitate to shoot their way out of trouble when challenged. On occasions the IRA even targeted certain policemen for death whom they considered too 'enthusiastic'. A total of twenty-two policemen would be killed during the first quarter century of the new state including thirteen Oriel House and Special Branch detectives. During the same period, seven IRA men were killed in exchanges of fire with Special Branch officers while six others were executed. The detectives' methods were often brutal and sometimes they had scant regard for legal niceties, but, nevertheless, they were ruthlessly effective. Supported by stringent security measures, including military courts and sweeping powers of arrest and internment, the IRA was virtually crushed by the end of World War Two.

Chapter 1

TERROR AND COUNTER TERROR, 1922-1923

'Salus Populi Suprema Lex.'
[The safety of the people is the highest law].

Cicero

Following the War of Independence and eventual truce on 11 July 1921, the Anglo-Irish Treaty was ratified by Dáil Éireann by sixty-four votes to fifty-seven on 7 January 1922. A large section of the IRA refused to accept the democratic will of the Irish people, plunging the country into civil war the following June. Eamon de Valera, leader of the anti-Treaty faction, added fuel to the fire in a speech in Thurles in March 1922 during which he thundered that the Volunteers, 'would have to march over the dead bodies of their own brothers. They will have to wade through Irish blood', though he would later claim he had been misrepresented.[1]

An election was held on 16 June 1922, effectively a referendum on the Treaty, and the results were even starker for the anti-Treatyites – fifty-eight seats for the pro-Treaty TDs and thirty-six for de Valera and his supporters. Civil war broke out on 28 June when government troops shelled the Four Courts which had been occupied some weeks earlier by anti-Treaty forces. The government introduced emergency regulations on 27 September 1922 giving the army extraordinary powers.

These included sweeping powers of arrest and the setting up of Military Courts with authority to impose penalties ranging from fines of any amount, imprisonment for any period, or even the death sentence. About 11,000 republicans were interned without trial by the end of the civil war.[2] William T. Cosgrave, soon to be Chairman of the Provisional Government, was very specific in his attitude when he said, 'those who persist in these murderous attacks must learn that they have got to pay the penalty for them, a penalty greater than internment.'[3]

On 11 September 1922, General Eoin O'Duffy was appointed commissioner of the new police force which was at first called the Civic Guard. On 31 July 1923, however, the name was changed to An Garda Síochána.[4] The prickly O'Duffy soon came into conflict with his political masters when he began appointing police duty instructors without reference to the Department of Home Affairs. When departmental secretary Henry O'Friel took him to task for this, he forwarded a withering reply saying:

> I am at a loss to know if they exercise the same vigilance over other Departments where hundreds of civil servants are employed at handsome remunerations who come in, in the morning at 11 o'clock, take an hour or two for lunch and leave sharp at 5 o'clock, with a half-day on Saturday and not one of whom perhaps ever did a day's work or lost an hour's sleep for Ireland.[5]

It had been originally planned to arm the newly established (uniformed) Civic Guard, but there was a change of heart following the so-called Garda Mutiny in May 1922 when recruits to the new force (mostly ex-IRA men) refused to work under former RIC officers. Following the resulting O'Shiel report into the matter, it was decided that an armed force would have looked uncomfortably similar to the recently disbanded RIC.[6] McGarry suggests that the decision to leave the force unarmed was a tactical one, which would render any potential attacks by the IRA as both unjustifiable and counterproductive in terms of public support.[7]

During the civil war, the army was the main bulwark against armed crime. Once the war was over the government felt that the use of the army to combat banditry, whether politically motivated or not, was not appropriate in peace time. Michael Collins, first chairman of the provisional government, quickly realised that he needed a special squad of police to investigate crime and to deal with political opponents without involving the army. In addition, he needed a protection squad to safeguard himself and his ministers, as well as to confront the increasing outbreak of criminal violence and banditry that was then reaching epidemic proportions. In Dublin in 1922, there were twenty-three murders, 479 armed robberies, 234 other robberies and attempted robberies and 917 cases of malicious damage.[8]

This prompted the setting up of a new squad of armed detectives in August 1922 officially called the Criminal Investigation Department (CID). It was originally based in Oriel House before moving to 88 Merrion Square in February 1923. Among republican circles it would be contemptuously referred to the 'Oriel House Murder Gang'. Many were former members of The Squad commanded by Michael Collins during the War of Independence and remained fiercely loyal to him. They were joined by remnants of the so-called Republican Police, a pro-Treaty force of IRA men who carried out police duties in the absence of the RIC. This latter group was not held in high esteem by Collins who described them as 'the wretched Irish Republican Police system and … the awful personnel attracted to its ranks.'[9]

Though nominally part of the Department of Defence the new squad reported directly to Collins and was under his absolute control. In September 1922 (weeks after Collins' assassination), responsibility was transferred to the Department of Home Affairs.[10] It had close links with Free State Army (FSA) intelligence as well as the 100-strong Citizens' Defence Force (CDF)[11] and also a small Protective Officers Corps.[12] Captain Patrick M. Moynihan controlled Oriel House and the Protective Officers Corps, while Captain Henry Harrison led the CDF. The latter two groups were used for the protection of government buildings as well as intelligence gathering.[13]

The CID was initially under the command of Liam Tobin, who was given the title, Director of Intelligence. Tobin was Collins' former Chief of Intelligence who controlled many of Collins' spies in Dublin Castle and the DMP during the War of Independence.[14] He was replaced by Joseph McGrath in February 1923 taking over control of Oriel House along with the Protective Officers Corps and the Citizens Defence Force.[15] By June 1923, however, the Protective Corps was amalgamated with the CID bringing their combined strength up to 350.[16] They included women who were officially 'typists' but were in fact utilised for 'special duties connected with the detection of women engaged in hostilities against the government.' It was originally intended to have a military rank structure, but the 'privates' were soon given the rank of Detective Officers.[17] The DMP also used the term Detective Officers to describe constables attached to the G-Division.

The CID quickly earned itself a reputation as a ruthless, though efficient unit that carried out their task with gusto. Their approach was often unorthodox if not downright illegal and there were regular allegations of mistreatment of prisoners. However, the new government was not overly concerned with legal niceties. It was struggling to retain control of a lawless country with a large minority of disaffected gunmen intent on bringing it down. O'Higgins and his family (along with other ministers) had to move into Government Buildings after shots were fired into his home in Terenure. This was not completely safe either, as one night he went on the roof for a smoke and when he lit a match a sniper shot the cigarette out of his hand.[18] In the absence of an effective nationwide police force there was a staggering level of lawlessness and banditry in the country and the new government was determined to root it out by whatever means necessary.

Within weeks the new detectives began to suffer casualties. On Friday 25 August 1922, a team was on the way to make an arrest when they were fired at by snipers in Deansgrange. The driver John J. Murray (28) suffered serious leg injuries and was removed to St Vincent's Hospital in a serious condition. The leg became gangrenous and had to be amputated. He died the following evening from cardiac failure.[19]

Detective Officer Anthony Deane was shot and killed on Sunday 17 September 1922 when the IRA launched an attack on Oriel House. Four men drove up to the building at 9.45 p.m. and two of them entered saying they wished to report the theft of a car. As Inspector Michael Finn prepared to take the report, one of the men drew a revolver and fired a shot which embedded itself in the woodwork of the wall. A second raider fired another shot which struck Deane, who was standing behind the counter smoking a cigar, killing him instantly. The shooting attracted other officers in the building, and they rushed to the scene. The attackers fled, pursued by detectives who arrested four men nearby. A car suspected of belonging to the raiders was found near Westland Row Station with sledgehammers, a quantity of cotton wool and a large supply of petrol.[20]

In his autobiography, Ernie O'Malley claimed that he led the raid on Oriel House. He said that a friendly CID man gave him details of the positions of sentries, rooms, telephones and routines. He was particularly interested in the fifty rifles and small arms that were stored there. His raiding party included Paddy Mannion (son of an RIC inspector) and Seán Lemass (later taoiseach). He decided the best time for a raid was in the evening when they had finished their evening meal. They would gain entry on some pretext, hold up the military guard and the main party would rush in and seize firearms and documents. However, as they approached the building the advance group encountered more detectives than they expected, and an exchange of shots followed. Realising something was wrong, he abandoned the raid.[21]

The government issued a proclamation on 3 October 1922 offering an amnesty and free pardon to all persons surrendering their arms by 15 October.[22] Apparently there was little response to the offer and, on 17 November 1922, four men were summarily executed by firing squad at Kilmainham Jail. They were Peter Cassidy, 7 Usher Street, Richard Tuohy, 1 Connor's Buildings (off James St. Harbour), John Gaffney, 3 Usher Street, and James Fisher of 1 Echlin Street.

The four were found with loaded revolvers in Dublin city on 23 October, eight days after the expiry of the amnesty offer. Defence Minister Richard Mulcahy told the Dáil:

> These men who were executed this morning were found on the streets of Dublin at night carrying loaded revolvers, and waiting to take the lives of other men. Everyone who goes around with a loaded revolver in his pocket in the street to take the lives of other men must be made to face the fact that by doing so he forfeits his own life.[23]

Oriel House became a target of almost nightly attacks by snipers and there were a number of attempts to bomb the building. At 9 p.m., on Monday 30 October 1922 four landmines were placed in the basement at the Merrion Street side of the building but only one exploded, injuring three civilians and a boy manning the telephone exchange. Widespread damage was caused and numerous windows were broken in nearby buildings. The other three mines were made safe by Captain Moynihan who cut the wires leading to the batteries. Captain Ennis was talking to a colleague on the steps at the front door of the building on Westland Row around the corner when the bomb went off. They were both blown off their feet and then came under rifle fire from attackers on the other side of the street but escaped uninjured. About twenty attackers were involved and they fled on the arrival of troops. Detectives quickly arrested three men armed with revolvers on the corner of Westland Row. O'Higgins complimented the CID men on the 'splendid courage and coolness' they displayed on the occasion.[24]

The arrested men were Joseph Spooner of 67 McCaffrey's Estate, Mount Brown, Patrick Farrelly of 67 Chancery Lane and John Murphy of 56 Belview Buildings. On 14 November they were charged before a Military Court with offences including possession of a revolver and bombs. All were found guilty and executed by firing squad at Beggar's Bush Barracks on the morning of 30 November 1922.[25] These executions along with four others on 17 November clearly displayed the ruthless determination of the government to suppress the Irregulars by any means necessary. Within a few months seventy-seven 'official' executions would be carried out in all parts of the country though as we shall see, there were also many unofficial executions. In 1959 Ernest Blythe told a radio programme that the actual figure of official executions was eighty-three, or possibly eighty-four.[26]

In November 1922, the IRA denounced the newly formed Civic Guard as a 'Police Force of a semi-military character' and 'a continuation of the old RIC'. They warned of 'drastic action' after 1 January 1923 if the guards did not return to their homes or to civil employment and offered 'a note of safe conduct' to any guard who gave a written undertaking 'not to take up arms against, nor to assist in any [way] the enemies of the Republic.' It was signed 'A. Murphy, Brig. Gen. O/C Kerry No. 1 Brigade.' The proclamation was sent to the superintendent in Tralee and was also posted up on poles in the area.

An identical proclamation was issued in Cork, signed this time by 'O. Holland, O/C Cork No. 3 Brigade.' Superintendent O'Duffy of Bandon (no relation of the commissioner) forwarded it to O'Duffy on 13 December with a brief note which included the words, 'the men are somewhat restive since its publication.' An unimpressed O'Duffy responded with a brusque minute saying that the note was a lie, adding that 'some people are ready to swallow anything, and amongst the gullible ones, so far as I can gather from your statement, are some of the Civic Guard themselves. There is no place in the Guard for men who are uneasy or restive or discontented.' He was prepared to accept the resignation of all such men irrespective of rank at short notice.[27]

Though the IRA regularly exchanged shots with armed detectives, they generally refrained from carrying out shootings of unarmed uniformed gardaí who would have been extremely vulnerable to such attacks. They probably realised that shootings of unarmed policemen, all Irishmen and almost all former IRA men, would not play well with the people or indeed with many of their own volunteers. If they had been ruthless enough to shoot the gardaí out of hand at every opportunity, it would have plunged the country into a spiral of bloodshed and death, the consequences of which can only be imagined. As was foreseen at the time, the brave decision to have an unarmed uniformed force was inspired and undoubtedly saved many lives.[28] As happened earlier with the RIC, an armed force would have been the target of regular attacks on stations and individual policemen to secure arms resulting in many fatalities.

As it happened, there were dozens of attacks on stations all over the country though usually without the guards being shot at. In most cases, the station was either burned or badly damaged and, in all cases, the raiders took as much personal property as they could find especially cash and bicycles. In December 1922, there were attacks on stations in Askeaton, County Limerick along with Thomastown, Callan and Mullinavat stations all in County Kilkenny. Thomastown barracks was burned down by the raiders while the other two were partially burned. During the same month, Liscannor barracks in County Clare was attacked and the raiders took some bedding and clothing along with bicycles belonging to three guards before setting the station alight.[29] Between December 1922 and November 1923, a total of 106 stations were attacked, some of them twice if the building was not properly destroyed on the first attempt.[30]

On 22 December 1922, Assistant Inspector Matt Daly (27) of Oriel House was shot and seriously wounded at Queen Street in Dublin and he died a week later. He was accompanied by Detective Officer Doyle and two protective officers named Joyce and Keegan. They went to Queen Street where Daly wanted to visit Lynch's shop and told his colleagues to wait for him around the corner. While waiting on nearby Arran Quay for a few minutes, they heard shots coming from Queen Street where they found their injured colleague. They saw four men running in the direction of Haymarket and one detective fired several shots at them, but they escaped. Daly was carried into a nearby shop by troops and civilians who arrived on the scene, and he was later removed to the Richmond Hospital.[31]

At the inquest at the Meath Hospital on 30 December, Constable Thomas Weldon of the DMP said that while on duty at Queen St Bridge (now Mellows Bridge) he was held up by two men, one of whom had a revolver, who told him he would 'plug him' if he moved. They brought him to Garrison Lane nearby and held him there for several minutes. One of them said he was sorry for having to do this but believed he was 'doing right'. On being allowed to leave he saw the injured Daly outside McGarry's public house. Dr Vivier said that the deceased had three bullet wounds – one in each thigh and one in the buttock. Death was due to shock and gangrene caused by bullet wounds.[32] Daly, a former member of the Irish Volunteers, was a native of Roundfield, Monivea, Athenry, County Galway.[33] He was engaged to be married to Alice Lynch from Ardcath, County Meath and the ceremony was due to take place a week after his death.

In December 1922 detectives raided 3 Harold's Cross Road and recovered ten bombs, two .45 Smith and Wesson revolvers, two Webley revolvers, a Martini rifle and assorted ammunition along with a box of fake CID badges. Oriel House issued a warning in newspapers that robber gangs were at work displaying silver-coloured badges and purporting to be CID men. It pointed out Oriel House men did not wear badges of any kind and sightings of any cases should be brought to their notice.[34]

However, there were plans to issue badges for the CID. The Department of Home Affairs wrote to the Department of Finance on 11 October 1922 seeking sanction for 200 badges for the CID at a cost of 4/9d (about fifty-four cent) per badge and this was approved.[35] On the evening of 5 December 1922 the Irish Jewellery Company at 47 Lower Kevin Street was raided by three gunmen who took 205 CID badges in the final stages of manufacture of which 150 were numbered. Superintendent Tumbleton of the CID reported that 'it is evident there must have been considerable collusion between the staff engaged on the premises and the raiders.'[36]

In a particularly vicious incident fifty armed men descended on the town of Ballyconnell in County Cavan around 8.00 a.m. on the morning of 6 February 1923. They went on a rampage, smashing windows and shooting up the town with rifles and revolvers, stealing stock and cash from shops, and cleaning out all the money they could find from the Ulster Bank. They held up a train heading for Ballinamore and brought it back to Ballyconnell where they forced the stationmaster to hand over keys to the station and took all the cash. A young Irish teacher, 23-year-old Sean McGrath, and a shop assistant, William Ryan, were shot dead and several others wounded. The gunmen walked up Main Street shouting, 'This is the month's mind for Cull.' (This was in reference to the shooting by the military of a hold-up man named Michael Cull, who, with an accomplice, robbed the post office in Ballinamore on 6 January). Elsewhere they burned a motor dealer's premises and drove away with several cars. Kevin O'Higgins told the Dáil, 'It was not a natural thing to expect that a body of Irishmen would descend upon a little town and proceed to murder their fellow-citizens. The only way to deal with anarchy was by the way of force.'[37]

President Cosgrave made the government's attitude clear in a statement released on 16 February 1923 when he noted:

> The government is determined to put down this revolt against democracy, regardless of the cost. Let no man be deceived. If anyone continues this unnatural war against his own people after the expiration of the stated period of amnesty, he must be prepared to pay the price in full for there will be no going back upon this. The guns and ammunition which the Irregulars have been trying to borrow or buy from Russia may add to the destruction.[38]

Cosgrave's announcement brought a swift denial from Monsieur Klishko, Assistant Official Agent of the Soviet Government in Great Britain saying the Soviet Union had not supplied such weapons nor was there any attempt at such.[39]

On Thursday 22 February 1923, Oriel House men backed up by troops carried out a large number of searches and arrests in Dublin city. In one incident detectives raided a house in Harrington Street, the home of an IRA quartermaster. The man fled from the house but was shot and injured by police and taken to Oriel House. Seven men described as Irregular Leaders were arrested in Phibsoro. They included Seán Fitzpatrick who was described as the Officer Commanding of the Dublin Brigade. The arrests and searches resulted in high praise for the Oriel House men in a piece in the *Freeman's Journal* lauding their achievements. The article proclaimed that 'their vigilance and activity have been incessant and some of the most important captures have resulted from their efforts. For all this the citizens are, and have good reason to be, grateful to the men from Oriel House.'[40]

In July 1923, Ernest Blythe, Minister for Local Government, told a public meeting in Tullamore to loud cheers that the government would allow 'no pack of bullies and ruffians to filch the people's property.' 'We will give them the lash', he added to loud applause. A voice from the crowd shouted, 'The firing squads.' 'Yes', replied Blythe, 'the firing squad if necessary. We are the servants of the people, and we will do the people's work.'[41]

He continued this theme in a speech in Castleblayney when he said:

> It was necessary for the Government to show that the fellow with the gun could not go and shoot and burn - the only risk being taken to prison to be kept on a spring bed and get bacon for his breakfast. It was necessary for the Government to show that there was a bigger risk. We were not very long at it until the fellows who were captured began to tell where a rifle could be found and other things to save their skins. That was what the executions did. Any fellow who went out with a gun and petrol tin deserved the firing squad and no man got it except those who deserved it.[42]

A favourite type of CID operation was known as the 'sit down raid'. CID officers (including women searchers) would quietly enter the home of a suspected republican, unknown even to his neighbours. After searching the house and its occupants they would hold the family incommunicado in a back room for a day or two while, (according to O'Malley), helping themselves to any food, drink or souvenirs they found there. Any callers to the house would be seized, searched and similarly detained.[43]

Detectives called them 'Mouse Trap Raids' and considered them to be a highly effective system for nabbing Irregulars. The selected property would be quietly entered at an early hour and all residents in the house detained along with any visitors that happened to call. After a few hours everyone would be brought to Oriel House where they were interrogated, and any wanted persons were transferred to military custody. They insisted that interrogations were always carried out humanely but that 'Irregular propagandists had spread such lying reports about these interrogations that the average Irregular really believed that the terrors of the Spanish Inquisition were mere lullabies [compared] to the treatment meted out to prisoners of the CID'.[44]

Another Oriel House man, Thomas Fitzgerald (22), was shot and killed on 19 October 1923 following a raid by three men at Rathborne's Candle Factory in Castleknock, Dublin. They made their escape on bicycles with £43.10s cash. Three members of staff followed them on bicycles towards Finglas. Oriel House men were quickly on the scene and found Fitzgerald's body in the car. One of the raiders, James McDonald, was also shot dead by detectives while a further two were captured. All three were Free State Army soldiers.[45]

At the inquest on 20 October Superintendent Finian O'Driscoll said he, along with Inspector John Mooney[46] and Detective Officers Kirwan, O'Keefe and Fitzgerald, were at the scene. They caught up with the raiders on Dunsink Lane and after an exchange of shots, arrested a man named William Downes. They left Downes in the car with Fitzgerald and ran off in pursuit of the remaining culprits. Somewhat naively they had not searched Downes, nor had they handcuffed him. As Fitzgerald turned the car, Downes drew a pistol and fired four shots at him before fleeing across fields. On returning to the car the detectives found Fitzgerald's body still in the driver's seat. O'Driscoll said, 'Tom, speak to me,' but Fitzgerald just half-opened his eyes, smiled, and died in a few seconds. He checked Fitzgerald's pistol and found it had not been fired.

Detectives later searched Downes' home at 4 Leitrim Place and Detective Peter Doran[47] arrested him. Downes tried to draw a pistol, but Doran struck him on the head with his revolver and retrieved the pistol that had a round in the breech. Medical evidence revealed that Fitzgerald had four bullet wounds and the heart, liver and lungs were perforated. The jury found that Fitzgerald died from bullets fired from a revolver by William Downes – wilful murder. The coroner complimented the Oriel House men and mentioned that Fitzgerald was a captain in the old IRA during the War of Independence and had been involved in defending Oriel House against two attacks.[48]

On 22 October 1923, Downes along with George Cullen appeared in court charged with robbery and murder.[49] Inspector John Mooney produced Downes' statement in which he described how the three of them planned to rob Rathborne's. When arrested, the driver [Fitzgerald], ordered him into the car.

> The driver then reversed the car as if to go back to his comrades to effect the arrest of McDonald and Cullen. As the car was about to move off, I noticed that the driver put his gun in his pocket. I then stood up and got out on the footboard of the car, and pulled my gun and fired a number of shots at the driver, who fell back on his seat. I then ran away across a field.[50]

Inspector Mooney denied a suggestion from defence counsel that the prisoner was badly beaten in Oriel House and that his confession was 'wrung from him at the point of four revolvers.' He added that the injuries on the prisoner's head had been caused when he was struck by Detective Doran to prevent him drawing his pistol at the time of his arrest.[51]

Downes claimed that Fitzgerald had fired two shots at him and had he not returned fire he would have been killed himself, though earlier evidence had shown that Fitzgerald's pistol had not been fired. He added that the treatment he received in Oriel House terrified him and he had been forced to sign the statement at the point of four revolvers. In the highly-charged atmosphere of the time, it is highly likely that Downes' interrogation was a none-too-gentle affair and that plenty of duress was involved. His statement has all the hallmarks of police jargon such as 'as if to go back to his comrades to effect the arrest of …' and later, '… pulled my gun and fired a number of shots…'

Downes was sentenced to death and was executed on 29 November 1923 by British executioner John Ellis. He had the dubious distinction of becoming the first man to be executed in the Irish Free State after being sentenced by a civil court.[52] When the usual notice was posted up outside Mountjoy Prison informing the public that the sentence was carried out a young woman tore it down, shouting angrily, 'Scandalous, scandalous'.[53] His co-accused George Cullen pleaded guilty to armed robbery and sentenced to five years imprisonment along with twenty strokes of the 'cat'.[54]

The Free State government was utterly ruthless when dealing with the challenge to their authority and was prepared to fight fire with fire. Scores of executions were carried out during the civil war period, often on the flimsiest of pretexts and sometimes without the slightest pretence of legality. The most infamous of these was the execution without trial of four republican prisoners, Rory O'Connor, Liam Mellows, Joseph McKelvey and Richard Barrett, in Mountjoy Prison on 8 December 1922 as a reprisal for the IRA killing of Cork Teachta Dála (TD) Seán Hales on the previous day. A second TD, Pádraig O Máille from Mayo was seriously injured in the same incident. Many years later author and playwright Ulick O'Connor established that the shootings were carried out by an IRA man named Owen Donnelly. The anti-Treaty IRA Chief-of-Staff Liam Lynch earlier issued a directive that pro-Treaty TDs were to be shot on sight and Donnelly carried out the shooting on that basis.[55]

In this highly-charged atmosphere the government was clearly prepared to turn a judicious blind eye, if not actually encourage, the extra-curricular activities of Oriel House and the army. On the date of the executions,

Kevin O'Higgins told the Dáil, 'Where the existence of the nation is at stake there can be but one code … though it sounds a grim code, *Salus Populi Suprema Lex.*' [The safety of the people is the highest law.][56]

In the same vein, President Cosgrave said, 'if we have to exterminate ten thousand republicans, the three million of our people is bigger than this ten thousand'.[57] While this figure can be dismissed as hyperbole there is no doubt that he and his government were willing to carry out whatever executions were necessary to restore order. Richard Mulcahy, Army Commander following the death of Michael Collins, regretted such draconian actions but blamed it on de Valera and Liam Lynch, who in November 1922 had ordered the assassination of pro-Treaty TDs. He felt that the execution of the four prisoners and threats of further executions brought a sudden cold sense of realism to his opponents.[58] Mulcahy was proved correct as there were no more attacks on government TDs. On 12 August 1922, President Cosgrave, contemplating the real possibility of his own assassination, wrote:

> Even if the members of the Government are shot and die, others will be found to take their place. None of us could be indispensable. The country has not yet discovered the true worth of our successors. The people must discover them; I believe Genl. Collins is one of the greatest men Ireland has produced.[59] A statesman and a soldier – and there are others also in the Government and the Army. My place will be easily filled. I am sorry for my people, my wife and children, my mother and family…I willingly forgive those who think I should be shot and those who take part in such shooting and I ask forgiveness of all those I have offended.[60]

As we have seen, the Oriel House detectives acted with the utmost ruthlessness when dealing with the IRA, many of whom they shot out-of-hand leaving the bodies in isolated locations. In 1922 and 1923, the killings were carried out both by Oriel House men and Free State troops, (often referred to as the 'Murder Gang' by Republicans) working separately or in unison, as the following examples will demonstrate.

Many in these state forces believed they had carte blanche for shooting IRA men at any and every opportunity. This was a belief that was possibly reasonably held owing to the lack of any meaningful investigation or condemnation by the government. In many of the examples, it is not clear which group carried out individual killings but, because of their fearsome reputation, Oriel House men were blamed for most of them. It demonstrates the poisonous animosity that existed between them and their former anti-Treaty colleagues with whom the fought side-by-side in the 1916 Rising and the War of Independence, a few short years earlier. Many of them had been badly traumatised by their experiences in the War of Independence resulting in what might now be diagnosed as Post-Traumatic Stress Disorder. Whatever their mental state, they were almost certainly brutalised by their experience of conflict.

On Saturday 26 August 1922, two men were shot 'under revolting circumstances' at the Yellow Lane, Drumcondra. They were Vice-Brigadier Seán Cole (19) of 22 Lower Buckingham Street and Commandant Alfred Leo Colley (20) of 113 Parnell Street, both members of the Dublin Brigade IRA. Witnesses said that a large open car travelling at speed swerved off the Puckstown Road and men in trench coats ordered women and children away from the scene at gunpoint. There were six men in the car while two other men were struggling to get away and one of whom screamed, 'What's it for'? The two men were taken from the car, put up against the piers of a gate and shot several times. The car then drove off, leaving the two bodies at the scene. Cole had four bullet wounds, one in the head and three in the body while Colley had one bullet wound to the head, another in the spine and two others in the body.[61]

The body of Lieutenant Bernard Daly (26) Dublin Brigade IRA, from Drogheda, was found near Swords, County Dublin on Saturday 25 August 1922, the same evening as the Cole/Colley shooting and probably carried out by the same group. He was employed at Miss Hogan's pub at 2 Suffolk Street, Dublin, and was engaged to be married. Three men entered the pub and asked for him by name. When a barman enquired what they wanted him for, one of the men produced a revolver and threatened to also arrest him if he was impertinent. On locating Daly, they searched him, brought him out to a waiting Ford car and drove off. His body was later found by civilians in a ditch full of briars and nettles at St. Doulagh's near Malahide and they notified the army. He had three bullet wounds in his chest and two in his head. Daly was described as an 'active Irregular' who had fought in the Four Courts.[62]

Edward Leo Murray (19) of 19 Charlemont Avenue, and Charles Joachim Murphy (22), both of Deans Grange, both active IRA men, were shot and killed by troops on 2 September 1922. Along with James Nolan (19) and Andrew O'Neill, they were sleeping at Newpark Lodge in Stillorgan when, in the early hours, it was raided by troops who were looking for Murphy who had previously escaped from custody. Murray first heard shots and shook Murphy awake. Murphy took up a gun and there was a volley of shots. Both men were killed. Nolan later told the inquest at St Michael's Hospital that troops told him to say his prayers as he was also going to be shot. Murray's mother told the inquest that her home had been raided the previous Wednesday by CID men who she could identify. They were looking for her son who was not there and they told her they would riddle him and make her a present of his dead body. The jury returned a unanimous verdict that both men met their deaths at the hands of the military in the discharge of their duty.[63]

Interestingly, the British army, still present though confined to barracks, submitted weekly intelligence reports to their authorities on the ongoing situation in Ireland. For the week ending 16 September 1922, Major-General Boyd included the following (inaccurate) sentence about the killing of Murray and Murphy, 'The reason for the alleged murder of Rodney [*sic*] Murphy and Leo Murray of Deans Grange by CID men is that they were the men who ambushed Michael Collins near Foxrock just prior to his death.'[64] The Foxrock incident refers to an ambush on Collins' car near Stillorgan on Friday 18 August (though Collins was not on board) when several gunmen threw a hand grenade and fired twenty to thirty shots at the vehicle as it drove towards the city. Two of his drivers, named Rafter and Quinn, were on board and returned fire.

Rafter was wounded on the hip and was later treated in Baggot Street Hospital.[65]

On 3 September 1922, a badly-wounded John Joseph (J.J.) Stephens (28) from Belleek, County Fermanagh, was found near Blackhorse Bridge, Inchicore, Dublin. He had four bullet wounds and was barely alive. Stephens was in the Fermanagh Brigade of the IRA during the War of Independence and after the Treaty was in the 1st Battalion of the Dublin Brigade of the anti-Treaty IRA.[66] He was found at 7 a.m. by a passing cyclist named John Carroll of Templeogue who notified the police. Stephens was able to relate what happened to the first policeman at the scene, Constable Timothy O'Connor of Inchicore Station.

He told the constable that he was asleep in his lodgings at 7 Gardiner Place when several men knocked loudly on the door around 3 a.m. demanding admittance, shouting, 'Open! Open at once!' and waking up some neighbouring residents. The landlady, Mrs Jane O'Donoghue, stuck her head out of an upstairs window and asked what was up. They ordered her to come down immediately or they would smash down the door, so she hurried downstairs and admitted them. They asked for Stephens by name and, on being shown his room, roused him saying, 'Come on quick.' They ushered him down the stairs at gunpoint, put him into a waiting car and drove away. On arriving at Naas Road, Inchicore, they ordered him out and shot him four times, before driving off and leaving him for dead. He was removed to Dr Steevens' Hospital but later died of his injuries. At the inquest Dr Wilson said the deceased had bullet wounds in the right flank and right leg. Death was due to shock and haemorrhage.[67]

On Friday 22 September 1922, the body of IRA man Michael Neville (22) of Lisdoonvarna, County Clare, was found with numerous bullet wounds in a disused graveyard in Killester in north County Dublin. He was described as a grocer's assistant, employed at Mooney's pub on Eden Quay. At the inquest, Mr Terence McCaul, manager of Mooney's, said three young men called to the pub at about 5.30 p.m. on Friday and asked for Neville by name, stating they were going to arrest him.

He noted they were three tall men and one of them wore a trench coat. They brought Neville upstairs for his coat before taking him away. Earlier that afternoon, a bomb was thrown at a military vehicle on Eden Quay killing one soldier, Private James Kennedy, and injuring three other soldiers and several civilians. McCaul said he was aware that a bomb had been thrown but denied that Neville was responsible, saying they were both working in the pub at the time. His body was brought to his native Lisdoonvarna for burial.[68]

The bodies of three young IRA men were found at Monastery Road, Clondalkin at 7 a.m. on Saturday 7 October 1922 by a Patrick Brien from Inchicore. They were Edwin Hughes (17) of 107 Clonliffe Road, Brendan Holohan (17) of 49 St Ignatius Road and Joseph Rogers (16) of 2 St Brigid's Road, all in Drumcondra, Dublin. All three had bullet wounds. Residents heard 'a lot of shooting' around midnight, though this was not unusual at the time. Others heard a car leaving the scene. The bodies were removed to the mortuary at Tallaght aerodrome and later to the city morgue.[69]

The inquest was held on Monday 9 October and Mr M. Comyn KC, appeared for both the next-of-kin and the IRA and declared that all three youths were members. Witnesses told the court they observed a vehicle with Free State Army officers on Clonliffe Road that night and identified two of them as Patrick O'Connell and Charlie Dalton (one of Michael Collins's Squad and who took part in the Bloody Sunday shootings of British agents in November 1920).[70] A witness who was in school with Dalton said, 'Charlie, don't you know me?' but Dalton did not reply. Summonses were issued for Dalton and O'Connell to attend but Superintendent Prenderville gave evidence that when he called to Portobello Barracks, 'I did not get beyond the gate.'[71]

Another witness, Leah Sandross of Clonliffe Road, said that she was driven home that evening by three Free State Army officers whom she named as Comdt. Dalton, Comdt. Seán O'Connell and Captain Nicholas Tobin. As she entered her home, she could hear shooting and, on looking back, she saw three men getting into the car and driving away with the officers. Mary Nolan of Naas Road told the inquest she returned home at about 11.20 p.m. on the night of the shootings. When she went to lock up, she heard a most terrible scream – the scream of a man – once only. The man tried to scream again and then there was silence. Shortly afterwards she saw a car with Free State soldiers on board leaving the area. All three died from numerous bullet wounds.

The jury returned an open verdict which declared, 'death from gunshot wounds inflicted by some person or persons unknown.'[72] Charlie Dalton was clearly involved in these, and almost certainly many other killings. He was briefly arrested for murder but was subsequently released and resumed his military duties.[73] He later suffered a mental breakdown and by 1941 he was a patient in Grangegorman psychiatric hospital. He had a pension based on his 'delusional insanity.'[74] A medical report in April 1941 certified that he had a serious mental breakdown and was in constant fear of being shot. He was also hearing voices accusing him of murder. On 7 November 1941, the High Court declared him to be 'a person of unsound mind and incapable of managing his person or property' and gave his wife Teresa control of his affairs.[75]

On 5 November 1922, IRA Lieutenant James Spain (22) from Geraldine Square, Dublin, was shot by Free State soldiers after an attack on Wellington Barracks, South Circular Road. A parade of 140 soldiers was taking place on the square when a party of IRA men, including Spain, opened fire on them with a machine gun killing Private Thomas Murphy and injuring about twenty others. Troops chased a group of men running away from the scene and opened fire. A badly wounded Spain made his way to the gate of 22 Donore Road, home of Mrs Doleman and said, 'for God's sake let me in.' He fell inside the gate and she assisted him to the sofa inside. She asked him why he was running, and he said he was blamed for an attack on the barracks. He died later and large crowds, including a guard of honour from Cumann na mBan, attended his funeral from Whitefriar Street church. Three volleys of shots were fired over his grave at Glasnevin Cemetery.[76]

At 9 a.m. on 29 December 1922, the body of Frank Lawler of 3 Raglan Road, Dublin, was found at the junction of Churchtown Road, and Green Lane, Milltown, by a young man cycling to work. Lawler was aware that the CID were looking for him and went to live in a friend's house at Castlewood Avenue in Rathmines. However, at 12.30 p.m. the previous day, two men wearing trench coats and caps called to the house in Castlewood Avenue, knocked at the door and asked for him by name. When Lawler came downstairs he enquired, 'Who are you?'

One of them replied, 'You will have to come with us.'

Lawler said, 'I will not go until I know who is taking me.' They took him one on each arm and pulled him out of the house saying they were 'the authorities.' Other residents assumed the visitors were Oriel House men. A postmortem examination revealed he had been shot numerous times. There were two entrance bullet wounds in the right side of his head and two exit wounds on the left side of the head along with several other bullet wounds on his body.[77]

On Friday 23 March 1923, IRA man Captain Thomas O'Leary (22) of 17 Armstrong Street, Harold's Cross, was found shot dead at Upper Rathmines Road. His mother, Mrs Jane O'Leary, told the inquest that her house was raided between 1 a.m. and 2 a.m. on the previous Sunday by military who said they were looking for her son. They told her they would give him until Wednesday to surrender and if he did not, she would find him shot in Clondalkin or Bluebell. The next time he was brought to her would be in a wooden box. The medical evidence was that O'Leary had twenty-two bullet wounds.

His brother William said there was another raid about two weeks earlier when all the raiders were in civilian clothes and wearing trench coats. One carried a rifle and the remainder had revolvers. He agreed that Thomas was a member of the IRA for about eight months before the Truce. A military witness said no raid was carried out by the military on Mrs O'Leary's house that night.[78] The jury returned a verdict that O'Leary died on 23 of March 1923 'from shock and haemorrhage following numerous gunshot wounds caused by armed forces unknown.'[79]

On Thursday 29 March 1923, IRA Commandant Robert Bonfield (a dental student) of 103 Moyne Road, Ranelagh, (Quartermaster and acting Officer Commanding of the Dublin Brigade of the IRA) was arrested at Leeson Street by men from President Cosgrave's bodyguard[80] and his body was found the next day at Dowling's farm, Newlands Cross, Clondalkin. It was at the bottom of a ditch 400 yards from the public road. At the inquest a youth named Arthur Mowan of 58 St Alban's Road said that on that evening he was at the junction of Stephen's Green near St Vincent's Hospital when he saw Bonfield, whom he knew, with two men in civilian clothes, walking towards the Shelbourne Hotel inside the railings. He saw one of the men strike Bonfield. The jury returned a verdict of murder against person or persons unknown.[81] Bonfield was the gunman who murdered former Cumann na nGaedheal TD Seamus Dwyer on 20 December 1922 at his shop in Rathmines. Dwyer, a close confidante of Michael Collins, was a member of the first Dáil and had been Secretary of the committee that negotiated a pact between Collins and de Valera aimed at averting civil war. That pact ultimately failed and led to the death of Dwyer.[82] The identification of Bonfield by the men of Cosgrave's bodyguard, who were staunch pro-Treaty Oriel House men, was always likely to have a fatal outcome.

On Tuesday 3 April 1923, the bodies of two anti-Treaty IRA men, both of whom had been shot to death, were found at Cabra Road. They were Christopher Breslin (25) of 9 Mount Temple Road, Manor Street and Joseph Kiernan (19) of 40 Mercer Street. At the inquest, Breslin's aunt, Mary Margaret Breslin said on the previous night there was a knock on her door at 11.30 p.m. Christopher opened the door and three men in civilian clothes entered and told him to dress and come along with them. They searched his room and one asked him if he was a brother of Peadar Breslin. On replying that he was, one of the men said, 'you're another good thing.' They told his aunt they were taking him to Portobello Barracks and they drove off in a car. She recognised one of the men as having been on a previous raid on the house, but he had been in army uniform on that occasion.

Joseph Kiernan was seized in Wexford Street that same evening by men in a powerful touring car who drove off with him inside. The same vehicle was seen later on Cabra Road, shortly before the bodies were found.[83] At the inquest, Margaret Byrne of 4 Bishop Street said she was 'keeping company' with Kiernan for six months and had been speaking to him at Redmond's Hill on Tuesday night at 11.15 p.m. She saw a greenish-grey touring car, 'like what officers go in', pass by, going toward George's Street. An officer in the car roared 'halt' and three men in civilian attire got out. One of them said to Kiernan, 'come on with me' and struck him in the jaw while a second man struck him with the butt end of a revolver, knocking him to the ground. They put him in the car and drove toward George's Street. When she protested to the men one of them said, 'we know him long enough'. The jury returned a verdict of wilful murder against persons unknown.[84]

At 11 a.m. on Sunday 22 April 1923, the body of Martin Hogan (32) of Dromineer, Nenagh, County Tipperary, was found in a small stream in a field at Grace Park Road, Drumcondra. He had a total of eleven bullet wounds, including one through the heart and another through the forehead. Local residents reported hearing five or six reports the previous night around 10 p.m. which they presumed were from a car backfiring. Hogan had been living at 26 Temple Cottages in Broadstone.[85]

At the inquest a female witness said that on Saturday night she saw Hogan on Dorset Street with another man who was wearing a trench coat. The man told her to go away, or he would 'plug' her. He appeared to be menacing her with a revolver in his pocket though she did not see it. They both got into a car and drove away. There were about eight people in the car. She said Hogan was a captain in the IRA. The following day she went to Oriel House to enquire about him as she thought they looked like CID men and they told her they knew nothing about him and to check Mountjoy Prison. On her way to the prison, she saw a crowd at the Mater Hospital and learned that he had been brought in dead. The jury returned a verdict of wilful murder against some person or persons unknown.[86]

On 3 August 1923, the body of Henry McEntee (27) of 22 Lennox Street was found on Dubber Road near Jamestown Road, Finglas. He had been shot to death. Oriel House men were looking for him and called to his home and place of work several times. On their final visit to his home on 3 August they told his wife they were going to 'riddle him' when caught and that 'he would be probably found in a ditch'. His body was found later that same day.[87]

Detective Officer Horan told the inquest he was given the task of arresting McEntee. He visited several addresses with other officers looking for him but insisted he had nothing to do with his death. He denied he had told Mrs McEntee that if her husband was arrested, they would find him shot in a field or somewhere else. Other officers who gave similar evidence were Detective Officers McCabe, Cullen, P. Derry, and W. McEnerney.[88]

In the most notorious case of the period, on 12 October 1923, the badly decayed body of IRA man Captain Noel Lemass (brother of future taoiseach Seán Lemass) was found in the Featherbed Mountains in Dublin. There were signs of torture on the body.[89] Three months earlier on the afternoon of Tuesday 3 July, Lemass was having lunch with a friend named John Devine in the Wicklow Hotel in Wicklow Street. At about 2.30 p.m. they walked to Exchequer Street and were approached from behind by two strangers brandishing revolvers. One of them struck Devine on the jaw with the revolver while the other told Lemass that he wanted him saying, 'come here 'till I see who you are.' Both men struggled but were overpowered. One man led Lemass away and Devine did not see him alive again. Meanwhile Devine's captor led him along several streets to the corner of Westland Row (near Oriel House). The man looked towards Oriel House and said, 'I will not go over there. There are people about I don't want to see.' Before releasing him, the man warned him not to mention the matter to anyone. Devine went towards Capel Street to inform Lemass' parents of what happened but on reaching Grattan Bridge he saw two men leaning against a bank wall near the Lemass home. As they looked like the men who accosted them earlier, he turned back.[90]

The matter was not reported to the CID until the 16 July by his father Mr. John T. Lemass, a tailor and outfitters of Capel Street, Dublin.[91] On 12 October 1923, an anonymous letter arrived at Garda HQ giving information on the whereabouts of the body. A party of guards from the Phoenix Park Depot was sent to the Dublin Mountains and, after a three-hour search found his badly decayed body in a heather ditch not far from the Hellfire Club. He had suffered a bullet wound in the left temple. His parents were only able to identify him from his clothing.[92]

Lemass took part in the 1916 Rising and was on the anti-Treaty side in the Civil War. At the inquest on 15 October 1923 the Coroner, Dr Brennan, told the jury that Lemass was taken from the streets on 3 July that year and certainly brutally murdered somewhere. 'It would appear that his teeth had been brutally torn from his jaws and some hairs were lying beside him, suggesting barbarism the most pitiless savage would be ashamed of,' he noted.[93]

A witness named Richard Broderick said he was arrested on 15 September by five Free State Army intelligence officers one of whom was personally known to him as Captain James Murray. He was driven to Stillorgan and questioned about various men 'on the run.' When he failed to answer he was punched and kicked and forced to say prayers. He was severely beaten with revolvers and a shot was fired. He said that Captain Murray boasted he had already shot Noel Lemass and Henry McEntee. He was then driven to Portobello Barracks where he said Comdt. Neligan[94] gave him another beating. He was held overnight and released the following day after being warned not to tell anyone he had been beaten or he would be finished.[95]

On 23 October the jury returned the following verdict:

> We, the members of the jury agree that the remains are those of Noel Lemass; we also agree with the medical evidence that he was brutally and wilfully murdered. We have not sufficient evidence produced to satisfy us who the actual perpetrator was. Arising out of this inquiry, we are

> convinced that armed forces of the State have been implicated with the removal and disappearance of Noel Lemass from the streets of Dublin.[96]

While Oriel House men were well capable of carrying out this killing, they were probably not involved. Captain Murray and his associates looked like the more likely candidates having already carried out a vicious killing of a military policeman named Noel Bergin who was suspected of supplying information to the IRA. Murray was later convicted and sentenced to death for his part in this murder though it was commuted to life imprisonment.[97] Durney's *Civil War in Kildare* suggests that Captain Murray led a renegade group of FSA troops who were responsible for murders during the Civil War period including that of Noel Lemass.[98]

Apart from being involved in many of these killings, the Oriel House men were also regularly accused of brutality towards prisoners – justifiably in many cases. In July 1923, four men arrested by detectives for a robbery at Boland's Mills appeared in Dublin Police Court. Dominic Hudson of Enfield, County Meath, a member of the Free State Army, told the court he was pleading not guilty and any statement he made was provided under duress. He said Inspector Hughes and Superintendent O'Driscoll had arrested him in Kingsbridge on 26 June and brought him to Oriel House. There he was taken to the basement, told to take off his coat and Hughes gave him five minutes to tell him about the Boland's robbery. After two minutes O'Driscoll fired a shot just past him and threatened to take him to the Red Cow to shoot him. The two detectives told him they were going out to get drunk and he knew what to expect when they returned. On their return they brought him to the basement again where he claimed the two of them beat him for an hour or two. O'Driscoll allegedly then tried to choke him, and he lost consciousness.

A second accused, John Meade, made similar allegations. He said he was taken down to the basement and when he denied the charge was beaten for about thirty minutes. He was then taken up for his dinner, 'to make me strong for another beating.' He was unable to eat and after an hour was taken down and beaten again. John Tighe of Ring Street,

Inchicore, said he was also brought to the basement by Inspector Hughes and beaten for five minutes. When he continued to deny his involvement, he was beaten again and kicked on the floor and Hughes called him 'an English bastard.' A second detective held a bar three-quarters of an inch thick over his head and he was so frightened he made a statement. His eyes and lips were swollen, and his gums were bleeding. Later in Mountjoy Prison a doctor told him one of his ribs was fractured.[99] Hudson was later sentenced to ten years imprisonment along with fifteen strokes of 'the cat' while John Meade got ten years, John Tighe got seven years and James Meade got three years.[100]

There is no doubt that CID men were involved in many of these killings and regularly dished out serious beatings to prisoners but some of the lurid tales being told about the alleged horrors suffered in Oriel House are not credible. Coogan quotes IRA man Michael Fitzpatrick as saying that while being interrogated he was forced to walk up and down in a cell and every so often a detective would fire a .45 pistol at either side of his head and that he was so traumatised that he had decided to turn his head into the path of the bullet to end his torment.[101] It would be highly dangerous for a detective to fire a gun in such a confined space as he himself would be in mortal danger from a ricochet though it is possible that he was using blank ammunition.

The anti-Treaty forces, outnumbered and outgunned, were completely routed by May 1923 and the civil war ended officially on 24 May 1923 with de Valera's call to the 'Soldiers of Liberty – Legion of the Rearguard', to dump arms. A second document signed by Frank Aiken was published in newspapers. It was a bullish call to 'All Ranks' and read:

> Comrades! The arms with which we have fought the enemies of our country are to be dumped. The foreign and domestic enemies of the Republic have for the moment prevailed. But our enemies have not won. Neither tortures nor firing squads nor a slavish Press, can crush the desire for independence out of the hearts of those who fought for the Republic, or out of the hearts of our people. Our enemies have demanded our arms. Our

answer is: We took up arms to free our country, and we will keep them until we see an honourable way of reaching our objective without arms.[102]

Thousands of anti-Treaty prisoners languished in detention camps throughout the country and by 30 November 1923 they numbered 5,581.[103] The Court of Appeal issued a decision in July declaring that the state of war had ended and, therefore, the continued detention of internees was illegal. Catholic primate Cardinal Logue also expressed the hope that internees would be free by Christmas. The CID began to screen those deemed suitable for release (i.e., those considered to be no longer a threat to the state) and they were gradually set free throughout the autumn and winter of 1923.[104] A government statement issued on Christmas Eve 1923 announced that 3,487 prisoners were released in the first twenty-three days of December leaving 2,037 still in custody. However, some well-known names remained in custody for several more months including Eamon de Valera, Austin Stack and Ernie O'Malley.[105] The last prisoner to be released was de Valera, who was freed on 16 July 1924.[106]

The CID men were hugely successful in suppressing the activities of the anti-Treaty IRA by the simple expedient of striking terror into them. The irony was that, to a man, they were former IRA men and included many who had been Collins' most ruthless gunmen during the War of Independence. Their strength lay in the fact that they knew most of their opponents including their safe houses and habits. Their highly unorthodox tactics along with military courts, internment, and wholesale executions, both official and unofficial, swiftly brought the civil war to an end, though it left a decades-long legacy of bitterness.

They were hated with a passion by anti-Treaty republicans such as Todd Andrews who wrote;

...some of them wanted to show how 'tough' they were, while a few were psychopaths. The terror took the form of torturing prisoners under interrogation, which is to say they were beaten and battered sometimes into

> a state of unconsciousness. Some republican activists, real or suspected, were picked up on the streets and never got as far as Oriel House. They were shot out of hand.[107]

He claimed that 153 men were killed in 'unauthorised killings by the Free State murder gangs' – i.e., Oriel House men and Free State Army men often operating in plain clothes.[108]

By September 1923, O'Higgins believed that the remaining opposition confronting the government was from a variety of causes, only a small number of which related to dissatisfaction with the Treaty. Much of the support for the Irregulars was from those who had 'vested interests in chaotic conditions.' These included people involved in land grabbing or who owed money to shops, for land annuities or rent and people involved in profitable, but illegal enterprises such as poteen-making. He added:

> I am of opinion that there should be executions in every county. The psychological effect of an execution in Dublin is very slight in Wexford, Galway or Waterford. The Irregulars in these counties, as a rule, do not know the men who are shot in Dublin, and the effect on their minds is very little more than if they were reading of an execution in a novel, or a history instead of a newspaper. I believe that local executions would tend [to] considerably shorten the struggle…summing it up, we must kill the active Irregular, tackle the passive Irregular [and] make friends with the rest.[109]

However, the era of wholesale executions had drawn to a close and while fifteen others (including one woman) would be executed during the remaining years of the 1920s these were all in relation to 'ordinary' murders unrelated to the civil war.

On 8 August 1972, a former Oriel House man, Seosaimh Ó Ceannaigh, of Woodpark, The Rise, Griffith Avenue, [Joseph Kenny, DMP No. 11998, born 1894, in Rathangan, County Kildare] wrote a letter to the Taoiseach complaining about inaccurate stories of events in Oriel House. He was part of Michael Collins' intelligence team during the War of Independence. Somewhat unconvincingly he claimed that prisoners in Oriel House were never spoken to roughly and were never assaulted. He said they had nice clean beds, were served three meals a day by official waiters from the Hammond Hotel and ate at the same table as their captors (a very dubious claim).[110]

Ó Ceannaigh recalled that on one occasion they plied a prisoner with drink, gave him his dinner and released him two hours later. The prisoner went straight to the *Irish Independent* newspaper complaining about the 'terrible beating he got in Oriel House.' On another occasion when the door of Oriel House was blown in, one of the guards, whom he named as Jack Grace, was injured. He said the prisoners could have walked away but did not – they went to Grace's assistance. He conceded that two 'dirty criminals' were assaulted by them before being handed over to the DMP. He added that Tom Derrig [anti-Treaty IRA man and later Fianna Fáil TD] was struck with a gun by a civilian guard and accidentally shot. That guard was instantly disarmed and sacked.[111]

During and after the civil war, Oriel House officers arrested over 500 IRA men and captured huge amounts of weapons and documents. As Kevin O'Higgins told the Dáil in 1923, 'we may take it that the three or four score of men were not selected according to any drawing room standards.' He added, 'they may not handle a cup of tea as gracefully as the Deputy, but they have saved this State at a time when the Deputy's efforts were rather in a contrary direction. Kipling said, 'Single men in barracks ain't exactly plaster saints."'[112]

The Oriel House detectives and Free State troops were battling men who, a few short years earlier, were their comrades in the War of Independence. The bitterness of the Civil War was alive and well, and their ruthlessness was actively encouraged by the government. President Cosgrave told the Dáil on 17 January 1923, 'the death penalty is a thing we cannot economise on when there is such destruction, such disorder, and such hopeless lack of morality through the country from one end of it to the other.'[113] In this ruthless atmosphere, at least seventy-seven official executions were carried out in less than a year – thirty-four in January 1923 alone. The Oriel House detectives took it for granted that there would be little outcry if they carried out a few extrajudicial executions on the side. All of them were former guerrillas who were bloodied during the War of Independence and now found themselves in an unfamiliar policing role.

With the defeat of Irregular forces and the new State relatively secure, the government issued an 'Irregular Campaign Indemnity' on 5 November 1924. This was an attempt to heal the bitterness of the Civil War period and effectively gave immunity to anyone involved in politically motivated crime. This included 'criminal acts committed or alleged to have been committed between 6 December 1921 and 12 May, 1923.' It applied to offences committed in connection 'with the state of rebellion and public disturbances created by the recent attempt to overthrow by force the lawfully established Government of Saorstát Eireann.'[114]

Kevin O'Higgins, the acknowledged strong man in the cabinet, summed up the position of the new government during the civil war when he noted, 'this is not going to be a draw, with a replay in the autumn.'[115] He continued, 'the Provisional Government was simply eight young men in the City Hall standing amidst the ruins of one administration, with the foundation of another not yet laid and with wild men screaming through the keyholes.'[116] During a Dáil debate on 1 March 1923 he said, 'we cannot make omelettes without breaking the eggs. We cannot build up a disciplined and self-respecting decent country without hitting pretty hard a head here and there to encourage the rest.'[117] Patrick Hogan, Minister for Agriculture, also told the Dáil, 'we are prepared to take rough and ready methods, the Irregulars must be beaten and terrorised by the utmost military activity.'[118] With the end of the Civil War, the army could now return to barracks but the need for an armed police unit to deal with IRA remnants still remained.

It is difficult to disagree with O'Halpin when he wrote, 'the CID succeeded in its task of suppressing small-scale republican activities in the Dublin area, not by the sophistication and efficiency of its intelligence work...but by the more direct method of striking terror into its opponents.'[119]

‹bove: Special Branch detectives at the scene of an arms find at Killakee in the Dublin Mountains on 3 June 1931. (Courtesy of the National Photographic Archive)

elow: Detectives examining the underground chamber in Killakee where weapons, ammunition and xplosives were seized on 13 June 1931. (Courtesy of the National Photographic Archive)

Above: Another view of the scene of the seizure of a weapons cache in Killakee on 13 June 1931.

Below: Kevin O'Higgins, Minister for Justice, pictured with Patrick McGilligan and Eamon Duggan at a police event in 1922. He was assassinated by IRA men on 10 July 1927.

bove: Funeral of Kevin O'Higgins leaving the church at Westland Row, Dublin. (Courtesy of the National hotographic Archive)

elow: Detectives at the scene of the assassination of Superintendent John Curtin outside his home at Fri-rsland House, near Tipperary town, on 21 March 1931. (Courtesy of the National Photographic Archive)

Above: Detectives at Friarsland House, home of Superintendent Curtin, near Tipperary town. (Courtesy of the National Photographic Archive)

Below: Gardaí carrying wreaths at Superintendent John Curtin's funeral. (Courtesy of the National Photographic Archive)

bove: Scene of IRA bomb xplosion at Special Branch HQ, ublin Castle, on 25 April 1940 ıat injured five detectives and a ɛmale housekeeper. (Courtesy f the National Photographic rchive)

ght: Scene of damage caused y a bomb at Exchange Court, eside City Hall in Dublin on November 1937. (Photo ɔurtesy of National Archives of eland (NAI) and its Director - /Justice File 2008/117/995)

Detective Garda Richard Hyland, shot dead by the IRA on Rathgar Road, Dub lin on 16 August 1940. (Photo courtesy of his daughter, Marie Hyland)

Portrait of Detective Sergeant Patrick McKeown, on display at Special Branc HQ in Harcourt Square, who was also shot dead in Rathgar on 16 August 1940. (With the kind permission of Det Chief Supt Justin Kelly of the Special Detective Unit)

.bove: Pall bearers carrying Detective Garda Hyland's coffin. (Photo courtesy of his daughter, Marie yland)

elow: Marie Hyland holds a photo of her late father Detective Garda Richard Hyland. (Photo by author)

Above: Scene of shooting of Garda Joseph Egan, at the junction of Lower Leeson St and St Stephen's Green East, on 12 May 1935. (Photo courtesy of National Archives of Ireland (NAI) and its Director - D/ Justice File 2008/117/793)

Below: IRA man John Joseph Reynolds from Dromod, Co Leitrim, who was charged with the murder of Ge ald More-O'Ferrall in Edgeworthstown, Co Longford on 9 February 1935. After two trials he and three others were later acquitted of the murder by a jury. (Photo courtesy of National Archives of Ireland (NAI and its Director - D/Justice File 2008/117/991)

ıssistant Inspector Matt Daly, Oriel House
etective officer, a native of Monivea,
ıthenry, Co Galway, who was shot dead
y anti-Treaty IRA men at Queen Street,
ublin, on 22 December 1922. He was
ngaged to Alice Lynch from Ardcath,
o Meath and the ceremony was due to
ıke place a week after his death. (Photo
ourtesy of Orla Murphy, granddaughter of
lice Lynch)

etective Garda John Brocklebank, one of
e "Broy Harriers" recruited into the Special
ranch in 1933, pictured in Irish Volunteer
niform. He shot IRA man Peter McCathy
ead on Clanbrassil Street, Dublin, on 15
ne 1937. (Photo courtesy of his nephew
atrick Brocklebank)

Above: Funeral of Detective Garda Michael Walsh who was killed in an exchange of fire with an IRA ma
in Mount Nugent, Co Cavan on 1 October 1942. (Photo courtesy of Michael Dalton)

Below: Gardaí at the ruins of their garda station in Rathfarnham, Dublin, destroyed by anti-Treaty IRA during the Civil War. (Courtesy of the Garda Síochána Retired Members Association)

bove: Oriel House, Dublin, headquarters of the riminal Investigation Department (CID) in 1922/23. Courtesy of the Garda Síochána Retired Members ssociation)

ght: Charlie Kerins, IRA chief of staff. He was inged in Mountjoy Prison on 1 December 1944 for e murder of Detective Sergeant Denis O'Brien.

Above: Party of Special Branch men in Tullamore, Co Offaly in 1924. *Left to right*: Detective Gardaí Michael Walsh (shot by an IRA man in Co Cavan on 1 October 1942), Michael Gill, D. McGuire, unknown & Detective Sergeant P.J. Duff on right. (Photo courtesy of Michael Dalton)

Below: Harry White, IRA Chief of Staff, being escorted from court surrounded by Special Branch men in October 1946 after being charged with the murder of Detective Garda George Mordaunt.

Chapter 2

THE NEW SPECIAL BRANCH, 1923-1927

A gang of police thugs...
Todd Andrews, IRA

In October 1923 Justice Minister Kevin O'Higgins sought the views of Colonel David Neligan on the future of the CID.[1] Neligan was the army's director of intelligence and was a former DMP man who acted as an agent for Michael Collins in Dublin Castle during the War of Independence. Neligan recommended that the unit be disbanded, and the most efficient officers transferred to the detective branch of the DMP. As a result, the Oriel House CID, consisting of seventy-two men, was disbanded on 29 October and twenty-eight of them were transferred to G Division of the Dublin Metropolitan Police.[2]

The *Freemans Journal* was gushing in its praise:

> The Irish public has heard with misgiving the decision of the Government to disband the CID. It is questionable if any force organised for the prevention and detection of crime has established so fine a record in so short a time. At the time they were formed most people had almost given up hope that any effective means would be found of stamping out the epidemic of

> armed robbery in Dublin. Inside a few weeks the CID had the bandits on the defensive, and ever since it has been keeping them on the run.[3]

Neligan was asked to take charge of the new unit with the rank of chief superintendent. His deputy was Captain Peter Ennis[4] who was given the rank of superintendent while two others, Superintendents Joseph Kinsella and Finian O'Driscoll were reduced to the rank of inspector. Six others were promoted to sergeant – Detective Officers McKeon, Lynch, Crimmins, Gibney, Cullinan and Currivan – while twenty-six were transferred with the rank of constable. The remainder, for whom there was no place in the new arrangement, were given four weeks' pay as a gratuity, along with assistance in obtaining other employment.[5]

In a speech at Dun Laoghaire praising the police forces on 29 October 1923 Kevin O'Higgins said;

> You are well aware of the good service given by the men of Oriel House during the last twelve months. They share with the Army the dangers and the toils of a peculiarly trying campaign, and their success in defeating and exposing the methods of the enemies of the State did much to hasten a return to more normal conditions. When Colonel Neligan has his branch under way, I will not hesitate if the situation in the country requires it, to seek the necessary powers to enable its members to deal with major crime in any part of the country.[6]

On 29 October twenty-eight former Oriel House men reported for duty at the G Division in College Street (now Pearse Street)[7]. A statement from the Ministry of Home Affairs read:

> In view of their past services in the Irish Volunteers and Oriel House all these specially selected officers and men are being taken into the new force, irrespective of the ordinary regulations as regards, physical disqualification etc. Another thirty were described as meriting 'special consideration' and should be paid a bonus in view of their good service if they were not

> employed elsewhere in the public service. The remainder were described as 'not recommended for any special consideration on disbandment.

No reasons were given explaining why less than half of the original force was considered suitable for transfer to the DMP. More than likely, it was felt that some of them were considered to be either borderline psychopaths or just plain useless. Despite the lavish praise from O'Higgins, it is likely that the government just wanted to get rid of the problem detectives while retaining the most efficient twenty-eight.[8]

The newly-amalgamated unit lost no time in making a name for themselves. On 19 November 1923, they confronted three men who robbed the Johnston, Mooney & O'Brien bakery in Ballsbridge and shot all three, killing one of them. The cashier, Ignatius Moran, was travelling in a side car to a nearby bank when he was held up by the gunmen who made off with £800. Waiting detectives, who were clearly tipped off, pounced on them and opened fire. Two of the gunmen, James Eaton (30) of 58 Pearse Street, and Joseph Mooney (18), from Finglas, were both injured. Patrick Kelly (21) of 225 Phibsboro Road, Dublin, died of his injuries the following day.[9] At the inquest the jury found that Kelly died from wounds caused by police officers in the execution of their duty. They exonerated the police from any blame and commended them for their prompt and efficient action.[10]

At 6.50 p.m. Friday 21 March 1924, a party of unarmed British soldiers attached to the Royal Garrison Artillery came ashore in a launch in Queenstown (now Cobh), County Cork from nearby Spike Island, where they were stationed under the terms of the treaty. Some were accompanied by their wives and children. A car described as a 'powerful Rolls Royce' with four men dressed as Free State soldiers on board, drove into the town at speed and pulled up near the shore where the soldiers were disembarking. Two Lewis machine-guns opened fire killing Private Herbert Aspinall (19) and injuring an officer and seventeen other soldiers along with five civilians, including two women. As they drove off at speed, they fired a further burst in the direction of a British destroyer *HMS Scythe* which was anchored in the harbour. A crowd of locals including doctors rushed to the scene and rendered what assistance they could to the injured. One of the injured soldiers, Gunner Mellor (19) had to have a leg amputated while Gunner Copestake (21) had his forearm amputated.[11]

This shooting made headlines worldwide and was a grave embarrassment for an administration under pressure from an enraged British government demanding a robust response. On 5 March, an angry President Cosgrave condemned the atrocity in the Dáil saying, 'the annals of savagery may be searched but I doubt if any worse instance of murderous cowardice can be found.' He announced a reward of £10,000 to anyone giving information leading to the arrest and conviction of those involved. Even the Cobh branch of Sinn Féin condemned the attack. Extreme anti-Treaty Sinn Féin TDs, Mary MacSwiney (sister of Cork Lord Mayor Terence McSwiney, who died on hunger strike in Brixton Prison in 1920) and David Kent (brother of Thomas Kent, executed after 1916 Rising) disassociated themselves from the episode.[12] According to MacEoin, however, the attack was approved by then IRA chief of staff Frank Aiken, who organised it along with Seán MacBride and others in a house in Ranelagh, Dublin. The idea was to provoke a British military response which would reignite the War of Independence and unite the country again.[13]

A massive garda investigation got underway and many houses all over Ireland were searched and numerous arrests made. On 11 April, Commissioner O'Duffy reported to Cosgrave that they had information from an IRA source that the attack was carried out by an out-of-control group of Irregulars known as the '1st Cork Brigade'. Two men named O'Donovan and O'Shea were believed to be in the attacking party. He added that Tom Barry (IRA commander in Cork) was not involved.[14]

On 7 May, gardaí issued a description of five men they wanted to interview about the shooting. These were Daniel 'Sando' Donovan,

Frank Busteed, Jim and Miah (Jeremiah) Gray and Peter O'Shea.[15] The five men, describing themselves as 'officers of Cork No. 1 Brigade', published an emphatic denial of their involvement on 19 May.[16]

In September 1924, a prisoner in Portlaoise Prison named Patrick O'Neill claimed to have first-hand knowledge of the shooting. He told detectives that the gunmen were Matthew Connolly, William Keane and Edward O'Rourke. Neligan was a bit concerned with some discrepancies in O'Neill's account believing he was 'sane but erratic and is given to making incoherent statements.'

Based on O'Neill's information, detectives led by Neligan and Superintendent Ennis raided a number of addresses all over the city and arrested seven men and charged them with conspiracy to murder and with the murder of Private Aspinall. They included those named by O'Neill, Matthew Connolly of Ballybough, William Keane of Rathmines, Edward O'Rourke of East Wall, along with Patrick Mullally of South Summer Street, John Byrne of Church Street, Arthur Kelly of Hanover Street West and John Harrington alias O'Brien of Camden Row.[17] On 29 October, they arrested Joseph O'Connor of Fairbrothers' Fields, Dublin and charged him also with complicity in the murder. They were remanded in custody but on 5 November 1924 all were discharged after witnesses failed to identify them.[18]

The arrests by Neligan's detectives prompted Commissioner O'Duffy to send a strident letter of complaint to Home Affairs on 3 November. The Detective Branch was then part of the DMP, a separate force under a separate Commissioner. O'Duffy was not informed of the planned arrests and was embarrassed when asked by the news editor of the *Irish Times* about 'the sensational arrests this morning.' O'Duffy replied that he knew nothing about it but that it was not in connection with the Cobh incident. The news editor replied, 'you are not in the know at all, they were charged this evening.' The furious O'Duffy complained he should have been first consulted, or at least informed of the proposed arrests.

He also complained of a second incident where armed men raided a house near Cork city and arrested a blacksmith named William Sheehan and his apprentice James O'Leary at gunpoint. Believing that Irregulars were involved, a huge garda operation backed up by military was put in place and searches were carried out over a wide area. It later transpired that the 'gunmen' were in fact DMP detectives. On 31 October, Sheehan and O'Leary were interviewed by Comdt. P. D. Scott of Collins Barracks about their detention and Sheehan told him they questioned the legality of their arrest and asked one of the detectives for his authority. The detective produced his revolver saying, 'this is my authority.'[19] Plans to amalgamate the two forces were then well in hand and O'Duffy sought an assurance that when that happened the Detective Branch would be under his control.[20]

The deputy secretary of the department replied to O'Duffy on 4 November, assuring him that the steps taken were prompted by 'the urgent circumstances of the case and not from any desire whatsoever to subject the garda to any indignity or humiliation.' He was also assured that in the amalgamated force the Detective Branch would be under his control. A barely mollified O'Duffy replied that he had no desire to prolong the correspondence but added (not unreasonably) that 'it is difficult to understand why I could not have been informed of the intended action on the private wire, or by a note, no matter how great the urgency.'[21]

Three years later in July 1927, the two Gray brothers, Jim and Jeremiah, were also charged with the murder of Private Aspinall but after a few remands the prosecution dropped the case and they were released.[22] These arrests marked the end of the case. Despite a lengthy investigation involving dozens of searches and arrests, the reward money was never claimed, and no one was ever convicted of the crime.

On 22 October 1924, gunfire erupted between hold-up men and detectives following the robbery of a post office motorcycle and side car on the Malahide Road in Dublin. Detectives sped to the scene and carried out a widespread search of the area. Detectives O'Driscoll and Byrne boarded a city-bound tram in Lower Dorset Street and when they went upstairs, they were fired at by two men. Women passengers screamed and threw themselves on the floor. The detectives returned fire and the gunmen fled down the front stairs and ran up North Circular Road as people scattered in panic. The detectives continued firing after the fleeing gunmen who fired several shots in reply. Shortly afterwards detectives visited the nearby Mater Hospital and found a young man named Michael McNamara of Mill Lane, The Coombe, being treated for a recent bullet wound. He was later removed to the more secure St. Bricin's military hospital. They also recovered a .45 Webley revolver and the proceeds of the robbery.[23]

On 30 October, McNamara was charged in Dublin District Court with conspiracy to commit robbery and attempting to murder Detective Officers O'Driscoll and Byrne. On 8 December, he was convicted in the Central Criminal Court and sentenced to five years imprisonment.[24] He was very lucky to escape with such a lenient sentence. Had he been arrested for a similar offence a year or two earlier he would almost certainly have faced the firing squad.

Kevin O'Higgins was anxious to amalgamate the Garda Síochána and the DMP to save on duplication of training facilities and administration. There were also tensions between both forces leading to some distrust and a lack of cooperation as demonstrated by the Cobh shooting investigation.[25] This led to the passing of the Police Forces Amalgamation Act in April 1925. On the date of amalgamation, the DMP consisted of one commissioner, two chief superintendents, seven superintendents, twenty-five inspectors, forty station sergeants, 145 sergeants and 925 constables – a total of 1,145 men. Commissioner O'Duffy now took charge of the combined force while DMP Commissioner W.R.E. Murphy was appointed a deputy commissioner in the Garda Síochána. The Dublin area became known to as the Dublin Metropolitan Area under Chief Superintendent Eamon Broy. Chief Superintendent David Neligan moved to Garda HQ in the Phoenix Park where he set up the garda

Special Branch as a national unit.[26] It was beefed up by 200 men drawn from An Garda Síochána and the Free State Army. They were given a six-month training course before being dispatched in groups of ten to twenty men to various garda divisions throughout the country.[27] Armed back-up for the uniformed force was now available throughout the country to confront the remnants of the IRA, many of whom had taken to banditry and other assorted criminality.

O'Higgins told an election meeting in Carrigallen, County Leitrim, 'you may take it, that the gunman, bank robber and the midnight thief will be met by men who will be as quick or perhaps quicker on the 'draw' than they are. Terrorism will be put down. The young fellow who thinks that with the aid of a gun he can get rich quick at the expense of his neighbour will find that there is a difficult time ahead for him.'[28] He was as good as his word. In March 1925, twenty detectives under Detective Inspector Finian O'Driscoll were sent to Ballinamore in County Leitrim armed with rifles and revolvers. They soon made their presence felt. They were armed with powers under the Civic Guard (Acquisition of Premises) Act, 1923 which allowed for the compulsory takeover of buildings to be used as garda stations. Each unit was supplied with a Ford car along with a supply of Lee-Enfield rifles and Thompson sub-machine guns and each man had a personal issue of a .45 revolver.[29] Dozens of arrests followed and soon the Arigna Mountains was cleared of gunmen. Similar sweeps were carried out in the Wicklow Mountains and other parts of the country.[30]

On 30 July 1925 detectives raided 68 Adelaide Road in Dublin and during a search found a cleverly concealed room being used as an IRA office. Detective Sergeant Mooney and Detective Garda O'Keefe later told the Central Criminal Court that during the search they came across a trap door and upon going through it, found a fully furnished office. Inside he found Michael Carolan (IRA Director of Intelligence) and Margaret Clancy sitting in the office. They found documents headed 'Headquarters, IRA' dealing with the organisation of battalions and divisions throughout the country.

Charges against Ms Clancy did not proceed but Carolan was charged with taking part in the formation of a body purporting to be a military force not established by law. He defiantly told the court he was a Republican and belonged to the Volunteer Army of the Republic where he held the rank of commandant-general and Director of Intelligence. He railed against what he said was an attempt to classify him and others with the criminals of Mountjoy Prison because 'they had tried all their lives to follow the teaching of Tone, and Lalor and James Connolly.' He was sentenced to twelve months imprisonment.[31]

On the night of 21 September 1926, detectives led by Superintendent T. McDonagh, evidently acting on a tip-off, lay in wait for a car at Galbolie near Bailieboro in County Cavan. They left a car in the centre of the road with the lights off, and, on hearing a car approaching switched them on. The suspect car stopped about twenty yards away and Detectives Conway and Cullen approached it with drawn revolvers. They instructed the five men on board to put up their hands. Conway searched Michael Reilly and found two unloaded revolvers, six rounds of ammunition and a mask. Cullen tried to search Patrick Corr who made two attempts to draw a gun, but Cullen restrained him and found a Parabellum (Luger Po8 pistol) in his hip pocket loaded with seven rounds with one in the breech. All five were arrested and brought to Bailieboro Station and charged with firearms offences. They were Bernard McPhillips and Patrick Corr from Ballinagh, Eugene Lee from Cavan, Michael Reilly from Lisnalea, and Patrick Clerkin. In March 1928, Reilly, McPhillips, Corr and Clerkin, were each sentenced to two years imprisonment with hard labour while Lee, whom the judge felt was 'led into the offence' was released on his own recognisance to be of good behaviour for two years.[32]

On 14 November 1926, the IRA carried out concerted attacks on twelve garda stations in five counties resulting in the deaths of two gardaí. The raids were intended as a means of securing arms and intelligence and were organised by Maurice Twomey (later chief of staff) with the approval of recently appointed chief of staff Andy Cooney.[33] Armed men knocked on the door at St Luke's Station in Cork city. When it was opened by the station orderly, he was confronted by a man with a revolver. The garda knocked the revolver out of his hand and slammed the door shut. A shot was then fired through the door killing Sergeant James Fitzsimons (2566).

Garda Hugh Ward (5663) was shot in a similar attack when he answered a knock on the door on Hollyford Station in County Tipperary. He was confronted by a number of masked men, one of whom shot him at point blank range. He staggered out the back door of the station to an adjoining house where he was cared for pending the arrival of a priest and doctor. Meanwhile the raiding party held up the only other garda in the station, Garda Martin McTigue (3439), and robbed him of £30 cash. Garda Ward was removed to Tipperary Hospital and later to St Vincent's Hospital in Dublin where he died two days later on 16 November.[34]

Ward was buried on 18 November amid pathetic scenes in his native Nobber, County Meath, in a funeral attended by Commissioner O'Duffy. Ward was a member of the old IRA in the War of Independence and later served in the National Army and in the Garda Detective Branch. O'Duffy told mourners:

> Standing by this open grave, I feel sad that people, in the name of patriotism, are still prepared to strike us down. I want to be charitable, and only hope and pray that God may give to the assassins a little more time to prepare for the Eternal Judge than they gave to Hugh Ward.[35]

Rathcormack Station in County Waterford was held up by thirty-five to forty armed men who stole station records, batons, handcuffs along with personal belongings of gardaí. In County Cork, Blackrock and Carrigtwohill stations were raided.[36] After an identification parade at Union Quay Garda Station on 17 November, Garda Patrick Fowley (2253) identified two men as being on the raid in Carrigtwohill. They were

Robert Aherne of 67 Evergreen Road, Cork City and Daniel Buckley of 13 Dublin Street, Cork and both were charged and brought before Midleton District Court. On 2 December 1926, Aherne was discharged. On 9 February 1927, Buckley was convicted of assaulting Garda Foley and stealing station records and given a six-month suspended sentence in the Central Criminal Court.[37]

In January 1927, Detective Sergeant O'Riordan arrested one Edward O'Reilly (25), of Rossmore, County Tipperary, for the murder of Garda Ward in Hollyford and conspiring to rob Garda Martin McTigue of a wallet containing £30. His solicitor told Dundrum District Court (County Tipperary) that his client had a complete answer to the charge and could easily account for his movements on the night. He said Father Willie Ryan and Father Maloney's housekeeper could verify his story.[38] The charge was withdrawn in June 1927 on the instructions of the Attorney General. Chief Superintendent James J. Hannigan of Thurles was not pleased by the decision. On 29 June, he reported to the Commissioner that, there was not the slightest doubt O'Reilly was involved as he was unmasked and had only a few daubs of black on each cheek and had been clearly identified by Garda McTigue.[39]

Twenty armed and masked men raided Kilmessan Garda Station in County Meath. The leader of the raiding party had two revolvers in his belt. Gardaí Kelly, Bredin and Harley were sitting by the fire in the station when the door was pushed open and six of the raiders entered while others stood outside the windows. The raiders asked for the records of 'touts and spies' and were told there was no such record. The leader asked where they kept the guns and when told there were no guns he said, 'we hear a lot about the unarmed Civic Guards but when we meet them, they are generally armed.' They took with them assorted handcuffs and other items along with a copy of *Fógra Tóra*. [An internal garda information booklet of crimes/wanted or missing persons etc]. Detectives led by Detective Sergeant Kirwan later raided the home of Christopher Moran of Kilmessan and found a box buried five feet deep in a field some 200 yards from the house. In the box they found two Lee Enfield rifles, two revolvers, around 100 rounds of assorted ammunition, training manuals, detonators and the missing *Fógra Tóra*. However, the justice refused to send him forward for trial saying there was nothing in the box connecting him to the defendant as the items could have been placed there by someone else. Moran was released from court but was immediately rearrested and interned.[40]

In the early hours of 20 November, Crumlin Garda Station in Dublin was also targeted by IRA gunmen. Garda Thomas Doyle responded to a knock on the door at 2.30 a.m. and asked who was there. Several shots were immediately fired through the door, one of which struck him on the arm, and he fell to the floor. He shouted to a colleague, 'Murphy, Murphy, I'm shot.' Garda Murphy crawled on his hands and knees to assist him but he said, 'don't mind me, but don't let them in.' Murphy reached into a drawer and picked up a revolver that was left there by a detective and fired back at the raiders who quickly fled. Outside, they found a bloodstained mask as well as bloodstains on the ground. There were about ten bullet holes in the windows and door, apparently fired from a revolver. A party of twenty armed detectives led by Superintendent Ennis was immediately dispatched to the scene and carried out intensive enquiries. They later arrested eight men including Archie Doyle and Timothy Coughlan of Inchicore, both of whom would feature prominently in future years.[41]

The deaths of Fitzsimons and Ward were the last straw for a force that since its foundation endured continuous threats and intimidation and suffered eight fatalities in their four years of existence. They considered it a particularly cowardly act to shoot down two unarmed, uniformed gardaí who had no involvement in the ongoing battle against the IRA. Most of the new force consisted of former pro-Treaty IRA men themselves and took a dim view of being targeted by their erstwhile comrades in arms. In Waterford Station, republican prisoners were severely beaten in their cells by relays of gardaí and detectives apparently after some of the prisoners jeered them on hearing news of the deaths. Following a major outcry, O'Duffy promised a full enquiry but O'Higgins was furious and demanded that those responsible be dismissed.[42]

In the quarrel that followed, O'Duffy threatened to resign, maintaining that the guards had suffered years of intimidation and provocation and insisted that discipline was his prerogative. O'Higgins told him that if he refused, he would be replaced with a commissioner who would dismiss them. In the end they compromised, and the guards were allowed to keep their jobs provided they paid a portion of the costs awarded to the injured men. Despite this bitter row which they quickly put behind them, O'Higgins was O'Duffy's only supporter in the cabinet as the remainder would have been glad to get rid of him. Notwithstanding O'Duffy's insolence and tetchiness, O'Higgins knew it would be difficult to find a replacement with similar drive and enthusiasm.[43] There were plans to dismiss him and a replacement was lined up in the form of Chief Superintendent Michael Francis Leahy. But this decision was overtaken by the events of 10 July 1927.[44] [See chapter 3].

A sworn enquiry was set up by O'Higgins chaired by Mr Charles Kenny BL, Dr D.L. O'Kelly from the Department of Local Government and Mr J. E. Duff BL from the Department of Justice. Of the ten who made complaints, the committee found that the charge of ill-treatment should be sustained in three cases. They recommended that James Doherty be paid £15, and Maurice Healy should receive £3. They also found in favour of James Crotty but made no recommendation for compensation as he refused to sign a document in advance agreeing to accept the findings of the committee. Responsibility for the assaults was fixed on Detective Gardaí Hartigan and Spain along with Detective Sergeant Shaw for his failure to prevent the assaults. In the other seven cases they found that the complaints were not established.[45]

There was a sequel in November 1927 when the three prisoners, whose allegations were sustained, took a civil action for assault against the three named detectives. The defendants were Detective Garda Thomas Spain (6682), Kilkenny, Detective Garda John Hartigan (996), Thurles, and Detective Sergeant John Shaw (1747) of Maurice Mills, County Clare.

The prisoners claimed they were grievously assaulted by all three detectives by being beaten and kicked at Rathgormack Station in County Waterford on 23 November 1926. The detectives denied the assault and said any violence used was in self-defence or to prevent the escape of the plaintiffs. Crotty said he was brought to the barracks and while there, was questioned by detectives Spain and Hartigan about the raids. When he denied it, he said, 'they started to beat me straight away. They kicked and beat me and the big fellow, Hartigan, had a baton in his hand. He kept digging me in the ribs, saying: 'Come on and tell.' Shaw was kicking me, and Spain was striking me in the face.' He said he was stripped naked and beaten on the back with a strap attached to a baton by Hartigan. He also claimed that Hartigan put a revolver in his mouth saying, 'I will blow your daylights out.' He pleaded with the gardaí to shoot him and Hartigan hit him in the ribs with a baton which made him vomit. He then got a blow on the head which knocked him unconscious. He said he was a member of the IRA but not since 1923 and did not approve of the barrack raids.[46]

James Doherty made similar accusations. He said he was beaten and kicked by Hartigan and Shaw. Hartigan asked him, 'are you going to cough?' He caught him by the hair and banged his head off the floor. He said that later he was made undress and Hartigan beat him with a leather strap saying, 'I'll make you cough' before picking up a baton and beating him again. He said Hartigan put a revolver in his mouth and then beat him with the butt. Maurice Healy gave a similar account of being beaten by the detectives. The station cook, Mrs Quinlan, said that she found the kitchen was covered in blood and Doherty stretched on the floor while Crotty was in bed with his mouth swollen and could not take any tea.[47]

Three doctors gave evidence about the men's injuries. Dr. N. Purcell said Doherty had bruises on his face, chest and left thigh and that two impressions on his back must have been caused by some instrument. In reply to the judge, he said his appearance was consistent with his having got a bad beating. Dr. C. Halpin testified that he found Crotty had a fractured rib, though curiously a Dr. V. White noted that when he examined Crotty, he could find no evidence of a fractured rib.

Defence Counsel Mr. A.E. Wood KC argued that it was significant that of the eighteen people arrested, only three had made complaints. If there was any violence by the guards, all of them would have complained. Detective Garda Hartigan gave evidence about the interview with Doherty. He said Doherty became very sarcastic and had a 'few words' with Spain. Spain slapped Doherty in the face and then picked up a baton and gave him a 'few strokes' of it. He said no revolvers were used and there was no blood at all. He also denied the allegations made by the other two prisoners. He claimed Healy made an obscene remark to him and he struck him with his open hand on the jaw. He added that Crotty fell backwards against a bicycle when he was leaving the barrack and he helped him up. Detective Garda Spain said that Doherty was abusive and attempted to hit him during questioning. He struck Doherty several times 'lightly' with a baton. He denied seeing any revolver being put into anyone's mouth.

The jury found against the three detectives, and they were ordered to pay Healy £3, Doherty £20 and Crotty £30. Judgement was also given against Detective Sergeant Shaw for not preventing the assaults though he was later exonerated by the High Court. In subsequent disciplinary proceedings, Shaw was severely reprimanded, warned for reduction (meaning he would be reduced to garda rank in the event of a future breach), reverted to the uniformed force and transferred from the division. Similarly, both Spain and Hartigan were 'severely reprimanded with record, warned for dismissal and transferred from the Division.'[48]

Elsewhere, wholesale arrests were also carried out in relation to the barrack attacks with twenty-five arrests in Dungarvan, twenty in Waterford, fourteen in Cappoquin, twelve in Dublin, twelve in Ballinamult, ten in Westmeath, five in Kilmessan and one each in Rylane and Midleton. In Tralee, County Kerry, detectives arrested John Joe Sheehy, captain of the Kerry senior football team. As a result, the Kerry junior football team refused to travel to Waterford for the semi-final of the All-Ireland Junior Football Championship game due to be played on Sunday 28 November.[49] In Kenmare they arrested John Joe Rice, former O.C. of the

3rd Kerry Brigade of the old IRA immediately after the burial of his father in the local graveyard.[50]

With characteristic bravado, a self-serving statement issued by Óglaigh na hÉireann appeared in *An Phoblacht* on 13 November explaining the purpose of the raids.

> The system of Imperial espionage directed against patriotic organisations in Ireland has been unusually virulent of late months. A regular persecution of our members has been going on in certain districts. Men rescued from jail and men otherwise on the run have been dogged with the utmost persistence. There has been abundant proof that selling information for money was being trafficked in to an alarming extent. It was decided that the most effective means of discouraging such work would be to have the confidential documents in police barracks seized, and thus convey to the persons concerned that there was not an effective cloak of secrecy for espionage. Raids were accordingly carried out in selected districts.
>
> In removing documents, it is quite possible that paper money may have been included. Such money will of course, be returned. The taking of money was no more the intention of the raids than the shootings that occurred. Not even the reports of the hostile Press could conceal the fact that documents only were sought, and they were sought for the purpose of discouraging the present campaign of espionage against the Irish Nation.[51]

Following the attacks on the garda stations, O'Duffy penned a strident eleven-page memo to the Minister for Justice Kevin O'Higgins on 6 December 1926. It was headed, 'State of National Emergency, The Garda – Armed or Unarmed.' He pointed out that, 'the police were placed in an impossible position in being required to enforce the principles of citizenship amongst a population, the vast majority of whom know or care little about such principles.' He said these attacks had 'roused the get-rich-quick merchant from his apparent slumber.' He complained that the force was now placed in an impossible position and that there was a failure to equip the policeman on an equal footing at least with the criminal.[52]

He feared that some members would resort to carrying firearms without authority and sought authority to issue the force with short .45 revolvers. There were daily reports of armed robberies throughout the country – sometimes two or three per day. There were no attacks on detectives (who were armed) and he referred to an incident in Ballymakeera [County Cork] where 'a number of local men who were overheard planning an attack on the uniformed force there, but these heroes would not dare interfere with the few detectives who had revolvers.' He recalled meeting police officers from other European countries recently 'who could not understand an unarmed, and at the same time, effective police force.' He had tried to explain but they were 'incredulous.'[53]

The secretary of the Department of Justice sent a memo to government on 3 January 1927 disapproving of any plans for a general arming of the force. It pointed out that the force was unarmed for the previous five years (apart from detectives) when the level of attacks was much greater. The support currently shown by the community to the garda would not be as great if the force was armed. The memo added that the fact that the armed RIC was a symbol of oppression and that such popular prejudices of this kind, however illogical, could not wisely be ignored. An armed force would also result in an increase in raids on stations for arms. At a meeting on 24 January, the government agreed and rejected O'Duffy's proposal.[54] A fully armed force had already been wisely ruled out since its foundation. It is certain that an armed force would have been the target of many more raids for arms on garda stations and the fatality rate would have been much greater. Despite some killings of unarmed gardaí, the IRA was reluctant to carry out wholesale shootings (as happened during the RIC days), probably fearing it would not have played well with the public or even their own supporters.

Remembrance Sunday (Poppy Day) in the 1920s and 1930s was always a tense affair as the IRA tried to disrupt proceedings, while clashes with gardaí and Special Branch officers were a regular occurrence. IRA supporters felt it was a provocative display of British imperialism and the sight of Trinity College students assembling in College Green waving Union flags and singing *God Save the King* was too much for many of them. Speakers at anti-Poppy Day demonstrations included leading IRA men as well as Fianna Fáil spokesmen, though when they entered government in 1932 there were no further appearances by members of Fianna Fáil.[55]

Todd Andrews, a former anti-Treaty IRA man who was attending UCD relates how fighting broke out at the 1924 demonstration between Republicans and British Legion supporters in Earlsfort Terrace. He spotted a man he took to be a British Legion supporter brandishing a revolver and instinctively grappled with him, giving him what he referred to as a 'Ringsend Uppercut', causing him to drop the gun. Andrews grabbed the revolver and hid it nearby. On returning to the UCD building he spotted a squad of Special Branch men lined up outside. One of them shouted, 'there he is' and rushed to grab him. It was only then he realised that the man he had punched was actually a Special Branch officer. Though he had no particular wish to return the revolver to what he described as 'a gang of police thugs', neither was he too keen to do another jail sentence. A friend of his, Joe McGilligan, began negotiating with the detectives and a deal was agreed. If the gun were returned, Andrews and three other students who were in custody would be released. And so, it happened – the gun was returned, the student prisoners were released, and honour was satisfied.[56] No doubt the detective would have been in hot water with his authorities if he had to report the circumstances in which he lost the gun.

At the November 1926 Remembrance Day ceremonies, gardaí and detectives were on duty at College Green when about 300 young men formed four deep and marched up Grafton Street to St Stephen's Green where they burned effigies of Black and Tans and Free State soldiers.

They returned via Grafton Street where gardaí tried to disperse them. IRA man George Gilmore from Killakee (OC of the Dublin Brigade), was one of the leaders shouting instructions to the crowd. Two men wearing Union Jack badges and a British Fascist badge were attacked by a mob. One of them, J. L. Twiney, was stabbed in the shoulder while both were relieved of their flags and badges. Detective Sergeant Lynch and six other detectives confronted Gilmore and on searching him found a dagger in his pocket. Gilmore ran from them and boarded a passing tram before getting off again at York Street. Detectives George A. Fennell[57] and Albert Jackson[58] caught up with him and in the struggle, Gilmore struck Jackson on the head with a stick. Fennell drew a revolver and fired a shot in the air before he and other detectives overpowered Gilmore and arrested him. Jackson was removed for treatment to Mercer's Hospital nearby.

In the District Court, Gilmore was charged with giving instructions to men performing military manoeuvres, attempting to evade arrest, and assaulting Detectives Fennell and Jackson. When District Justice Little offered bail Gilmore retorted, 'I am not a subject of your King at all and I don't recognise any authority of his agents in my country, except the authority of force'. He continued, 'I regard the Court as an illegal assembly, and every member of it is liable for treason to the Irish Republic.' At these words a woman cheered at the back of the court and was put in custody for contempt but was later released. Gilmore was remanded in custody. Twiney later identified Gilmore as one of the ringleaders but could not say if it was Gilmore who had stabbed him. In December, Gilmore was convicted of rescuing nineteen prisoners during a mass escape from Mountjoy Prison in November 1925, and with assaulting a warder. He was sentenced to eighteen months imprisonment with hard labour.[59]

By the end of December 1926, newspapers were hailing the success of the detective branch in drastically reducing the number of armed robberies particularly in the Dublin area. The *Irish Independent* reported that in previous years 'Christmas was a gunman's holiday in Dublin.' In December 1924, there were no fewer than thirty armed robberies in the city while in December 1925, the number was reduced to twenty-two. By December 1926, not a single armed robbery was reported. It added proudly, 'this is an achievement that the greatest detective force in the world might be proud of.' The piece concluded, 'we may well extend hearty congratulations to our police in stamping out this worst of our social evils.'[60] The arrival of armed detectives throughout the country in support of the unarmed force practically stamped out the armed robberies and banditry that was prevalent in many parts of the country. Prior to their arrival, gangs of armed gunmen (mostly former IRA men), were able to carry out their attacks with little hindrance or danger of arrest.

The young force paid a high price in the process. In just four years, thirteen gardaí and detectives were killed, eight by the IRA and the remainder by regular criminals. However, despite their successes the Special Branch could not rest on their laurels just yet.

Chapter 3

ASSASSINATION, INFORMERS AND INTIMIDATION, 1927–29

You are wrong, but I forgive you, I forgive you.
Kevin O'Higgins to his killers.

On Sunday 10 July 1927, Mr Kevin O'Higgins, Vice President of the Irish Free State and Minister for Justice, was walking to noon Mass in the parish church in Booterstown, Dublin. Just a few hundred yards from his home three gunmen approached and opened fire on him with revolvers. He managed to struggle on for a few yards before he collapsed. Sergeant Sweeney from Blackrock Garda Station was quickly on the scene and found O'Higgins being given the last rites by Canon Breen from Booterstown Church. Sweeney asked O'Higgins what happened, and he replied that while walking along Cross Avenue three men were waiting for him at the corner and shot him. He told the sergeant he was dying and added that he did not know the men.[1] Commissioner Eoin O'Duffy visited him and O'Higgins told him, 'I am dying at peace with my enemies. I die for my country; I go to join Michael Collins.' He was brought back to his home nearby and, remarkably, lived for a further five hours before passing away. He was struck by eight bullets, one in the right side of the head, four in the chest, two in the neck and one in the left hand. The IRA issued a denial saying, 'the Army Council and General Headquarters Staff of Óglaigh na hÉireann desire to state most emphatically that they have no knowledge whatever of this act, and repudiate any responsibility for it.'[2]

This would be the greatest challenge yet for the new Special Branch and led to wholesale searches and arrests. Despite the IRA denial, it was assumed they were responsible. Within days, detectives rounded up scores of IRA members suspected of involvement. On 12 July, ten men appeared before Dublin District Court and were charged by Detective Superintendent Ennis with conspiring to murder O'Higgins. The accused men were Frank Kerlin, 15 Lower Camden Street, William Roe, 142 Francis Street, George Plunkett, 40 Elgin Road, Michael Fitzpatrick of 6 Lower Tram Cottages, Phibsboro, Owen Donnelly, 30 Finglas Road, Brendan O'Carroll and Kevin O'Carroll of Washington Lodge, Rathfarnham, Joseph Reynolds, 47 Donnelly's Avenue, Mount Brown, and Aubrey and Henry Hunt of 86 Rathgar Road. They had a contemptuous attitude to the proceedings, and some laughed and lounged around with hands in their pockets. All denied the charge. They were discharged on 25 July when Superintendent Ennis said he did not propose to offer any evidence.[3] This was normal police procedure at the time which to modern police forces, may seem extraordinary. Without a shred of evidence, they would round up likely suspects, charge them with a crime, and then start looking for evidence. When no evidence could be found, they would return to court and tell the judge they had no evidence to offer.

Another example of this curious practice was the arrest of Seán MacBride for the murder.[4] Detectives entered his home 'in the middle of the night' and lodged him in the Bridewell. He recalled he was treated 'quite roughly' and was charged by Superintendent Ennis with conspiracy to murder Minister O'Higgins.[5] When he appeared in the Dublin District Court, Justice E.J. Little B.L. ordered that he be discharged as the Public Safety Act under which he had been arrested was not passed until 11 August and it was not retrospective. Superintendent Ennis and a squad of detectives waited in the courtyard and when MacBride emerged and he was immediately re-arrested. MacBride asked why he was being arrested and Ennis replied, 'conspiracy to murder.' MacBride protested saying, 'But I have been discharged on that charge. I…'. At this point Ennis interrupted and instructed a sergeant in uniform to remove him to the Bridewell.[6]

A Habeas Corpus application followed in the High Court on 8 September and Superintendent Ennis, when asked if anyone had picked out MacBride in an identification parade, replied, 'not so far.'[7] He was later put in an identification parade with about fifteen others and, though completely innocent, was picked out by O'Higgins' gardener and one other as being one of the gunmen involved.[8] Fortunately for him, at the time of the murder he was sailing to Belgium on business and on board met Major Bryan Cooper, a Cumann na nGaedhal TD for Roscommon. Cooper was able to verify that MacBride was in Brussels at the time of the shooting and without apology or explanation he was suddenly released from custody in October.[9]

There were many wild rumours about who carried out the killing, even including that the Special Branch did it to prevent disciplinary actions against themselves.[10] A Fianna Fáil TD, Seán T. O'Kelly (later president) told the Dáil on 9 May 1929 that:

> They [the government] have at the moment in their employment I believe the men who were responsible for the murder of the late Deputy Kevin O'Higgins. These men are harassing the IRA today. I do not object to them harassing murderers and assassins. What I would like to see them do is to harass more of those who are responsible for all the murders done in 1922 and 1923.[11]

This outburst prompted a visit by Chief Superintendent Brennan and Superintendent Kelleher who came to see O'Kelly in the Dáil on 11 May. O'Kelly admitted that he had no first-hand information but later brought Gerald Boland TD (former anti-Treaty IRA) to the room saying he had received the information from him. Boland said it 'leaked out' on the Friday before the murder that O'Higgins had intended to take 'drastic action' against certain members of the CID. This was allegedly resented by the higher authorities in the police. He said there was a prima facie case that CID men were involved and when pressed for a name Boland said, 'Neligan knows a great deal about it.' O'Kelly also thought it was significant that the detective who was guarding O'Higgins turned back to the house before the shooting but Brennan told him it was 'an unfortunate circumstance' but there was nothing in that suggestion. O'Kelly said he carried out enquiries from republican sources and was satisfied that the crime was not committed by them.[12] This wild conspiracy theory appealed to republicans as they had a virulent hatred of both the Special Branch and David Neligan.

In fact, O'Higgins disliked having a garda escort. On the morning of the shooting, he left his home on a bicycle at 9 a.m. for a swim in Blackrock baths, as was his custom. He was escorted by Garda Brian O'Grady (12175)[13] to and from the baths. At 11.40 a.m. O'Higgins asked O'Grady to go to Blackrock for cigarettes and on returning he discovered that the minister had already left the house for 12 o'clock Mass at Booterstown. As O'Grady hurried after him, he could hear shooting and, on reaching the Booterstown end of Cross Avenue he found O'Higgins lying on the ground with several people standing around him.[14]

Despite a massive investigation with wholesale arrests and questioning of suspects, no one was ever charged with the killing and it would be half a century later before the identities of the gunmen were revealed. Despite O'Kelly's assurances to the contrary, the killers were in fact IRA men. They were Archie Doyle,[15] a Dublin corporation employee Bill Gannon (who had been in Michael Collins' Active Service Unit during the War of Independence), and Timothy Coughlan. The IRA statement of denial was technically correct as it was not an authorised assassination, but an opportunistic killing carried out by the three IRA gunmen who by pure happenstance, spotted O'Higgins as they drove to a GAA match in Wexford.[16]

Years later O'Higgins' daughter, Una O'Higgins O'Malley, entered into correspondence with Bill Gannon's son Roger. Gannon told her that his father gave him a full account of the shooting on his deathbed in 1965. Gannon senior was involved in the Bloody Sunday shootings of British agents in Dublin in November 1920. He told his son he was haunted by the memory of the O'Higgins shooting all his life particularly, by the words of forgiveness uttered by his victim. There was no planning involved and on the day of the shooting, the three killers were going to a football match in Wexford in a stolen car. As they drove through Booterstown they spotted O'Higgins walking along on his own. They were surprised to see he had no bodyguard with him especially, as he was one of the most hated men in the government because of his role in the executions during the Civil War. They argued among themselves about whether or not it was O'Higgins and decided to go back for a second look to make sure. They drove back and saw that it was indeed him and they were 'taken over and incensed with hatred.' They began shooting at him from the car saying, 'we all shot at him; he didn't have a chance.'

They were instructed by Michael Collins when in the ASU that a victim was never to be left in agony. They were astonished to find that O'Higgins was still alive. 'This was against all the odds, it was multiple – we had all shot him', explained Gannon. He went on, 'I had never seen anything like it before. I have shot many, too many.' O'Higgins had somehow got his rosary beads into his hands. He recognised them and told them there had been too much killing in the country and that it had to stop, adding, 'you are wrong, but I forgive you, I forgive you.' They drove off and decided to carry on as if nothing had happened as they knew there would be a national alert and 'all hell would break loose.' However, they attended the match and returned to Dublin without encountering a road block and abandoned the car. They intended to engage in a shootout if they were stopped and did not expect to survive the day. None of them were ever arrested or questioned about the shooting.[17]

Una O'Higgins O'Malley and Roger Gannon later took part in an RTÉ radio programme about the assassination of her father. Gannon became emotional during the programme and choked back tears – still grieving over a killing his father carried out sixty years earlier. O'Higgins O'Malley organised a memorial Mass, not only for her father but also the three men involved in his murder. It was celebrated at the Church of the Assumption, Booterstown, Dublin on 11 July 1987. Roger Gannon attended that Mass as did relatives of the other assassins.[18]

In October 1985, Belfast republican Harry White gave the *Irish Press* further details of the killing. He said that Bill Gannon told him that he and Archie Doyle were involved. He added that ten years previously, Archie Doyle also told him of his involvement and laughed as he described how he shot O'Higgins. According to their account O'Higgins fell after the first volley of shots, upon which the three of them crossed over to where he lay and each fired a further shot at him, one to the head, one above the heart and one to the abdomen. Years later Doyle gave White the short Webley revolver he used in the killing.[19] White said O'Higgins was a murderer and deserved to be assassinated. He argued, 'as Minister for Justice he had ordered the murder of his former friends, Rory O'Connor, Liam Mellows, Dick Barrett and Joe McKelvey in Mountjoy Jail. That's why he was killed.'[20]

While this is the commonly held view, it is not accurate. O'Higgins was part of the cabinet, but he was very reluctant to endorse these executions and was the last to agree to it.[21] The fact that Rory O'Connor was best man at his wedding must also have weighed heavily on his mind. He took most of the flak for it in subsequent years though the actual execution order was signed by General Richard Mulcahy as head of the army.[22] Republicans show similar vindictiveness towards O'Higgins to this day as they simplistically see him as being almost solely responsible. He seemed to have had a premonition of his early death and frequently told friends and colleagues, 'of course, I shall be assassinated.' In a letter to Lady Lavery (with whom he was suspected of having an affair) he wrote, 'I feel a wall of hate closing round me.'[23] His last public act was to unveil a memorial to murdered gardaí at the force's headquarters. At that event he noted, 'I profoundly hope that there will be no addition to this

Roll of Honour, and that these men who were defending and upholding the people's peace have now found peace eternal.'[24] It would be a vain hope as we shall see.

On the night of 28 January 1927, detectives in Ballinamore, County Leitrim, shot and killed one of several gunmen raiding the local Ulster Bank. They had earlier been suspicious of a number of strangers hanging around the town near the bank. Detective Sergeant Christopher Jordan[25] spoke to the manager and arranged for them to be surreptitiously admitted to the bank. Jordan, along with Detective Gardaí Thomas Heaphey[26] and Clifford, went into the bank at 1.50 a.m. and concealed themselves. Later that night gunmen went to the nearby home of a bank cashier, Mr David Elliott, and demanded the keys to the safe. They forced him to accompany them to the bank. Three masked raiders entered the bank with Mr Elliott at 2.10 a.m. while others remained outside. The three detectives stood up, turned on flashlights, and shouted at the men to put up their hands. Elliott threw himself on the floor and one gunman turned and fired a shot, narrowly missing Jordan. The detectives returned fire and the raiders fled, firing more shots as they ran. Another man opened fire with a rifle from across the street giving cover as the raiders escaped. Shortly afterwards detectives found a man lying on the ground moaning. He was about twenty-five yards from the bank. His name was Patrick Crowley (35) from Ballinaboy, County Leitrim. Crowley had a revolver in his hand which was picked up by Detective Heaphey. It had three live and three spent cartridges. A priest and doctor were summoned but the man died shortly afterwards, and his body was brought to the local station.[27] Dr. Charles Dolan from Ballinamore told the subsequent inquest that Crowley had a gunshot wound on his right side and that death was due to shock and haemorrhage as a result of laceration of his internal organs.[28]

Shots were fired into a dancehall in Bweeing, County Cork on the night of Easter Sunday, 17 April 1927. The resulting investigation lasted for over a year. The problem arose as there were two dances on the same night in the same locality between Donoughmore and Blarney. The dance at Bweeing was well patronised with most of the locals attending. The second dance two miles away was poorly attended resulting in the displeasure of the proprietor, IRA man Cornelius 'Gunner' Healy (also known as 'The One-Eyed Gunner') from Grenagh. He closed down his dance and, along with some friends went to the rival dancehall and fired several shots into it. The gardaí arrived on the scene and quickly established who was involved. Healy went on the run and had several narrow escapes from arrest in the following months. On 1 August, Detective Garda O'Donnell cycled from Mallow to Donoughmore to the farm of a Mr Donovan where he spotted Healy standing at a gate. Healy drew a revolver and fired four shots at the detective who whipped out his own revolver and fired in reply. Healy fled and appeared to be limping but made good his escape. Reinforcements arrived to search for Healy and they found a notebook bearing the name Cornelius Healy in a blue jacket left at the scene of the shooting. There was no trace of the man himself.

On 16 October 1927, Detective Gardaí Barrett, Carrigy, Cronin and Maguire went to Ballymorrisheen, Grenagh, where Healy lived, in another attempt to arrest him. They took up positions around the house between 7 a.m. and 8 a.m. and waited. At about 11 a.m. Healy emerged from his home and headed towards his father's house nearby. Detective Barrett shouted at him to put up his hands and immediately Healy drew a revolver and fired two shots at him and then took off running. The chase continued across fields towards a marsh where Healy turned and fired two more shots at his pursuers and finally made good his escape. The following year, on 1 August 1928, during another attempt to arrest him, he again fired on approaching detectives. Detective Garda O'Donnell fired a shot in reply, hitting the gate behind which Healy had taken shelter but, unbelievably, he managed to escape yet again.

While the Healy case was still ongoing, one of the investigating detectives James Cronin (5375) was involved in a shooting tragedy when he accidentally shot and killed an unarmed poacher named Patrick MacSweeney in Bweeing, some ten miles from Mallow, County Cork, on the night of Saturday 24 November 1928. A distraught Detective Cronin told colleagues, 'this man and some more were poaching on the river. I fired, and unfortunately this man was struck. I thought I fired over their heads.' Cronin was charged with murder and on 26 February 1929 he pleaded guilty to manslaughter in the Central Criminal Court. The judge revealed he had no hesitation in saying that if the prisoner had pleaded not guilty, he would have received a verdict of not guilty. He was very much struck by the attitude of the prisoner and discharged him.[29] Cronin was suspended on 25 November 1928 and reinstated on 25 March 1929 following the court decision. He retired in 1953.

Meanwhile on 4 October 1928, detectives finally caught up with the elusive Gunner Healy. They brought him to Union Quay where they charged him with the attempted murder of Detective Garda Barrett on 16 October 1927. When detectives gave their evidence, he said to the justice, 'I refuse to recognise the jurisdiction of this court. I have no question to ask, but I reserve the right to make a statement in a minute when the evidence is all given, if I choose.'[30]

At his trial in December 1928, Healy denied he was 'on the run' for shooting at detectives, but instead for the attacks on the garda stations in 1926. He said detectives raided his house and threatened to murder him, and the detective who issued the threat lived up to his reputation and was currently under arrest for murder (a reference to the Detective Cronin case). Healy put it to Detective Garda Cronin that both he (Cronin) and Detective Barrett searched a Mrs Flynn's house with their guns drawn, hunting for him and asked, 'did you or Barrett then threaten to blow my other eye out?' Cronin replied, 'No fear; I never did.' Healy was convicted of shooting at Detectives O'Donnell and Barrett and possession of arms and sentenced to five years imprisonment.[31]

On the night of 4 November 1927, a team of detectives led by Detective Sergeant Mark Byrne[32] arrested leading IRA men Sean Russell (39) (later IRA chief of staff) of North Strand and Michael Price (31) from Killarney Parade. On being searched they found some highly incriminating documents firmly linking them to the IRA. On Russell, they found a document headed 'Óglaigh na hÉireann, No. 1 Area, Belfast', dated 29 October 1927, giving an account of weapons and equipment from 'Q.M., No. 1'. Other documents listed their arsenal as including one Thompson machine-gun, 113 rifles of various makes, eighty assorted revolvers, twenty-four Parabellums along with grenades, detonators and a staggering 220,000 rounds of ammunition.

On Price they found a prayer book in which were written the registered numbers of three cars belonging to detectives in Pearse Street. Both men were charged under the Treasonable Offences Act and Superintendent Ennis told the court that Russell was one of those who recently escaped from Mountjoy Prison. Remarkably both were acquitted by a jury at their trial the following July.[33] This was a common occurrence at the time where juries in the face of the most overwhelming evidence regularly acquitted IRA members, either through fear or perhaps sympathy with them. It would, in time, result in the introduction of non-jury courts both military and civil for dealing with republican extremists.

The long-standing IRA policy of having their members refuse 'to recognise the court' dates from an instruction issued in January 1928. It was entitled 'General Order No. 24 – As revised by General Army Convention, November 1927.' It stipulated how IRA volunteers should behave in various circumstances including when charged before the courts or being arrested and interrogated. As regards charges before the courts it read:

> A Volunteer charged in the so-called 'Northern Ireland' or 'Free State' courts with acts duly authorised by the competent Officers of Óglaigh na hÉireann shall, in all cases:
>
> (a) Refuse to plead in such courts
> (b) Refuse to pay any fine imposed
> (c) Refuse to give bail or any undertaking as to his future behaviour, as a condition of release or escape of punishment.

> Maximum penalty for breach of these orders shall be 'Dismissal with ignominy from the Army'.

There were exceptions for those charged with an act which might lead to the death penalty or when permitted by General Headquarters. In addition, even when not permitted to have legal representation, they were allowed to cross-examine witnesses or make a statement to the court.[34] When arrested volunteers were instructed to act as follows:

> INTERROGATION: If arrested and interrogated a volunteer shall:
> (a) Refuse to answer any questions put to him
> (b) Refuse to make or sign any statement.
> (c) Refuse to give any account of his movements, activities or associates.[35]

In time detectives would care little whether suspects answered questions or not as the introduction of Article 2A in 1931 and later section 52 of the Offences Against the State Act in 1939 made it an offence not to answer police questions or fail to give an account of their movements and invariably led to a prison sentence.

On 28 January 1928, a highly agitated President Cosgrave summoned Commissioner O'Duffy and Special Branch chief David Neligan to his office. He received word of a shooting incident in Dartry in Dublin where an IRA operative named Timothy Coughlan was killed. There was wild speculation that this was either an IRA vendetta or perhaps Special Branch men were taking the law into their own hands. Cosgrave assumed that Special Branch officers were involved and demanded an explanation. Neligan explained that the shooting was actually carried out by a Special Branch agent inside the IRA named Seán Harling.[36]

Harling was feeding Special Branch information about IRA activities but his cover was blown, and he was eventually provided with a police escort every day. He was even issued with a personal firearm. After being dropped home at Woodpark Lodge on Dartry Road on the evening of 28 January, he became suspicious of two men he spotted approaching his home with their hands in their pockets. He hid behind a wall with his gun drawn. When one of the men opened fire on him, he returned fire, killing Coughlan (one of Kevin O'Higgins' assassins, though it was not known at the time). When Cosgrave heard the details, he immediately brightened up and said, 'do you mean we have nothing to hide?'

'Not a thing' replied Neligan.

'Splendid', said Cosgrave, 'in that case we'll have an enquiry.'[37]

The cabinet agreed on 10 February and set up a tribunal consisting of three District Justices, George P. Cussen (Chairman), Seán Troy and Cyril J. Beatty. As expected, the gardaí were fully exonerated by the enquiry which found,

> The Tribunal is satisfied that Timothy Coughlan referred to in the Order of the Minister for Justice dated the 15th day of February, 1928, was killed by a bullet fired by Seán Harling from a Webley .45 revolver and that Seán Harling fired the shot on an occasion when he was being attacked by Timothy Coughlan and another man, and that his shot was fired by Harling, after shots had been fired at him, with intent to kill, by Timothy Coughlan.[38]

Afterwards, Harling wisely departed for the USA with assistance from the secret service fund.[39] However, according to a book by Noel Redican, (a nephew of Harling's wife) he actually went to Canada but after about a year moved to London, before eventually returning to Dublin. After several rejections he finally got a job in the civil service in June 1928, first as a low-paid messenger and in 1941 as a clerical officer. He retired on a small pension in 1966 and set up a sweet factory in a garage at the back of his house. Surprisingly, even though he was informing on the IRA and killed one member, he was never molested subsequently by them. He died on 20 August 1977.[40]

There had always been a steady stream of informers inside the IRA willing to give information to the police and the same is true of the criminal underworld. The reasons for informing were myriad. Usually, very little effort was required to recruit such informers – in police jargon referred to as 'agents', 'touts', or 'sources'. It could simply result from a detective's personal friendship with an IRA man, perhaps from knowing each other during their schooldays or on the sports field. A suspect, on being caught committing a minor offence would sometimes offer someone higher up in the food chain on condition his own offence was overlooked. This occasionally resulted in a build-up of trust between both parties. He might have run up debts from a gambling or alcohol addiction and would offer information for a fee. Other agents could be developed where an IRA member had feelings of guilt about what he was involved in and wanted to salve his conscience. Then there were the 'walk-ins'. An agent, who for whatever reason becomes disenchanted with the movement, would approach a policeman he knew and trusted with an offer of information.

In the late-nineteenth century, Inspector John Mallon of the G Division in the DMP was of the view that 'a good deal of that kind of patriotism can be bought for a five-pound note in this poor country.'[41] In a surprising number of cases, money was not a motivating factor. Payments were made from the Secret Service fund, however, where an agent supplied a stream of quality information. The amount and frequency of payments depended on the quality and regularity of the information received. It was a tricky area for the handler because if it became known who was supplying the intelligence it could, and sometimes did, have fatal consequences for the agent. The rules have changed in recent years but in those days a detective kept the identity of the agent secret, and he did not even have to reveal it to his superiors.

The level of quality information reaching the gardaí from inside the IRA was staggering. For example, a garda report in 1931 headed 'Return of the Personnel of Staffs of The Irregular Organisation Showing Approximate Numbers of Rank and File' gave details of the names and ranks of each of the IRA officers in practically every town and village in Ireland. In the Dublin area, it was broken down into members of 'General Headquarters Staff' which included Maurice Twomey as Chief of Staff and Seán MacBride as Adjutant General. It went on to give lists of names of officers including their ranks in the different battalions in the Dublin Brigade. It even listed the officers in each company including the name and address of each O.C., Adjutant and I.O. (Intelligence Officer) attached to each. It went on to catalogue each county in alphabetical order with similar lists.[42]

At 5a.m. on 11 November 1928 (Poppy Day), several explosions were heard around Dublin city. Bombs exploded at the statues of King William III in College Green, King George II in St Stephen's Green and the memorial fountain to King Edward VII in Herbert Park, Ballsbridge, causing minor damage at each location. In College Green a detective on special protection duty challenged two men acting suspiciously near the King William III statue shortly before the explosion. The men ran off and one of them turned and fired two shots at the detective who himself returned fire. They made good their escape.[43]

In 1925, the female IRA (Cumann na mBan) introduced their own flower symbol to honour the Republican dead as an alternative to the poppy. The flower they chose was the lily and thus, the tradition of the Easter Lily was born. The lily contained the colours green, white and orange (same as the Irish tricolour). For nearly a century the Easter Lily has become the must-have lapel badge of honour to be worn by Sinn Féin/IRA supporters around Easter, to celebrate the 1916 Rising.[44]

IRA suspects made repeated allegations to Fianna Fáil TDs (erstwhile colleagues who departed the IRA fold to form a new party under de Valera) alleging assaults and harassment by the Special Branch. Civil actions in the courts were also used in an attempt to keep the Branch men off their backs. On 7 November 1928, Seán Lemass, then a Fianna Fáil TD for Dublin City South (who would become Taoiseach in 1959), asked the Minister for Justice Fitzgerald-Kenney a series of questions alleging ill-treatment of suspects by the Special Branch in Leitrim. He said detectives visited the home of Thomas Shanley in Dromod on 15 October and threatened him with violence. There was a raid on the house the previous week and this was the reason for the second visit by Detective McCarthy. McCarthy threatened Shanley that 'if he published any more about it, he would kick him about the street and leave him in a way that would leave him unable to do any more writing, and warned him not to be seen outside his own door.' The minister replied there was no foundation to the allegation, adding that when the district officer investigating the allegation called to see Mr Shanley, he refused to make a statement or to cooperate.

On 17 April 1929, Thomas Mullins, Fianna Fáil TD for Cork West raised a question about the activities of a detective from Bandon. Mullins alleged that the detectives called to a premises masquerading as a member of the IRA. He alleged a series of raids by what he termed a 'gang of terrorists described as CID', who were using 'a systematic system of persecution in the village of Drimoleague.' On 28 March, Detective Garda Lavin called to the home of Andrew O'Donovan, chairman of the local Fianna Fáil cumann, in Drimoleague, County Cork. The detective claimed his name was Seán McGuiness and that he was chief organiser of the IRA. He handed them a letter which said that the bearer was Seán McGuiness, ex-TD, organiser-in-chief for Munster for the Irish Republican Army. It requested that he be given every facility. The bogus McGuiness asked O'Donovan for the names of six local men to form an IRA company.

It is not clear if Lavin was acting on instructions or on his own initiative, but this was an extremely foolhardy enterprise. In rural Ireland, strangers were treated with suspicion until their bona fides were established. Detectives would be quickly recognised by many IRA men. The ruse did not last long and on his second visit Lavin was recognised as a detective by an associate of O'Donovan who knew the real Seán McGuiness. Needless to say, Lavin's cover was blown. Mullins complained to the minister about sending out these 'agents-provocateur'. He added that on Easter Monday, Lavin, along with five other detectives, returned with a search order under the Firearms Act and he asked if this warrant authorised the tearing up of floors, breaking partitions and damaging ceilings. He said the detectives also raided a second house where they broke a window, tore wallpaper, broke the floor and raised all the stones on the footpath leading to the hall. He named the search party as including Detectives Burke and Reynolds of Macroom and Detective Kenny stationed in Bandon. Mr Fitzgerald-Kenney agreed that the searches occurred and complimented the detectives saying that while no arms had been found, 'a very great deal of interesting information' was gleaned.[45]

The incessant campaign against the IRA was frequently written about in disparaging terms in the Sinn Féin newspaper *An Phoblacht*. An issue published on 18 May 1929 in a piece headed 'CID Campaign Continues – New Cat and Mouse Phase', gave an account of the arrests of 'well known Republicans' who held 'distinguished records in the IRA during the Anglo-Irish War.' It named one of those arrested as Claude O'Loughlin [a member of the IRA's Dublin Brigade] whose home was searched at 6 p.m. on Sunday 5 May. The article claimed that the detectives had no warrant but insisted on searching nevertheless. When they could not find what they were looking for they asked 'if the dog licence had been paid.' The detectives returned at 6 a.m. on 11 May and this time arrested O'Loughlin and lodged him in the Bridewell along with three other suspects. The article added that there were about thirty detectives around the Bridewell and implied they were there to get a good look at the prisoners so they would know them again. This was probably true. Remarkably for *An Phoblacht*, the article said the prisoners were treated very courteously, noting that 'a feature of these arrests was the marked civility of the CID towards the prisoners.'[46]

Elsewhere in the paper they listed a long series of allegations against the CID including repeated arrests of republicans without charge, detention without food or exercise and numerous assaults. In one case, they claimed that a number of detectives, two of whom they named as Keyes and Larkin, entered the home of 70-year-old Patrick Burke in Cooraclare in County Clare. Burke was in bed while Mrs Burke and Pat Cahill were sitting by the fire. Keyes allegedly struck Cahill with a clenched fist, after which both Keyes and Larkin rushed into Burke's bedroom. Keyes held him down while Larkin repeatedly beat him about the head and shoulders leaving him bruised and bloodied. He was then dragged outside in the bitter cold and left standing for up to an hour. Keyes allegedly told Burke, 'I admit we are worse than the Black and Tans, but we must do something for our pound a day.'[47]

The IRA was now embarking on a sustained campaign of intimidation against jurors and witnesses, which included murders, shootings, threats, domiciliary visits by masked and armed men, kidnappings, assaults and beatings.[48] On 23 January 1929, two men called to the home of John White in Ashdale Road in Terenure. He was the jury foreman in a case the previous December where four men were tried for tearing down the Union flag from the offices of the Royal Insurance Company in Dame Street, Dublin on Armistice Day. When he answered the door one of the men asked for him by name. After White confirmed his name, the man drew a revolver and shot him in the stomach at point blank range. The attackers ran off and White collapsed on the doorstep where his wife found him groaning. He was seriously wounded but survived.[49] White, in his mid-fifties, had a business as a wholesale jeweller in Dame Street.

The four men charged with the flag incident were Patrick Stapleton, Patrick Fox, James Lyons and John Kinsella. When they refused to speak in court, they were found to be mute of malice by the jury. On 10 December, after a trial, the jury acquitted Patrick Fox and found the other three guilty of unlawful assembly. Mr Justice Sullivan ordered the latter three to be discharged saying they had been in custody since 24 August and that four months' imprisonment was adequate punishment for the offence.[50]

Albert Armstrong of 14 Madison Road, Kilmainham was an important witness in the same case and gave evidence against the men. He was

29 years of age and worked as an insurance inspector. On 20 February 1929, he told his family he was going to put his car into the garage at the rear of the house. A few minutes later his father heard noise and dogs barking and went out to investigate. His son's car was in the garage with the lights on and the engine running. He found Albert lying wounded and moaning saying, 'they have shot me, send for the ambulance.' Mr Armstrong and his other son Henry brought Albert into the house. He was removed to Dr Steeven's Hospital by ambulance but died there at 8.30 p.m. Inspector Curry found a spent bullet in the garage while Detective Sergeant Mooney found two other bullets embedded in the wall. Though nine men were arrested and questioned about the shooting, all were released without charge. No one was ever convicted of the crime.[51]

Armstrong earlier visited Robert Briscoe, a Fianna Fáil TD, at his business premises in 9 Aston Quay in Dublin. He knew Briscoe well and the men were on friendly terms. Armstrong informed him he was receiving police protection and sought Briscoe's advice on the matter. He did not expect he would be shot but feared he might perhaps be kidnapped. One of the accused in the flags case, John Kinsella, worked as Briscoe's election agent in the past. The TD undertook to speak to him about the matter. Three days later Kinsella came into the shop and Briscoe asked him if there was any danger to Armstrong. Kinsella replied he 'had done his four months' and 'the matter was over as far as he was concerned'. Investigating detectives were satisfied that the four accused in the flags case were not involved in the murder and thought it likely it was committed without their knowledge.[52]

Because of these ongoing threats and intimidation there was a marked reluctance by jurors to convict IRA men, even in the face of overwhelming evidence. In response, the government introduced the Jury's Protection Bill which included a prohibition on the publication of the names of jurors (thus making it difficult to intimidate them) and this did not please the IRA. On 5 May, a public meeting was held in Cathedral Street to protest against these new measures. Maud Gonne MacBride, whose son Seán was in custody at the time, made a fiery speech which included the words:

> The Juries Protection Bill is not being got up [*sic*] for the protection of jurymen. It is a British Coercion Bill set up for the purpose of indefinitely imprisoning the political opponents of the Free State government, under which people can be arrested and sent to prison without trial. Up to reading it I had an open mind as to who shot White and Armstrong, but since I read it, I have no doubt they were shot by the secret detectives of the Free State Government.

However, Detective Inspector McGloin and Detective Sergeant P. J. Kirwan were in the crowd carefully noting what she said. On 12 May, Detective Sergeant Byrne went to her home with an arrest warrant and took her to the Bridewell Station and charged her with making a seditious speech on 5 May.[53] She was tried in the Central Criminal Court in December but, not surprisingly, was found not guilty by a jury.[54]

The frequency of these 'not guilty' verdicts caused understandable chagrin among the embattled Special Branch men as well as Commissioner O'Duffy. Even with massive amounts of intelligence from IRA informers, which gave them chapter and verse on the identities, the ranks held by individual members as well as their activities, it was practically impossible to obtain convictions in the ordinary civil courts. Jurors were living in fear of the consequences and, apart from rare exceptions, were unwilling to convict, particularly after the wounding of John White and the murder of Albert Armstrong. However, changes were on the way. O'Duffy was about to submit a vigorous submission to the government on this issue which would lead to a drastic strengthening of the law. Life was about to become easier for the detectives - and a torrid time was ahead for members of the IRA.

Chapter 4

THE IRA UP THE ANTE, 1929-1932

One should reproach a man who is violent in order to ruin things, not one who is so in order to set them aright.

Machiavelli.

The late-1920s saw a resurgence of an increasingly confident IRA who did not hesitate to resist violently when confronted by the Garda Síochána. In the three-year period from 1929 to 1932, three members of the force were killed, two of them specifically targeted for death. County Clare was then a hotbed of IRA activity particularly under the leadership of Thomas Joseph (T.J.) Ryan, a farmer from Cranny. There was a strong tradition of militant republicanism in the county dating back to the War of Independence ten years earlier. Between 1919 and 1922, the Clare IRA killed thirty-two RIC men. This included six in one ambush at Rineen in September 1920 and five others in a second ambush near Sixmilebridge in January 1921.[1] There was intense Special Branch activity in the county and an increase in their numbers well above the national average. All leading IRA figures in Clare were under almost continuous surveillance and tension between the two sides was high, leading to serious clashes. Though the Branch had well-placed informers inside the movement, they had no advance knowledge of an IRA murder plot then in preparation. The IRA reasoned that a couple of dead Special Branch officers might scare them off or at least make them retreat.

On 11 June 1929, Detective Garda Timothy (Tadhg) O'Sullivan (6670)[2] was killed by a booby-trap bomb in Tullycrine, County Clare. Gardaí were lured to the area after receiving an anonymous letter which read:

> I found a box of ammunition and papers in a butt of hay in the haggard. The times are so dangerous I was afraid to keep it near the place. I threw it inside the ditch at Lahiff Cross in Ardill's meadow yesterday. I want you to take it away. I do not want to get into trouble with people around here. [Signed] Farmer.

Detectives and gardaí carried out a search and Detective Garda John O'Driscoll found the box and rather unwisely, put it on his bicycle and cycled off with it. While on the road to Kilrush, he met Detective Garda O'Sullivan and Garda Cusack. They discussed the box, which they decided to open, taking precautions. They fastened a piece of wire to it and concealed themselves behind a nearby hut. They pulled on the wire, but nothing happened except the box fell on its side. O'Sullivan remarked that there could not be much inside and caught it in both hands and tried to lift the lid. As he pulled on the lid the box exploded killing him instantly and injuring O'Driscoll and Cusack. At the funeral in his native Skibbereen, General O'Duffy gave a stirring oration where he spoke of O'Sullivan's service in the Irish Volunteers and in the National Army after the truce.[3]

The IRA could not have been certain who would respond to the anonymous letter which was addressed to Detective Garda O'Driscoll. O'Sullivan's parents were later refused compensation in the Circuit Court on the basis that it was only by chance that he happened to be in O'Driscoll's company when the box was opened. The judge, therefore, found there had been no malice against O'Sullivan. However, on 10 February 1930, the government decided to pay the family compensation out of the Contingency Fund.[4]

O'Driscoll, who was 27 years of age, was later awarded £400 at Ennis Circuit Court. Still recovering from his injuries, he hobbled into court with the aid of walking sticks. He told the court that since June 1928, his main duty was the questioning and searching of suspects for arms and documents and he was sure those activities had aroused ill-will against him.[5]

T.J. Ryan was, of course, the Special Branch's number one suspect for organising this murder. Shortly afterwards, Special Branch chief David Neligan was tipped off about a plot among detectives in Clare who were planning to take drastic action against Ryan. They had apparently acquired a boat and intended to kidnap Ryan and bring him on a one-way trip out to the Atlantic. Neligan quickly put a stop to the scheme.[6]

Local Branch men were determined, however, to keep Ryan under close scrutiny and make his life as miserable as possible. This intense attention was none too subtle and led to local TD and Fianna Fáil leader Eamon de Valera making a complaint in the Dáil on 31 July 1929. He said he had seen the marks of the beating and kicking that Ryan had received. He produced a copy of a letter he wrote to President Cosgrave which he read into the record. It is worth quoting in full as it paints a vivid picture of the tensions between the IRA and detectives in Clare at the time:

> To the President of the Executive Council.
> I wish to draw your attention personally to the following:
>
> > (1) On June 16th last, on his way from Bodenstown with five companions, Mr. T. J. Ryan, of Cranny, Kilrush, County Clare, was held up on the road between Clarecastle and Ennis by two members of the Detective Division, ordered to leave the car, and searched. On refusing to account for his movements (he had already been held up three times on the journey from Sallins), Mr. Ryan was pushed against a wall, threatened, and struck repeatedly on the stomach and chest. He was then ordered into the car, and, as he was entering, one of the detectives rushed at him and kicked him. When in the car he was again assaulted, one detective, taking hold of the iron starting

handle of the car, struck him with it on the legs, severely wounding him on the shin. The other detective rushed at him and struck him with his fist on the right eye, blackening it. Before he was let go threats of all sorts were made by the detectives, including threats to murder Mr. Ryan. He was treated for his injuries to his stomach, leg and eye by Doctors McAuliffe and O'Dea.

(2) On July 1st, Mr Ryan's house was raided, and a watch has been kept since by detectives day and night. No reason was given to Mr Ryan, either for the raids or for the constant surveillance to which he has been subjected.

(3) On Sunday, July 7th, about 3am Mr Ryan was called from the window of his bedroom and ordered to get up. He got up and opened the door. He was then pulled outside the house by two detectives, and pushed into an adjoining yard. He was repeatedly struck on the face and body, one of the assailants, with a drawn revolver, struck him with it on the body. The second lashed him with what appeared to be a belt on the body and legs. He was maltreated like this for some minutes before he was allowed back to his house.

(4) On entering, he went to the bedroom of his mother, who is old and an invalid. He was ordered by the detectives to get out of the room or he would be riddled with bullets.

(5) He then went to his own room and returned to bed. Some time later he was again ordered by a detective from the window to get up. When he opened the door, he was once more beaten and kicked. He was then allowed back to bed.

(6) He got up about seven or eight o'clock. It would appear that the detectives on watch had meanwhile been changed. Whilst preparing breakfast (he resides alone with his mother), he was again struck on the face by a detective. On saying that he would take legal proceedings, the second detective said he saw no assault.

(7) Mr Ryan next went out to milk his cows; he was again struck several times, knocked down, punched generally on the body and

stomach. This was repeated a number of times whilst he was endeavouring to milk the cows. His ears and hair were pulled, until finally he had to abandon the milking. The milking stool was thrown at him as he left. He was dazed with the beating and went to bed.

(8) About noon he was again ordered to get up. When he did not obey, the window of his bedroom was raised, and an attempt was made by one of the detectives to get in by it. Being unable to do so, this detective and his companion burst in the door which was on the latch. The two detectives rushed into Mr. Ryan's bedroom; they pulled him out of bed, struck him, threw him down and kicked him. He went back to bed, but was pulled out again and beaten and thrown on the floor. This happened three or four times. Whilst in bed he was throttled by one of the detectives, the other holding his hands. When lying on his back in the bed also they knelt on his stomach. These assaults were accompanied by abusive and threatening language. All this took place, roughly, between 12 and 1 o'clock. Mr Ryan's mother was witness to his being beaten in the bedroom.

Having been told of the assaults on Mr. Ryan, I went to Clare on Monday last; saw Mr. Ryan in his home, and learned from him the above details. As I was approaching Mr. Ryan's house I saw a man beside the house, obviously on duty. He accosted me as I was about to enter, asking my name, which I gave. When I entered, he followed; and when Mr. Ryan invited me into his bedroom, he accompanied us and was present in the bedroom whilst I took notes of Mr. Ryan's statements. On leaving, I asked this man his name. He showed me his police card and said his name was Mulkeen. When I reached the road, on leaving Mr. Ryan's house, two men with bicycles, whom I believed to be detectives, signalled me to stop. I was recognised and let pass.

Mr Ryan bears on his person marks of the ill-treatment he has received. One of his eyes is black and his shin has medical dressings on it, which I did not let him remove. He is being attended by Dr. O'Dea of Kildysart. He has also been visited by the local curate,

> Father Austin – both of whom can give evidence of Mr. Ryan's condition and of the condition of his invalid mother.
>
> The attention of the Minister for Justice has been called more than once to the conduct of some members of the Detective Force in West Clare. He was furnished with affidavits made by citizens who were assaulted by detectives who were named, and was called upon by the Clare Teachtai and by the Clare County Council to hold a public enquiry into the charges made; but he refused to hold an investigation or to take any disciplinary action. His attitude has been such as would encourage unruly members of the detective force to believe that their assaults on unarmed citizens had the approval of the Executive Council.
>
> May I ask why Mr. Ryan is kept virtually a prisoner in his own home; what legal authority there is for it; and whether you will have an enquiry held into the conduct of the Guards who have assaulted Mr. Ryan?
>
> (Signed) EAMON DE VALERA.

Replying, Mr Fitzgerald-Kenney (no doubt with a straight face and with his tongue firmly in his cheek) said that he had carried out enquiries into the allegations and that the gardaí concerned emphatically denied them. He added that on 7 July, while Mr Ryan was milking one his cows in the presence of the police on duty, he was knocked down by the cow and received the black eye as a result of this. Regarding the police surveillance on him, he said that 'Mr Ryan was well known as the leader of those people in West Clare who desire to upset the established form of government by violence and having regard to the nature of this conspiracy it was essential for the preservation of the public peace that Mr. Ryan's movements should be watched by the police and they had instructions to do so.' In the debate that followed Fianna Fáil deputies described the account of being kicked by a cow as a 'cock and bull story'.[7]

In January 1930, Ryan swore an affidavit giving some more details of his 'persecution by the Free State government.' He complained that for four months the police were a permanent presence in his life. They actually occupied his home where they:

> ...seat themselves on the kitchen table or occupy the chairs by the fireside. Frequently the police obtain books from a bookshelf and pass the hours by reading them and act generally as if the house belonged to them. Frequently the police amuse themselves within the house by whistling the latest music hall ditties and prancing with their feet in accompaniment.

Later he added, 'on a few occasions the police heaped turf on the fire. On one occasion I protested but without result until I quenched the fire. One night in December my mother was ordered away from the fire by a policeman to make room for themselves.' When he left the house, the police were always walking with him:

> On numerous occasions while being thus escorted I have been subjected to abusive and jibing comments by the police together with frequent murder threats. Those murder threats varied from poisoning to strychnine, boring holes through my body with bullets and burying me in a disused quarry, to tying me to a motor and dragging me along the public road.[8]

Assuming the allegations made by de Valera and Ryan were true (they probably were), it demonstrates the poisonous animosity that existed between detectives and IRA men in Clare at that time. The detectives were determined to make life as miserable as possible for them, especially their commander T.J. Ryan, whom they blamed for organising the recent murder of their colleague Detective O'Sullivan with a booby-trap bomb. There is no doubt that the government turned a 'blind eye' to what was going on but also recognised that the detectives' unorthodox tactics kept a firm lid on IRA violence in that county and elsewhere.

Elsewhere, IRA men resorted to the courts to pursue their claims of assaults and harassment against the gardaí. In January 1931, 32-year-old Patrick Fennell of Tullycrine, West Clare, sued two gardaí, William English and John Sands of Kilmihil Station for £40 damages for an alleged assault. The action was heard before Judge McElligot at Kilrush Circuit Court. Fennell alleged that on the night of 2 August 1930, he was stopped by English and Sands who asked him his name and address which he provided. He said Garda English was under the influence of drink. When they asked him where he was coming from, he replied, 'That is my business. I won't tell you.' He said they searched him and that Garda English kicked him in the back several times and he received one kick in the knee for which he was treated by a doctor. Both gardaí denied any assault, saying they stopped and searched him but that he refused to answer any questions. Finding nothing incriminating on him, they told him to go home.[9]

An article referring to the case appeared in the *Clare Champion* on 24 January 1931, quoting remarks made by Judge McElligot during the hearing. The judge said, 'I also believe that for one moment, English forgot himself and gave Fennell what he probably richly deserved – a kick – but unfortunately he did not give it to him in the right place.'

He added that as a judge in County Clare, he was aware of an atmosphere of intense hostility to the gardaí and that the action by the plaintiff reeked of ill-will. He said there was no foundation to the suggestion that English was under the influence of drink. He concluded that English used a degree of unnecessary violence under circumstances of extreme provocation. He did not believe, as alleged by the plaintiff, that he was kicked for hours by English and Sands. He gave a small decree of £4: 4: 0 against English and dismissed the claim against Sands. He added that he hoped it would not militate against English's character 'in the honourable force of which he is an honourable member.'[10]

In December 1929, barristers acting for leading IRA member George Gilmore (then OC of Dublin Brigade and unusually for an IRA man, a Protestant), applied to have summonses issued against two Special

Branch detectives Albert Jackson and Cornelius Coughlan and one uniform garda Thomas McElroy. He alleged that at 9 p.m. on 9 November, as he was about to board a tram in Westmoreland Street, he was seized by three detectives, knocked down on the road and kicked. He was taken to Pearse Street Station where he received a blow which knocked him unconscious. The following night, he claimed, he was seized by detectives in Harcourt Street and dragged across Camden Row to Camden Street where a crowd gathered around him. He said one detective said to another, 'pull out your gun and shoot him first if there is any chance of his escaping.' He received a blow to the back of the head which left him dazed. He was dragged along and received several more blows which rendered him unconscious. When he came around, he found himself lying on grass in the precincts of Kevin Street Station and was wet. He was put in a cell and where he was kept until his release at 1 a.m. He went to Mercer's Hospital where his injuries were treated. He said no charges were preferred against him on either occasion.

At the preliminary hearing on 20 December, defence counsel Mr J. Fitzgerald KC, asked Gilmore if he was the officer commanding the Dublin Brigade of the IRA. He replied he did not think that was a question he should be called on to answer. Fitzgerald said, 'I want to show that you are a most dangerous man, and a man who was likely to have firearms, and that it was for this purpose you were detained.' Gilmore declined to answer on the grounds he might incriminate himself. He admitted to being in charge of a party of men who rescued nineteen prisoners from Mountjoy Prison on 27 November 1925. He was convicted for this offence. He also admitted he was convicted of assault on Detective Jackson on 11 November 1928 but said Jackson ran at him with a revolver and he (Gilmore) broke a stick on his head. The three gardaí were returned for trial on charges of assault against Gilmore but on 31 January 1930 all were acquitted after a trial in the Dublin Circuit Court.[11]

In October 1931, John M. Fleming of Kilcummin near Killarney, County Kerry, took a civil action against Detective Garda David Tormey[12] of Killarney Garda Station for alleged assault. He alleged that Tormey and Garda Treacy, both armed with rifles, entered his home on 15 August stating they were there to search for arms. Fleming asked Tormey to show him the warrant and turned to get his glasses. Tormey asked his brother Thomas, who was sitting nearby, for his name and his brother replied, 'you know it well.' Tormey pulled away Thomas' chair knocking him to the ground. Fleming claimed that when he protested, Tormey struck him in the jaw. They searched the house and when completed Tormey said to him, 'I hope you won't resent the stroke I gave you.' He said that as a result of the blow his jaw was sore, his teeth were loose and he was deaf for a week afterwards. Detective Tormey told the court he and Treacy had entered the house with the warrant which he read out quite distinctly. He said Fleming replied he would not let anyone search the house and got up and made a grab for his rifle. He said he stepped back and gripping the rifle in both hands pushed Fleming back with it. He denied punching Fleming in the jaw or saying 'I hope you won't resent the stroke I gave you.' He said he had nothing to do with his brother Thomas and did not see him on the floor.[13]

On 28 October Tormey was ordered to pay Fleming five guineas for the assault.[14] In the Dáil on 5 November Mr P. J. Little TD, asked the Minister for Justice, Mr Fitzgerald-Kenney, if he proposed to dismiss Detective Tormey. The Minister, (clearly a man of few words), replied, 'The answer is in the negative.' Little was not happy with the reply and pressed the minister further asking him if he would direct the attention of the Attorney General to the evidence in the case with a view to an action for perjury against Tormey. The minister replied, 'No.' Little then asked if the minister was prepared to condone perjury when committed by a member of the Civic Guard. Again, the reply was, 'No'.[15]

On Monday 13 October 1930, Special Branch detectives stumbled across a bizarre IRA plot that could have caused serious embarrassment to the government. They visited a yard belonging to the Skin and Fat

Stores at 17 Chapel Lane, Dublin, owned by Matthew Stafford of 55 St Patrick's Road, Drumcondra. They described him as an 'extremist' and became curious about a large box sitting in a donkey cart in the yard. On examining it they found that it was designed to imprison a man. It had a hole on top for his head and included chains and padlocks so that the intended target could not easily be freed. The British admiral, Earl Jellicoe, then president of the British Legion, planned to visit Dublin that month. The plot was to kidnap Jellicoe and imprison him in the box with a bag over his head. The box was screwed to the donkey cart which was then to be driven to O'Connell Street and at a strategic moment the bag would be pulled from his head to make him the subject of ridicule. There were to be placards with the words 'Earl Jellyfish' ready to be placed on the side of the box. The timely intervention by the detectives ensured the plan could not be put into effect.

A sarcastic article in *An Phoblacht* afterwards read, 'the 'land admiral' Jellicoe, the warrior who lost the battle of Jutland and won it subsequently in the British press, would now be protected by Dublin Castle detectives: 'Tommies in plain clothes' who resented having to give up their Sunday.' Numbers of IRA men assembled at Amiens Street Station and the Mansion House as part of the kidnap plot but due to the large numbers of detectives detailed to protect Jellicoe, the plan never had a realistic chance of success and the visit went ahead without incident.[16]

On 30 January 1931, IRA man Patrick Carroll (27), described as an 'IRA captain', of 36 Anner Road, Kilmainham, was shot dead by the IRA at Captain's Lane in Crumlin, Dublin, for giving information to the police.[17] At his funeral in Glasnevin cemetery two detectives were attacked by a hostile mob that booed and jeered them. They were pelted with stones and one detective drew his revolver to no effect. He was grabbed around the arms by a woman and he passed the weapon to a colleague and they were then forced to retreat under a hail of stones.[18] At the inquest Superintendent Peter Ennis confirmed that Carroll was a police agent.[19] No one was ever charged or convicted of the murder. Later the Carroll family were given an ex-gratia payment of £100 at the recommendation of Commissioner O'Duffy though he was annoyed by their attitude as they had, 'embarrassed the police considerably by their venomous attacks... and that they were directly responsible for our having to expose the fact that deceased was an agent.'[20] It is not explained why they had to reveal that Carroll was a police agent which is considered a bad practice. The normal routine would be to neither confirm nor deny that someone was working for the police.

Intense pressure was maintained on the IRA with Special Branch activity continuing throughout the state. This resulted in a sharp increase in charges for IRA membership and illegal drilling. In Tipperary, 28-year-old Superintendent John Curtin (783) was very active against the movement and was instrumental in bringing about many arrests and subsequent charges. A native of Meelin, Newmarket, County Cork, he was active in the IRA during the War of Independence. In February 1931, he oversaw a case against four men who were charged with armed drilling, taking part in an illegal military operation, and setting fire to the home of Michael Kelly in Cappawhite on 30 January. One witness, James Ryan, made a statement implicating some of the accused in drilling but in court he rowed back on this, claiming the information was false and forced. He said he was taken out of the house and into a barn by four detectives where he was beaten with a rifle by Detective Kelly. He said he refused to give them information and added, 'when they had enough kicked on me, they left me.'

Another witness, Timothy Buckley, said he was arrested by detectives after being held up on his bicycle on the road. They brought him to an outhouse where they hit him three or four 'pucks' of a revolver in the stomach. He was taken to Tipperary barracks where he made a statement after being 'knocked about a bit' by Superintendent Curtin. When asked what did the 'knocking about' consist of, he replied that Curtin told him if he did not tell the truth, 'he would paste me against the wall.' When pressed further he agreed he was not 'pasted' against the wall but made a statement as he was in a state of fear and panic. He denied the truth of the statements. They were all acquitted by the jury and discharged.[21]

Curtin was driving to his home, Friarsfield House near Tipperary town on the night of 21 March 1931, after carrying out late night inspections. The gates leading to his home were normally left open but on approaching, he found the left-hand gate was closed. As he stopped to open it he was shot by gunmen concealed nearby. He was struck by five bullets and died a short time later. Scorching on his clothing showed that several bullets were fired from point blank range.[22]

Shortly afterwards, a poster appeared in Tipperary issued by Cumann na mBan which read, 'the men of Tipperary, true to the traditions of their forefathers, proud of the lead they gave in 1919, in an ambush have shown that they will not allow a Free State Superintendent to stand between them and freedom.' Curtin's widow Maureen (nee O'Connor) gave birth to twins on 18 April but neither child survived. She was later awarded £6,000 compensation in Tipperary Circuit Court. She passed away in 1975.[23]

This was the highest-ranking garda and the only superintendent to be murdered since the foundation of the state. The Tipperary county board of the GAA refused to adopt a resolution condemning the murder. To his credit, the chairman, Rev. John Meagher CC, drafted the resolution but he could get no one to propose it apparently on the grounds that it was 'political.' Fr Meagher then intended to resign from the board in disgust but was dissuaded from doing so by the Archbishop of Cashel, Dr Harty.[24] Clearly, the county board were either IRA sympathisers or perhaps just in fear of IRA retaliation if they passed such a resolution.

This was an officially sanctioned IRA murder and was one of the few cases where a member of the force was targeted specifically for his anti IRA activities. It is not clear why they picked on Curtin as he was doing the same as many other superintendents throughout the country. IRA commander Frank Ryan gave an interview which was published in the English edition of the *Daily Express* on 24 August 1931 explaining their rationale for the killing.

> Take the case of Supt. Curtin. As you say, he was shot after he had conducted a prosecution for illegal drilling. But that is not all the story. Supt. Curtin belonged to the Civic Guards, which is supposed to be an unarmed force that does not concern itself with political affairs. Supt. Curtin exceeded his duty. He went out of his way to persecute the IRA. We draw a distinction between members of the Civic Guard and the men of the CID. The Civic Guard have no right to interfere in matters that do not concern them. If they ask for trouble they must not be surprised if they get it.[25]

It resulted in many superintendents and chief superintendents carrying a personal issue of a revolver both on and off duty for many years afterwards.[26] Despite an intensive investigation no one was ever charged or convicted of the crime though information became available that IRA HQ authorised the South Tipperary unit of the movement to carry out the assassination.

On 21 July 1931, four months after the Curtin killing, the body of 24-year-old John Ryan, a witness in one of Curtin's cases, was found shot to death on a roadside at Ayle, midway between Tipperary, Cappawhite and Limerick Junction. A note on the body bore the words, 'Spies and Informers beware. IRA.' He previously received a threatening letter purporting to come from the South Tipperary IRA informing him he had been found guilty of treachery and ordering him to leave Ireland before 17 May. He did not take it seriously. In a drilling prosecution against four men at a court hearing in Tipperary town the previous February, he testified about his own membership of the IRA, providing details of various meetings he attended. Two men called to the house of the farmer for whom he was working just after midnight on 21 July claiming to be detectives and asked for him. He told them he did not know them and asked why they were not accompanied by a local guard. They replied that it was alright as they often took men out like this and gave the names Detective Officers Lavin and Cullen. They brought him away and his body was found some five hours later with seven bullet wounds. Despite intensive searches and enquiries led by Deputy Commissioner Coogan and Chief Superintendent Neligan both murders remained unsolved.[27] 'He was nothing but a traitor', Frank Ryan would tell reporters later.[28]

On 10 June 1931, detectives led by Detective Inspector Mooney and Detective Sergeant Mark Byrne carried out a search of the banks of a stream in the Killakee estate in the Dublin Mountains. Byrne found a hole in the bank and a trap-door covered by undergrowth. On forcing the trap-door open they entered and in a chamber found rifles, small arms, ammunition and a number of documents including four photographs of George Gilmore. The well-constructed chamber was nine feet high at the front, six feet nine at the back, and was eight feet long by nine wide and there were two air pipes on the roof.

Commandant Daniel Stapleton, an Ordnance Officer with the army discovered that a landmine was placed with the intention of detonating when the trap door was opened. He also found four tins of explosives known as 'Paxo' along with other assorted explosives, all of which weighed about 300 pounds. He said one tin of 'Paxo' was sufficient to demolish a three-storey building. They recovered twenty-nine rifles, 4,939 rounds of ammunition, a Lewis gun with two magazines, seventeen assorted pistols and revolvers, four stone (25.4 kilos) of gelignite and fifty hand grenades. The dump was perfectly dry and in 'a wonderful state of preservation.' The Gilmore family lived within yards of the find. Along with the parents, were three sons George, Charles and Henry, all well-known IRA men. George was O.C. of the Dublin Brigade at the time.[29]

On 9 July 1931, George Gilmore was charged in the Dublin District Court with offences under the Treason and Firearms Acts in relation to the find. A lifelong republican activist, he had been 'out' in 1916 and took part in the War of Independence. His brother Charles was charged later while a third brother, Henry, was also sought. George Gilmore told the court, 'I do not plead either guilty or not guilty. It is strange for me to be tried for treason by a court founded on treason.' As he was led from court in custody several women rushed forward and kissed him.[30]

In December 1931, George and his brother Charles Gilmore appeared before the Military Tribunal charged with organising an unlawful military force, possession of firearms and ammunition, and conspiracy to taking part in the organisation of an unlawful military force.[31] When the state concluded their case, both declined to give evidence or to call evidence on their own behalf. George was admonished by the president of the court for referring to the state counsel as the 'crown prosecutor' but he insisted that no insult was intended as he understood the king was still head of state. He said that in his sixteen years in the republican movement he never heard of a trap mine being used to guard a dump adding, 'I have never tried to conceal the fact that I am admittedly hostile to British imperialism and international capitalism.' He was sentenced to five years imprisonment while Charles got three years, but three months later, on 10 March 1932, both brothers were among those released from Arbour Hill prison by the new Fianna Fáil government.[32]

In September 1931, a new political party called Saor Eire (Free Ireland), consisting of left-wing members of the IRA, emerged on the political stage. This short-lived group was set up at a meeting of 150 delegates in Iona Hall in Parnell Square and the main movers included Seán MacBride and Peadar O'Donnell.[33] MacBride declared, '*Saor Eire* has been founded to organise and consolidate the Republic of Ireland on the basis of the possession and administration of the workers and working farmers, of the land, instruments of production, distribution and exchange, and to restore and foster the Irish language and culture.' They adopted a number of resolutions including protesting against the treatment meted out to political prisoners and sending fraternal greetings to the USSR.

The Special Branch kept a close watch on proceedings and at least a dozen detectives were posted in the vicinity of the hall in two cars and three motorcycles, while others kept watch on Saor Eire offices at 44

Parnell Square. They also carried out raids on the homes of some of the party notables including Frank Ryan and Seán Russell (both of whom later became IRA chiefs-of-staff), along with Michael Price and Claude O'Loughlin.[34]

MacBride went to Kerry in the autumn of 1931 to address political meetings and drum up support for Saor Eire and found himself being closely monitored by Special Branch detectives. On one occasion while travelling towards the home of Tom Daly in Firies, his car was stopped by detectives carrying rifles. They were led by Superintendent O'Mahony who (MacBride alleged) threatened that he would be shot unless he left the county at once. He was allowed to continue on his way to Firies, where the detectives took up duty around his lodgings and remained there all night. Over the next few days, squads of heavily armed detectives followed him wherever he went, and they finally arrested him and brought him before Listowel District Court.[35]

He and a number of others were charged with offences including assisting the formation of an organisation purporting to be a military organisation not established as such by law, and unlawful assembly. At the preliminary hearing, evidence was given by Superintendent Dunphy and Detective Officer Donovan of Listowel and other gardaí that they found about 200 men, among them MacBride, drilling on the road to Ballybunion. When they searched the house in which MacBride was staying, they found several documents including the Draft Constitutional Rules of Saor Eire. At the end of a long court sitting, the justice discharged MacBride and a number of others though four were sent forward for trial.[36] Of these, three were convicted in the Military Tribunal in December 1931. They were Patrick O'Callaghan, James Leahy and John M. O'Connor. All were bound to the peace for two years and as O'Callaghan was a teacher, they recommended that he would not lose his job as he could have done under Section 31 of the Constitution (Amendment No. 17) Act, 1931.[37]

On Thursday 17 September, MacBride arrived in Listowel followed by two cars loaded with detectives who waited outside while he visited a solicitor's office. The previous night in the village of Newtownsandes (since renamed Moyvane), three young men named Walsh, Lyons and Finnucane were stopped in their car and arrested by detectives carrying rifles. According to the *Irish Press*, they dragged Walsh along the road by the hair and beat Lyons with rifle-butts. It went on to report on the 'feeling of tense uneasiness' in the area as parties of detectives with rifles and revolvers were continually scouring the countryside in cars night after night.[38]

Further pressure was brought on the IRA and Saor Eire in October 1931, when a pastoral letter signed by Cardinal MacRory along with three archbishops and twenty-four bishops, condemned the 'growing evidence of a campaign of revolution and communism, which, if allowed to run its course unchecked, must end in ruin of Ireland, both soul and body.' It was particularly scathing of *Saor Eire* which it described as 'Bolshevistic and Communistic'.[39] Under pressure from church and state the movement quickly faded away and did not feature in the political landscape again until the late-1960s.

Between 1929 and 1931, Dublin Circuit Court heard several actions against members of Special Branch for damages for assault and false imprisonment. Though the IRA did not accept the legitimacy of the new state, it was not slow in using its institutions when it suited. It was also a useful mechanism to harass Special Branch members in the hope that they would back off – a vain hope indeed. In each of the following examples the state fully backed the Branch men even though adverse findings were made against them.

John Sugrue v Detective Sergeant Mark Byrne and Detective Garda William Donegan.

Sugrue claimed he was arrested at 1.30 a.m. on 26 March 1929, on suspicion of being concerned in the murder of Albert Armstrong who was a witness in an upcoming trial for the shooting of a juror. During his interview in the Bridewell, he refused to answer any questions and was released without charge after forty-six hours. The jury held he was detained for an unreasonable time, and he was awarded £40 and costs.

O'Donoghue v Thomas Rogers.
Rogers arrested O'Donoghue at 10.45 a.m. on 27 August 1929, on suspicion of the murder of Albert Armstrong and lodged him in the Bridewell. At around 6 p.m. O'Donoghue told the jailer that if he was not charged or released before 6.30 p.m. he would break the windows of his cell. At 6.30 p.m. he broke the windows and was charged with malicious damage. The jury held he was detained for an unreasonable time and awarded him £50 and costs.

McKee v Detective Gardaí John Sherlock, Francis Corry and James Hussey. The detectives arrested McKee on suspicion of the murder of Albert Armstrong on the instructions of Superintendent Ennis. In evidence, they were unable to give any grounds for the suspicion other than the instructions received from the superintendent. Ennis gave evidence that he had reasonable grounds for believing McKee was involved in the murder but refused to disclose those grounds. The judge ruled that the fact the detectives were acting on the orders of their superior officer did not give them a defence to the proceedings and the jury awarded McKee £75 and costs.

O'Neill v Detective Gardaí Michael Gill, Robert Stubbins and George Mordaunt.
Detectives arrested O'Neill at his home on Ben Nevin Road at 7.30 a.m. on 30 June 1929 when he failed to answer questions. They brought him 300 yards along the road to where a group of about thirty men were being detained. He was kept on the roadside until 11.30 a.m. when he was removed to the Bridewell where he was released without charge at 12.30 p.m. the following day. He denied he was going to a meeting of the IRA. He declined to answer when asked, if he was a member of the IRA saying the answer might incriminate him. He was awarded £80 and costs.

In every case the damages and expenses were paid by the state and no disciplinary action was taken against the detectives. The assistant secretary of the Department of Justice wrote, 'the officers in question were acting under orders and the cases were test cases as to the extent of police powers in the matter under the ordinary law. In my opinion no blame whatever attaches to these officers.'[40] While recognising the branch men's tactics to be both crude and often illegal, clearly the state understood the tactics were highly effective. The state stood by the men.

Commissioner O'Duffy clamoured for extra powers to deal with the deteriorating situation in the country and sent a fifteen-page memo to the Minister for Justice on 7 October 1931. In it, he listed a series of concerns including the failure of juries to convict in the face of overwhelming evidence, threatening letters being sent to jurors, jurors grievously wounded, the recent murder of a garda officer [Curtin], the murder of witnesses [Ryan & Armstrong], and the existence of a 'treasonable organisation' with 5,000 members that rendered impossible the administration of justice through the ordinary courts. This organisation, he said, was at war with the state and the gardaí were unable to cope. He also suggested an increased arming of the force and the setting up of an expanded Special Branch throughout the country, as 'presently raiders have nothing to fear'.[41]

Probably as a result of pressure from O'Duffy, the Constitution (Amendment No. 17) Act was passed on 17 October, introducing Article 2A into the Constitution. It conferred sweeping new powers of arrest and search on the gardaí as well as trials before Military Tribunals where the normal rules of evidence often did not apply. These tribunals consisted of five senior military officers as judges who could impose any punishment up to and including the death penalty. It provided that any civil actions taken against the police when enforcing these powers would be automatically dismissed in the courts. It also banned the Irish Republican Army, Cumann na mBan, Fianna Éireann, and Saor Éire, along with a number of small left-wing groups sympathetic to Soviet Russia.[42] At that time, the Free State constitution could be amended by legislation, without the necessity of a referendum, making it invulnerable to constitutional challenge.

This was a hugely important piece of legislation which empowered the Special Branch to deal more effectively with the IRA. In one stroke, it avoided jury trials for the IRA. An absence of jurors to intimidate would quickly lead to a string of convictions. Equipped with these new powers, the Special Branch swept into action, making wholesale arrests of IRA suspects throughout the country including in Dublin, Clare, Kerry, Waterford, Wexford, Mayo, Cork, Leitrim, Galway and Laois and charged them with various offences. High on their list of targets was their nemesis, T.J. Ryan from County Clare who was swiftly arrested and jailed.[43]

The government designated Arbour Hill prison as a military prison as it was convenient to Collins Barracks and could hold up to 150 prisoners. Captain Bernard Dunne was appointed as governor of the new prison and a team of soldiers was appointed to act as warders.[44]

The Tribunal held its first sitting on Monday 30 November 1931, with some twenty-eight prisoners awaiting trial. Cases included membership of the IRA or Saor Éire, robbery under arms, possession of firearms, contempt of court (for refusing to plead), and unlawful drilling. The defendants made regular complaints about being assaulted by detectives during arrest, or threatened with being shot. The courts paid no heed.[45] One of those imprisoned for contempt of court was the well-known IRA commander Frank Ryan (then editor of *An Phoblacht* and a member of the IRA army executive) for refusing to plead. Addressing the court in Irish he harangued the judges about convicted prisoners being treated like 'galley slaves' and that un-convicted prisoners were treated like 'common criminals' in Arbour Hill prison. The judges sentenced him to three months imprisonment for contempt and adjourned the principal charges against him. These included membership of the IRA, as well as refusing to give information about arms or documents under his control or about his association with the IRA, Saor Éire or other unlawful associations.[46] By the end of January 1932, twenty prisoners were serving sentences for political offences but all (including Ryan) were released in early March in a general amnesty by the incoming Fianna Fáil government who entered office on 9 March.[47]

Allegations about the circumstances of the death of 27-year-old IRA man James Vaugh of Drumshambo, County Leitrim following his arrest by detectives caused considerable controversy. Detectives arrested Vaugh and another man on 5 December 1931 and brought them to Ballinamore Station. Following his release two days later, he told friends he was beaten by detectives while in custody. He died eighteen days later on Christmas Day.[48] Medical evidence at the inquest revealed that he was suffering from influenza and measles and was in bed for a week when detectives called to arrest him. One doctor said Vaugh told him he was badly beaten while in custody in Ballinamore Barracks even though there were no marks of violence on his body.[49] An obituary in the *Leitrim Observer* on 2 January 1932 described Vaugh as 'an active IRA man'. An annual IRA commemoration for Vaugh was held by the IRA in Drumshambo for several years afterwards.[50]

On 14 February 1932, there was a further police fatality when Detective Garda Patrick McGeehan was shot dead in Ballinamore, County Leitrim, although the IRA was not involved.[51] A Cumann na nGaedhal election candidate, Patrick Reynolds TD, was on the campaign trail in Ballinamore, escorted by Detective McGeehan. Reynolds had just called to the home of Joseph Leddy to canvas for votes. An altercation broke out and Detective McGeehan and others intervened to break it up. As McGeehan and Reynolds walked to their car, Leddy appeared at his door with a shotgun and fired at McGeehan, hitting him in the chest. He fell to the ground. The shooter declared, 'Reynolds, take that' and shot the TD in the chest. Reynolds fell to the ground saying, 'a priest, a priest', but died shortly afterwards. Barry Tynan-O'Mahony BL, a Cumann na nGaedhal election worker was nearby while Leddy was laughing maniacally. The killer at first thought Tynan-O'Mahony was a detective and threatened to shoot him also.[52]

Gardaí quickly arrived and Detective Sergeant Peter Kenny and Detective Garda Patrick Shelly entered the house and found the double-barrelled shotgun and cartridges near the fireplace. A witness at the scene handed them McGeehan's revolver. They arrested Joseph Leddy (ironically an ex-RIC man[53]) and later charged him with both murders at Ballinamore Barracks.[54]

At his trial in the Central Criminal Court in February, Leddy gave evidence that he welcomed Mr Reynolds to his home and both men shook hands. Reynolds accused him of canvassing against him for another candidate, which he denied. Reynolds allegedly responded, 'you're a liar, you cur', and attempted to strike him and threatened to shoot him.

Leddy replied, 'if you come in to kill me Paddy, I will shoot you.' Both his wife and Detective McGeehan intervened to separate them. He said McGeehan drew his revolver saying, 'keep quiet you Leddy.' As the men left, he fired at Reynolds' leg while McGeehan covered the TD with his gun. Leddy fired at the detective's revolver. He added he was afraid he was going to be shot and had not intended to kill anyone.[55]

When other detectives arrived at the house, one of them came up to him 'with a running kick on the back and used foul language' and another said, 'put them up'. In the car on the way to Ballinamore Barracks, the detective beside him held a revolver in his hand with which he was punched in the ribs 'about twenty or thirty times'. He said the detective who was driving took his right hand off the steering wheel and with his clenched fist, struck him on the face. On arrival at the barracks two or three policemen caught him by the collar and dragged him inside. He alleged they kicked him along the hall into the cell and that two uniformed men came running from the guardroom, striking him at least twice on the side of the head. In the cell six or seven men started kicking him and boxing him for about ten minutes. One of them said, 'take out the bed, he will get nothing but cold flags'. The bed was removed from the cell.[56]

In his address to the jury, defence counsel O'Connor painted a bleak picture of the situation in County Leitrim where he said there was a 'reign of terror' and referred to 'the ill-treatment of prisoners by the detectives in barracks.' He said that Leddy:

> Had fallen into the hands of men who used revolvers. Reynolds on entering the Leddy household was met with a welcome, and in return poured forth violent abuse on Leddy. If a blackguard of the domineering type of Reynolds, who had attained certain characteristics on the docks of New York, came into one of our houses and polluted the ears of your wife and children would you not feel that you would revenge yourself? It is rather hard to understand that we are living in the year 1932 – ten years after we have got freedom – to find McGeehan, a police officer, entering a house and taking the part of an aggressor and assailant.

The jury were clearly sympathetic to Leddy's version of events and found him not guilty of murder but guilty of manslaughter with a recommendation for mercy. Judge Meredith said he agreed with the verdict and sentenced Leddy to twelve months imprisonment on each charge to run concurrently. He added he would write a letter to the Minister for Justice conveying the jury's recommendation in the hope that Leddy would not lose his pension.[57]

Years later, there was a poignant sequel to the case. Around 2005, a woman from Monaghan town laid a wreath on McGeehan's grave in Fintown in County Donegal. She revealed that her late aunt was engaged to McGeehan at the time he was killed. When the old woman died two years earlier her family opened her trunk and discovered a wedding dress and letters she and McGeehan had exchanged. She said her aunt never spoke about him and 'had never looked at another man.'[58]

The first ten years of the new state were turbulent for the young police force. However, they had massive successes against the IRA and in the period 1923-1931, seized no less than 985 rifles, 1,156 revolvers, 185 pistols, 2,979 shotguns and nine machine guns. These weapons were either discovered in dumps or seized in assorted raids. Their seizures included about 130,000 rounds of assorted ammunition along with huge amounts of explosives and 1,262 bombs.[59] During the same period, fifteen policemen were killed, eleven members of the Garda Síochána (including two Special Branch men) and four Oriel House detectives. Ten of those killings were carried out by the IRA. Despite their successes, however, the killings did not come to an end and in the coming decade, six more Special Branch men would die violently – all at the hands of the IRA.

bove: Oriel House detectives pictured with an rmoured car in 1922. (Courtesy of the Garda íochána Retired Members Association)

ight: Page from diary of Detective Garda ames Crowley (a Broy Harrier) with entries howing sightings of Tom Barry and other IRA uspects at Glanmire Railway Station (now Kent tation) in Cork City. (Courtesy of his daughter, elen Coakley)

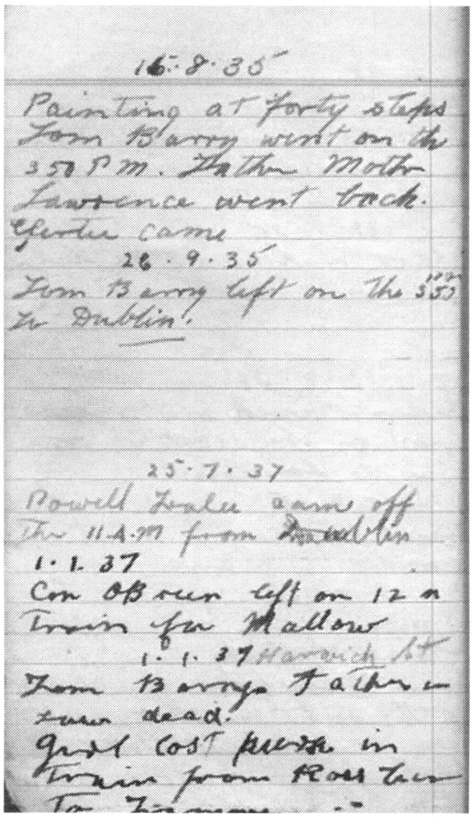

16.8.35
Painting at Forty steps
Tom Barry went on the
3 50 P.M. Father Mother
Lawrence went back.
Gertie came
26.9.35
Tom Barry left on the 5.55 [illegible]
to Dublin.

25.7.37
Powell Foale came off
the 11 A.M from Dublin
1.1.37
Con O'Breen left on 12 [illegible]
Train for Mallow
1.1.37 Harwich [illegible]
Tom Barry's Father in
law dead.
[illegible] Cost [illegible] in
Train from [illegible]
[illegible]

Left: Detective Garda Michael Brady, shot and seriously injured on Rathgar Road on 16 August 1940 in confrontation with IRA men during which two of his colleagues were killed. (Courtesy of his granddaughter, Elaine Warren)

Below: Pictured with their Scott Medals at Dublin Castle on 25 August 2021. *Left to right*: Orla McKeown, grand-niece of Detective Sergeant Patrick McKeown; Frank Brady, son of the injured Detective Garda Michael Brady and Marie Hyland, daughter of Detective Garda Richard Hyland. Standing are Justice Minister Heather Humphreys TD and Garda Commissioner Drew Harris. (Photo by Patrick Hugh Lynch)

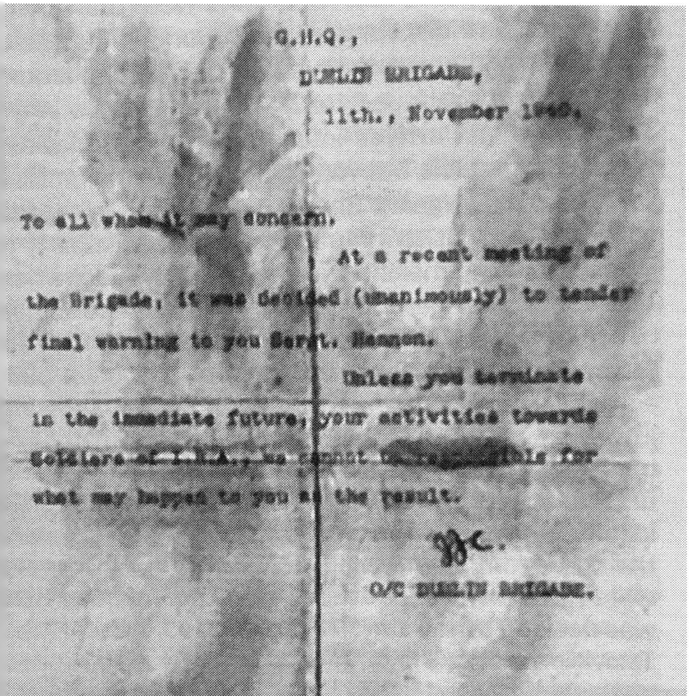

G.H.Q.,
DUBLIN BRIGADE,
11th., November 1940.

To all whom it may concern,

At a recent meeting of the Brigade, it was decided (unanimously) to tender final warning to you Sergt. Hannon.

Unless you terminate in the immediate future, your activities towards Soldiers of I.R.A., we cannot be responsible for what may happen to you as the result.

O/C DUBLIN BRIGADE.

To all whom it may concern, At a recent meeting of the Brigade, it was decided (unanimously) to tender final warning to you Sergt. Hannon. Unless you terminate in the immediate future, your activities towards soldiers of I.R.A. we cannot be responsible for what may happen to you as the result. *(copy of above letter)*

bove: Copy of threatening letter sent to a Detective Sergeant Hannon in Dublin Castle in 1940. (Courtesy f Maurice Kavanagh and his son Brian Kavanagh)

elow: G Division of the DMP pictured in Dublin Castle in February 1922. (Photo courtesy of Military rchives.)

Above: A Garda photograph of the scene of the fatal shooting of Detective Sergeant Patrick McKeown and Detective Garda Richard Hyland and the wounding of Detective Garda Michael Brady on 98A Rathgar Road, Dublin, on 16 August 1940. The bullet holes in the windows can be clearly seen. (Published with kind permission of the Garda Commissioner)

Below: Six Special Branch men who were presented with Scott Medals for bravery by Justice Minister Gerald Boland on 9 October 1941. (Published with kind permission of the *Garda Review*)

D/Sergeants Shanahan, McSweeney, Collins, D/Gardai Teahan, Mullally, Wilmot.

ıbove: Special Branch men in
)ublin Castle on the 15th Octo-
er 1947. Seated in the front row
ıre several men mentioned in the
ext. 5th from left, D/Sergeant
dward (Ned) Fergus; 6th, D/
ıspector Michael Gill; 7th,
)/Chief Superintendent Sean
Gantly; 8th, D/Chief Superin-
endent Michael Wymes (later
Garda Commissioner). (With
ıe kind permission of Detective
Chief Superintendent Justin Kelly
f the Special Detective Unit)

ight: Retired Detective Garda
eter Byrne pictured in the late
990s shortly before his death.
Ie was one of the detectives
ho were fired at by IRA man
ıckie Griffith in July 1943.
yrne returned fire with his
hompson SMG, killing Griffith.
Photo courtesy of Noel Hynes)

Left: Detective Garda John Brocklebank, (centre), one of the 'Broy Harriers' recruited into the Special Branch in 1933, pictured wit two companions. He shot IRA man Peter Mc Cathy dead on Clanbrassil Street, Dublin, on 15 June 1937. (Photo courtesy of his nephew Patrick Brocklebank)

Below: Detective Officer Thomas Fitzgerald of Oriel House (L) who was shot dead on 19 October 1923 and William Downes (R) who was hanged for the murder on 29 Novembe 1923. (Photo courtesy of Jim Herlihy)

James Crowley, from Kinneigh, Co Cork, pictured in Irish Volunteer uniform circa 1920/21. He joined the Garda Special Branch in 1934 as part of the 'Broy Harriers' and was given the Reg No 8590. (Photo courtesy of his daughter Mrs Patricia O'Brien).

Detective Chief Superintendent Sean Gantly, head of the Garda Special Branch from 1941 to 1948. He tragically lost his life when he was accidentally shot dead by one of his own men on 21 January 1948. (Photo courtesy of his son-in-law, Noel Hynes)

Superintendent John Curtin (on the right) pictured with an unknown companion in Killarney, Co Kerry circ 1929/30. He was shot dead by the IRA outside his home in Tipperary town on 21 March 1931. (Photo courtesy of his nephew, Sean Moore)

ight: Assistant Commissioner Aichael Finn lays a wreath t the scene of the murder of uperintendent John Curtin luring a commemoration ceremony at Friarsfield House, ipperary town, on 21 March 022. (Photo courtesy of atrick Hugh Lynch)

elatives of Superintendent John Curtin pictured at the scene of his murder during a ceremony at Friarsfield ouse on 21 March 2022. Left to right: Catraoine Ó Lionáin (grand-niece); Ultan Ó Lionáin (grand-nephw); Michael Curtin (nephew); Kay Phelan (nee Curtin) and Joan Ó Lionáin (nee Curtin) – nieces; and rothers Oliver Moore and Sean Moore (nephews). (Photo courtesy of Patrick Hugh Lynch).

Above: Wedding photo of Superintendent John (Jack) Curtin and his bride Maureen O'Connor of Ardmachree, Killarney, Co Kerry. They were married in St Mary's Cathedral, Killarney, on 3 June 1930. (Photo courtesy of his grand-nephew, Ultan Ó Lionáin)

Chapter 5

'UP DEV', 1932-1933

I'm telling ye that fella [de Valera] will be as bad as Cosgrave, he'll hang ye when he gets in, mark my words he'll hang ye.
Michael Conway, IRA.

The arrival of the Fianna Fáil party, who took up the reins of government on 9 March 1932 with the support of the Labour Party, was greeted with dismay by many in the Garda Síochána and in particular, the Special Branch. The new cabinet included several former anti-Treaty IRA gunmen and in the minds of many in the force they were seen as little better than the IRA. They included former IRA hardmen such as Seán Lemass (Industry and Commerce – and later taoiseach), Thomas Derrig (Education), Frank Aiken (Defence), and Gerald Boland (chief whip). The IRA supported Fianna Fáil's election campaign even though de Valera split from Sinn Féin in 1926 to form his new party. Prior to the election, Ernest Blythe TD, Minister for Finance, warned that, 'if the Fianna Fáil party were in power, and if it were not prepared to go out and imprison, and if necessary, shoot the members of any illegal armed organisation, then that government would last no time.'[1] His fears proved to be groundless as, in time, Fianna Fáil governments displayed an equal, if not a greater streak of ruthlessness in dealing with the IRA.

The February 1932 election campaign was a lively affair with fiery speeches, violence and baton charges a common occurrence. In

Ballinrobe, County Mayo, James Fitzgerald-Kenney TD, of Cumann na nGaedhal struggled to make himself heard above shouts of 'Up de Valera' and a persistent interrupter was approached by detectives who removed him. Detective Garda James Hernan (3150) was punched in the face and other detectives rushed to his aid. There were shouts of 'good boy' and 'give it to him' while others joined in the fray and Hernan drew his revolver. Patrick Hogan TD shouted, 'government by Fianna Fáil is government by the rowdy and the blackguard.'[2]

A large noisy crowd followed the detectives as they brought their prisoner to the station under a hail of missiles. Later Joseph Daly of Bowgate Street, Ballinrobe was charged with assaulting Detective Garda Hernan, and with acting in a disorderly manner. He appeared before Ballinrobe District Court on 22 March 1932. Daly claimed in court that it was Hernan who caused the trouble 'going around bumping and pushing everyone.' He claimed he saw Detectives Hernan and Conway assault an old man named Crean. When he intervened, Hernan asked him what it had to do with him and hit him on the chest. Daly said he made no attempt to strike the detective but hit back when Hernan hit him. However, other witnesses said that while they saw Hernan twisting Daly's arms, they saw no blows being struck. The old man, Thomas Crean, gave evidence that he was walking up the street and shouted 'up de Valera' when Detective Hernan pushed him and he fell to the ground and while down, he was kicked in the head. The justice said as the election was now over it would be better not to bind anyone to the peace but awarded Detective Hernan twenty shillings (£1.00) expenses.[3]

During the election campaign, the IRA assisted Fianna Fáil with massive vote-rigging especially in Dublin.[4] IRA volunteers were supplied with voting lists and many votes were even cast in the names of corpses and immigrants. As Bowyer Bell put it, 'some active Volunteers tripped from booth to booth judiciously casting fifty ballots.'[5] The IRA and their supporters were cock-a-hoop at Fianna Fáil's success as many of them considered de Valera to be one of their own, the new messiah who would lead them to a united Ireland. However, a more discerning IRA man, Michael 'Micksie' Conway, was more sceptical. 'I'm telling ye that fella will be as bad as Cosgrave, he'll hang ye when he gets in, mark my words he'll hang ye', he claimed. His prophesy was to prove more accurate than he realised as he himself would later narrowly escape the gallows.[6]

According to Brady, who interviewed David Neligan in later years, Commissioner O'Duffy was very concerned when Fianna Fáil came to power after the February 1932 election as he considered them little different from the IRA. Prior to being appointed commissioner, he was chief of staff of the Free State Army during the Civil War and still had many friends in the top ranks. Neligan claimed that O'Duffy canvassed the opinions of military officers with a view to establishing a military government led by himself. O'Duffy showed Neligan a proclamation that was prepared calling on the citizens of Ireland to stand behind this government, explaining the reasons why the democratic process had been suspended. A startled Neligan told him, 'you don't expect me to have anything to do with this.'

A concerned Neligan later spoke about it to Professor James Hogan, Head of the History Department of UCC, and a mutual friend of both himself and O'Duffy. Hogan went to O'Duffy and, after an all-night meeting, persuaded him to abandon the plan. O'Duffy also mentioned the matter to army chief of staff Lieutenant-General Michael Brennan who took swift action. First, he transferred a few officers he suspected might be in league with O'Duffy and then returned to Garda HQ and told him that if he made any attempt to stage a coup he would be immediately arrested by the army.[7] At least two other army officers were involved in the plot. Major-General Hugo MacNeill and Colonel Michael Hogan both approached a horrified former defence minister, Richard Mulcahy, seeking his support for the coup.[8] Brennan's decisive intervention had put a stop the conspirators' plan and nothing more was heard of it.

It is quite plausible that O'Duffy would have considered staging such a coup. In the 1930s, several European countries – Germany, Spain, Italy,

Portugal and Hungary – were already being ruled by right wing dictators. O'Duffy was a great admirer of Hitler and Mussolini and believed that political parties had outlived their usefulness.[9] On a train journey in Holland he announced to his travelling companion, James Dillon TD, that he was the third greatest man in Europe after Hitler and Mussolini, a clear indication of his nascent megalomania, not to mention his blustering buffoonery.[10] He was also an ardent admirer of Italian style corporatism and hoped to set up a similar corporate state in Ireland. He supported Italy's invasion of Abyssinia and would later lead an Irish brigade to support Franco during the Spanish Civil War.[11] His barely concealed contempt for democracy was heightened by (as he saw it) the lack of support from the judiciary, especially the failure to convict IRA suspects brought before the courts, even in the face of overwhelming evidence.

The emboldened IRA resumed intensive drilling and recruitment and often paraded openly through the streets. They quickly got thousands of extra recruits, convinced it was the road to a position with a pension in the new republic. Garda fears were soon realised when no sooner than the election was over, de Valera lifted the ban on the IRA. The new Minister for Defence, Frank Aiken (a formidable IRA commander along the border counties in his time) and Justice Minister James Geoghegan, summoned the secretary of the Department of Defence from his home to inform him they intended to release all IRA prisoners sentenced by military courts in Arbour Hill Military Prison. They went to the prison and ordered the governors of Arbour Hill as well as Portlaoise and Mountjoy prisons to release all the IRA men. Within days, seventeen were released from Arbour Hill, two from Portlaoise and one from Mountjoy. The released prisoners included leading IRA members Frank Ryan, George and Charles Gilmore, as well as T.J. Ryan from County Clare. There was huge rejoicing and they were greeted by cheering crowds with bands, torchlight processions, bonfires and welcoming speeches.[12] On 27 March, the newly-released prisoners attended an Easter Week Commemoration

Concert in the Theatre Royal and were even seated in a specially reserved 'Royal Box'.[13]

De Valera hoped that by appeasing his former friends in the IRA, he could wean them away from the gun and take the political route, as he had. Shortly after his election victory, he met two leading IRA members, chief of staff Maurice Twomey, and George Gilmore, at the home of Dr. Fannin in 5 Merrion Square, Dublin. He soon came to realise that his efforts were in vain and this would, in time lead to a hardening of his attitude towards them.[14]

Article 2A of the Constitution, which gave sweeping powers of arrest and detention, was suspended as was the Military Tribunal. Membership of the IRA and Saor Eire was no longer an offence and the ban on *An Phoblacht* was lifted. These developments left detectives with no option but to go back to the somewhat useless Treasonable Offences Act which resulted in few or no convictions. Before a prosecution could be instituted, files had to be submitted to the Attorney General where they languished usually without a reply. The mood music from the new government was clear – they wanted the gardaí to back off the IRA.[15]

Around the country gardaí were harassed, jostled and spat at in the streets and in some cases, were approached by jubilant IRA supporters and ordered to leave the station as they expected that 'Republican Police' would shortly be appointed to replace them. When an IRA delegation entered Listowel Garda Station in County Kerry, the sergeant ordered an impromptu baton charge causing them to swiftly scatter.[16] In one infamous incident while de Valera was on a visit to Skibbereen in County Cork, the local gardaí drew up a guard of honour while the local IRA drew up one of their own nearby. Incredibly, de Valera ignored the lawful police force of the state and inspected the IRA guard of honour.[17]

The unbelievable difficulties now being encountered in bringing prosecutions against IRA members is illustrated in a case taken in July 1932. Gerald Dempsey of Darley's Terrace, Donore Avenue, Dublin was charged in the Dublin District Court with possession of two revolvers, a rifle and seventy-three rounds of revolver ammunition. The armaments were found in his home by Detective Garda Leonard on 19 June. Dempsey was not at home at the time of the search, but was later arrested by Detective Mordaunt in Lower Gardiner Street on 5 July.[18]

Leonard gave evidence that when Dempsey was brought to the garda station he told the station sergeant, 'I take responsibility for that stuff. It is all my stuff. As far as I am concerned, all the stuff has been stolen from my place.' When the judge advised him that he should have legal representation he replied, 'what defence could I put up when I claim the right to have the arms?' He went on, 'it would be absolutely ridiculous for me to have a solicitor. I am a soldier of the Republic, and I cannot recognise the right of this Court to try me on a charge of having those arms.' Despite this overwhelming evidence he was acquitted by the jury at his trial in the Circuit Court even though they were sent back twice to reconsider their verdict by the incredulous judge. The clearly exasperated judge told Dempsey:

> You have heard the verdict. How you regard that verdict I do not know. Possibly you have the same contempt for it as I have. I have a duty apart altogether from the jury. When you appeared before me, you refused to recognise the court and that is an offence according to the statute which I must deal with. I sentence you to three calendar months in the second division.[19]

Several public meetings were held protesting against the sentence and within days he was released from prison by order of the Minister for Justice.[20]

In the IRA hotbed of County Clare, tensions were still high between Special Branch officers and the local IRA, resulting in regular confrontations. On the night of 5 September 1932, Detective Gardaí Hanley, Muldowney, Mulkeen and Carroll of Ennis Garda Station were returning to their station when they were fired at from three different positions.

The detectives took cover behind a wall running beside the River Fergus and returned fire. After an exchange of shots lasting ten minutes, the attackers left the scene and miraculously no one was injured. In a follow-up search, they recovered a Lee-Enfield rifle and ammunition clips in a nearby field.[21]

Matters took a very serious turn in the county during a bitter labour dispute in Kilrush in 1932 involving business owner Daniel Ryan. Ryan's workers sided with him over a dispute with the Irish Transport and General Workers Union (ITGWU) and formed their own union. Other traders in the town supported the ITGWU as they felt Ryan's activities were a threat. The IRA got involved on the side of the workers employed by the other traders and there followed a series of bomb explosions, arson attacks, assaults, threats and intimidation on a wide scale.

On 15 August 1932, Detective Garda Myles Muldowney (5728) and Detective Garda Michael Carroll (6777)[22] were on protection duty at Daniel Ryan's business premises in Kilrush. Following an altercation with a crowd of republican supporters, they opened fire with revolvers injuring two IRA members, George Gilmore and their old adversary T.J. Ryan. At a special court in Kilrush District Hospital, both men were charged with the attempted murder of the two detectives and obstructing the gardaí in the course of their duty.[23]

However, a week later the charges against the men were dropped and the two detectives were suspended from duty pending an official enquiry. Gilmore claimed that while in hospital, the detectives 'bashed' both himself and Ryan with revolvers.[24] Ryan said he had also been 'hammered' by three detectives. A doctor came to the station to treat his wounds and ordered that he be removed to hospital.[25]

An official enquiry was set up consisting of Clare-based Patrick Lynch, K.C., (chairman) along with Daniel J. Browne, solicitor from Tralee and John G. Magrath, a solicitor from Fermanagh.[26] It opened in Kilrush courthouse on Wednesday 7 September 1932. In his opening remarks O'Connor, representing Gilmore and Ryan, set the tone when he described the CID as 'the lineal descendants of Oriel House in its political activities and seems to spend a great deal of its energies and time in goading and provoking well known Republicans particularly in lonely country districts.'[27] Several witnesses gave evidence that on the night prior to the shooting they were putting up posters in Kilrush with the words 'Boycott British Goods' when they were approached by detectives including Detective Muldowney who said to T. J. Ryan, 'hello Tommy, this is what you're at, you poor old fool.'

Dr Richard Counihan said he saw Ryan and Gilmore in a car outside Kilrush hospital with two men, one of whom repeatedly struck Ryan on the head with a revolver. Dr John T. Coughlan examined Ryan and found eight head wounds along with a bullet wound in the leg. Nurse Agnes O'Connor stated she attended Gilmore's room in the hospital in the early hours of the morning and found three CID men sitting on his bed. Gilmore complained they were tormenting him, and she asked them to leave the room which they did. She added that 'the three CID men smelled terribly of drink.'[28]

Daniel Fleming of Kilrush told the inquiry that he went with three others to Kilrush Station to give a shirt to T.J. Ryan. Superintendent Feeney and several CID men told him to leave and five or six CID men rushed at him, and allegedly kicked him, knocking him to the ground. As he ran off, he received several more kicks from Detective O'Leary.[29]

Detective Muldowney gave evidence that he saw a group of about sixteen men in military formation walking towards them and some jeered with remarks such as, 'hello cows', a reference to the assaults on T. J. Ryan, and 'beware of the little black box', a reference to a booby trap bomb which killed Detective O'Sullivan in 1929. He claimed the crowd attacked them and both Ryan and Gilmore punched him in the head. He drew his revolver and fired at them. Detective Garda Carroll gave similar evidence.[30]

The enquiry found that Ryan and Gilmore were ill-treated by the detectives and both Muldowney and Carroll were dismissed from the force while Mulkeen was transferred to the uniform section and moved to the garda depot. Special Branch later got wind of an IRA plot to shoot both detectives regardless of the findings of the inquiry and arrangements were made for their protection, but the threat was never carried out.[31]

Commissioner O'Duffy and Special Branch chief David Neligan were furious at the tribunal findings. Neligan insisted the detectives were subjected to years of provocation and intimidation and saw colleagues murdered. With O'Duffy's approval, Neligan organised a nationwide collection for them, something that did not please the government who wrote to O'Duffy saying it was 'grave indiscretion.' O'Duffy responded with a bitter minute outlining how 'no other man in Saorstát Eireann today has laboured more zealously or more conscientiously since I accepted a position which I never sought. It is the first official rebuke I have ever received in my career, and being only human, I feel it very keenly.'[32] Carroll joined the army in 1940 in response to an appeal for manpower for the duration of the Emergency. He sought readmission to the force on 3 October 1944, saying that apart from the Kilrush findings, he was never subjected to a disciplinary charge. Both he and Muldowney were reinstated in 1945.[33]

In September 1932, several newspaper reports suggested that the government was considering reducing if not abolishing the Special Branch completely, while leaving a small plain-clothes section for dealing with ordinary crime.[34] While it was not disbanded, a severe cull of the numbers got under way. From an original strength of about 400 men, between 1932 and 1934 a total of twenty-nine sergeants and 273 guards were removed and transferred to ordinary duties.[35]

First to be removed was Special Branch chief David Neligan. In December 1932, the government decided to sack him, and O'Duffy sent him a memo informing him of the decision. He was granted three months holidays with full pay from Saturday, 17 December 1932. Neligan replied with a strongly worded memo on 24 December pleading his case but was bluntly informed that the Executive Council desired his resignation and if he resigned, he would be appointed to the Civil Service but if not, he would be dismissed. He bowed to the inevitable and submitted his resignation from the force on 16 March 1933.[36]

On 18 March, he was given a job as a higher executive officer in the Land Commission while still on the same pay as a chief superintendent.[37] This did not meet with the approval of departmental mandarins. His salary was £500 per annum plus bonus for duties of a standard normally carried out by a clerical officer (maximum salary £200 per annum). They said his appointment was not in accordance with existing legislation and that it should be on condition that it did not block promotion for any other staff member. The government agreed and on 19 March, appointed him as a staff officer (a reduction of two ranks) in the Land Commission but still with pay of £500 plus bonus but he would not be eligible for promotion.[38] Arriving on his first day he walked into an office with three desks and announced to the lone clerk Thomas Lavin that one of the desks was his. He asked Lavin if he knew who he was and Lavin replied, 'yes, you're Neligan.' Neligan surveyed the room and selected a desk facing the door and placed two revolvers in separate drawers, one at each hand. With a legacy of bitterness still around there was no point in taking chances with a potential assassin.[39] For the next thirty years he was left in the office on his own with nothing to do.[40] No doubt, Lavin felt it prudent to move to a different office.

A further sensation followed on 22 February 1933, when O'Duffy was himself dismissed and replaced by Chief Superintendent Eamon Broy. O'Duffy was offered a similar deal to Neligan's – the post of Commissioner of Prices at the same salary but he declined. He was awarded an annual pension of £520 and was also entitled to a military pension of £160 per annum.[41]

De Valera was not satisfied to allow O'Duffy continue in office as he was too closely associated with the previous administration. He believed he would not get the support of 'large sections of the community', namely IRA/Fianna Fáil supporters. On 14 March 1933, he told the Dáil, that O'Duffy was offered a position as Controller of Prices with a salary 'so he would not suffer in a monetary way' but that O'Duffy declined the offer.[42] O'Duffy was not held in high esteem by Fianna Fáil though he received a very generous severance package. Their attitude towards him could be summed up by Seán Lemass who described him as 'an exotica-seeking rural twit.'[43]

On 15 March, an angry O'Duffy issued a statement which read in part, 'I consider that I have been treated with the greatest ingratitude by the representatives of the people, for whom I have worked so hard in building up a police force for this State.' Regarding his refusal to accept another position in the Civil Service he remarked:

> The office of the Commissioner of the Garda Síochána is one of the most responsible and trustworthy in the State, and, as I have carried out the duty of that office fearlessly and impartially, I could not accept a less responsible and trustworthy position without stultifying my future. Fair play and gratitude among a people soar far above any other consideration.[44]

O'Duffy's unassailable belief in his own greatness combined with his hatred of the IRA and Fianna Fáil rendered him a danger to the impartiality of the police and to democracy. In all the circumstances, it is arguable that de Valera showed admirable restraint in not removing O'Duffy on his first day in office. Instead, he waited until February 1933 to side-line the commissioner. By replacing O'Duffy with a pro-treaty Collins-man in Eamon Broy, he effectively depoliticised the police in Ireland. If he had opted to install an anti-Treaty commissioner immediately on his election in 1932, it may well have set a precedent for future governments to install a party favourite.

Eamon Broy was heading the Special Branch for just a month when appointed as O'Duffy's successor. Though only a chief superintendent he was promoted over the heads of the assistant and deputy commissioners and no doubt, they were not too pleased. His deputy commissioners were Eamon Coogan and W.R.E. Murphy while the assistant commissioners were Eamon Cullen and Patrick Walsh. Broy met with them all on 23 February where he informed them of his plans for the force.[45]

He continued in his role as head of Detective Branch until he was replaced by Chief Superintendent Brennan in July.[46] In May, Detective Superintendent Ennis was transferred out of Special Branch and sent to Kevin Street as a uniform superintendent, switching places with Superintendent Patrick O'Connell who took up Ennis' former role.[47] On 26 February 1934, Chief Superintendent Brennan was moved from Detective Branch to Crime Branch while newly-promoted Chief Superintendent Thomas Woods was appointed to lead the Detective Division.[48]

Meanwhile the purge of the old guard continued with the shafting of two of the most efficient detective sergeants in Special Branch, Michael Gill and Philip McMahon. They were reverted to uniform, transferred to rural stations and allocated desk jobs which kept them away from anti-IRA activities. In time, both were installed as heads of Special Branch under Fianna Fáil administrations.[49]

De Valera's campaign of retribution against O'Duffy's old guard did not always run smoothly. On 19 February 1933, Inspector Edward M. O'Connell, Neligan's second-in-command in the Special Branch, was sensationally arrested along with Colonel Michael Hogan of Army HQ. Both were charged with offences under the Official Secrets Act and remanded in custody, though they were released on bail some days later. It transpired that O'Connell sent samples of pamphlets that were seized by detectives to Hogan's brother James Hogan, professor of European and Irish history at University College Cork. They were working on a booklet about Communism. These circulars and pamphlets were issued by the Communist Party and other left-wing groups.

At the trial in March, Detective Garda Michael Carberry gave evidence that while working as a clerk in Inspector O'Connell's office at the Detective Branch HQ on 6 February, O'Connell gave him an envelope of documents addressed to Colonel Hogan and asked them to deliver them to Hogan at Portobello Barracks saying they were 'very important.' O'Connell warned him to say nothing to Broy (who had just taken charge after Neligan's removal) as 'if he knew anything about it there would be a row.' Carberry took fright on seeing what the documents were about and brought them to Broy who in turn informed O'Duffy. Broy told Carberry not to tell O'Connell that he had the documents. When Hogan did not receive the documents, O'Connell got worried and kept asking Carberry if he had delivered them and Carberry pawned him off saying he had delivered them to Portobello Barracks. O'Connell berated him saying did he not know Hogan was not in Portobello but at Army HQ telling him, 'you're an awful idiot.'[50]

On 29 March 1933, before the defence concluded their address to the jury, the foreman handed a note to the judge who read it and said, 'the jury wish to bring in a verdict, as they have arrived at a unanimous conclusion.' After retiring for five minutes, they returned and acquitted them both.[51] The presiding judge Mr Justice Johnston suggested to the Attorney General that he should pay the defence costs as he felt a mistake had been made.[52] However, their costs were not paid which in O'Connell's case was £250.

In an attempt to justify himself, De Valera asked the Dáil, 'was the government to stand by while State files of secret documents were handed out – even if it was for the purpose of writing a book? What right had any State servant to give out any public document?'[53] This was a particularly petty and vindictive prosecution as the files in question were not 'secret documents' by any stretch of the imagination but communist party leaflets that were being handed out on street corners to anyone who wanted them. The jury's decision to bring in a not guilty verdict even before the case had concluded and the judge's comments afterwards, clearly showed they were sympathetic to the defendants and appalled that the state brought such a prosecution. It was obviously part of the purge of the Special Branch then underway and also an attempt to 'put manners' on Colonel Hogan because of his suspected involvement in the coup plot with O'Duffy in 1932.

Hogan resumed his army career and took charge of the Army Equitation School and was later Director of Infantry during World War Two. He retired in 1945 with the rank of major-general. O'Connell was less fortunate. He was removed from Detective Branch and reduced in rank to sergeant as he had been promoted to inspector by O'Duffy though had not passed the prescribed examinations. O'Duffy made these promotions (O'Connell was not the only one) on the basis that they would be reverted to their former rank if at any time they ceased to serve in Detective Branch.[54] It was over twenty years later before he got his old rank back in 1955 under John A. Costello's inter-party government.[55]

De Valera's policy of tacit appeasement of the IRA began to look increasingly threadbare as his old comrades repeatedly let him down by undermining the state he served as president. The Juries (Protection) Act 1929 was enacted to protect jurors from intimidation and provided that lists of jurors would no longer be published and available to the public. However, jurors were still subjected to intimidation by the IRA and Cumann na mBan. In December 1933, Special Branch discovered that forty members of a jury panel before that month's sitting of the Central Criminal Court received a circular issued by Cumann na mBan. The circular was dated 13 November 1933 and told members of the jury panel they might be selected in the trials of a number of 'Republican political prisoners' named as Patrick Fleming, Michael O'Leary, Patrick Kissane, Cornelius and Joseph McCarthy and Edward Myers, all from the Killarney area of County Kerry. The tone of the circular was not particularly threatening but explained that the men were charged with 'petty charges' of removing advertising signs for British ales. This was in connection with an IRA 'Boycott British' campaign intended to stop the import of British goods into the country. The circular went on to say that the trial was moved from Kerry to Dublin 'in the hope that you – citizens of Dublin – could be prevailed upon to become jailers of republicans of Kerry.'

Detectives believed that Sheila Humphries, who was Director of Publicity for Cumann na mBan, was the brains behind the project. She was in court for the trial of the men and was seen to note down the names of jurors as they were called. Whether as a result of the letters or not, the jury found all five not guilty and they were discharged. The judge ordered that they be paid their expenses for the journey back to Killarney.[56]

By late 1933, with relations between the IRA and Fianna Fáil rapidly cooling, the IRA paper *An Phoblacht* came under serious scrutiny. On 20 December 1933, acting on instructions from Garda HQ, detectives went to the Longford Printing and Publishing Company in Market Square, Longford and asked for a copy of *An Phoblacht* then in preparation. The manager refused but detectives got a warrant and Detective Sergeant Bernard McDonald (2936) along with Detective Gardaí Thomas Corr (7406), John Chatten (684) and several uniformed gardaí returned and took six copies of the paper and left Chatten on duty until they had time to examine the contents. They returned to the station and read the articles in the paper and decided that a number were seditious. They returned to the printing works and seized all 10,770 copies.[57]

On 3 January 1934, gardaí returned to the same printers and this time they seized all 4,175 copies. The Republican Press Ltd subsequently took an action against Commissioner Broy and Detective Sergeant McDonald. The application sought to restrain the gardaí from interfering with their business of printing and publishing *An Phoblacht*. On 16 January, the High Court refused the application.[58]

An Phoblacht had its own troubles in September 1934 when it increased the wholesale price of the paper to newsboys by three pence per dozen. The newsboys refused to pay the extra tariff and a mini-riot broke out at the offices at Frederick Lane during which windows were broken and several people injured. The IRA marshalled the troops and some hours later gardaí spotted about fifty men marching in fours along Parnell Square towards the offices. On arrival at the offices, they formed up in lines across the lane and drew sticks from under their coats. Fighting broke out between the two groups and a number were removed to the Mater Hospital with head injuries. Gardaí rushed reinforcements to the area and peacefully restored order. When the injured men were later interviewed at the hospital, they refused to give their names or give any information on how they got their injuries.[59]

In November 1934, the Department of Justice complained to the Commissioner that an issue of *An Phoblacht* dated 17 November was allowed to proceed though it contained an article which read,

> Dismissal from IRA.
> The Adjutant General of Óglaigh na hÉireann writes stating that Patrick Hickey, West Clare, has been dismissed with ignominy from Óglaigh na hÉireann.

As Óglaigh na hÉireann was the official title of the army, using this term to describe the IRA was clearly seditious. It was made clear that this was not to happen again and that any reference to the IRA should be viewed with suspicion apart from bona fide historical allusions.

This memo resulted in even closer scrutiny of the paper and any copies with words casting the slightest aspersion on the state or its agencies were seized. Several further issues were confiscated in November and December. The 9 March 1935 issue was deemed seditious merely because the word 'Dáil' was used with inverted commas and all 8,100 copies were seized.1,000 copies of the 13 April issue were seized as it had the words 'Free State' in inverted commas.[60] New instructions were issued to the gardaí in June 1935 to the effect that there should be no further seizures of the paper until the Military Tribunal had declared it seditious. A superintendent should call to the publishers and warn them that if any more offending material was printed, they would be prosecuted for seditious libel in front of the Military Tribunal.[61]

The garda actions clearly had an impact. An IRA document seized in July 1934 read in part, 'you will have observed that owing to enemy action publication of *An Phoblacht* has been suspended for the present.'[62] It was eighteen months before it re-appeared. On 26 February 1936, it was announced that *An Phoblacht* would be on sale again from Friday 13 March, adding that 'heavy losses had been incurred through seizures' and that 'consequently financing the re-issue of the paper is a heavy burden.'[63]

On assuming power, De Valera hoped that by love-bombing the IRA with prisoner releases and repealing anti-IRA legislation he could tempt them towards the Fianna Fáil fold. In a very shrewd move, he introduced the Military Service Pensions Act 1934, providing pensions for anyone who was in the Irish Volunteers, the IRA, the Irish Citizen Army, the Hibernian Rifles, Fianna Eireann or Cumann na mBan between 1916 and 1923. The earlier 1924 act specified the dates for 'active service' as being from 23 April 1916 to 1 July 1922. The 1934 act extended it to 1 October 1923 which now included the anti-Treaty IRA involved in the Civil War whether or not they were involved in the 1916 Rebellion or the War of Independence. The prospect of a pension for life proved very tempting and brought many potential troublemakers into the fold. In total, 82,000 applications were made under both acts although only 15,700 were successful.[64]

This caused understandable chagrin amongst the hardcore IRA who fully understood that de Valera's benevolence would tempt many potential recruits from their ranks. They viewed themselves as the true inheritors of the second Dáil of 1921[65] and held both the Cosgrave and de Valera regimes as apostates and traitors to the cause. They issued a statement on 10 September 1934 directing their members not to accept service pensions 'by virtue of military service to the Republic.'[66] At least 4,000 men left the IRA in order to avail of the pensions, not to mention the over 300 who joined the Broy Harriers.[67] In addition, the creation of a part-time militia known as the Volunteer Force in April of that year along similar lines to the British Territorial Army led to thousands of young men joining up. The temptation of military training and the provision of a smart uniform along with some cash proved too much for many who might otherwise have joined the IRA.[68]

Barely a year after winning a snap general election in January 1933, with an overall majority, the Fianna Fáil government decimated the Special Branch. They released all IRA prisoners and repealed anti IRA legislation. There was no love lost between several senior government ministers and the Branch detectives. Several ministers were former anti-Treaty IRA who had bitter memories of their encounters with detectives in the previous decade and this was payback time. The education minister Thomas Derrig, lost an eye after being shot by an Oriel House detective in 1923.[69] In March 1924, detectives threatened Gerald Boland (then OC of the Dublin Brigade of the IRA) that if any more detectives or other policemen were shot, he (Boland) would be peremptorily shot.[70] As an opposition Fianna Fáil TD in March 1929, Boland referred to them as 'political CID men, those survivors of the murderers of 1922.'[71] Following the O'Higgins' assassination in 1927. both Sean T. O'Kelly and Gerald Boland alleged that the assassination were carried out by the Special Branch and specifically named David Neligan as having been involved. (See Chapter 3).

It was no surprise then that once the purge started, Neligan was first to go, and he was followed by the transfer of over half of the rank-and-file Branch men to uniform duties. These included two of their top investigators (Gill and McMahon) who were transferred to rural stations and several senior officers were also transferred from the unit. The prosecution and subsequent demotion of Inspector O'Connell was seen as particularly harsh and vindictive. The remaining Branch men were, henceforth, answerable to local divisional officers (i.e., chief superintendents). As the *Irish Independent* forecast at the time, 'the Special Branch as such will disappear.'[72]

But the Special Branch was not about to disappear, and the realities of office soon had a sobering effect. Within a few short years, it was becoming obvious to de Valera and his government that the IRA was not responding to their blandishments. The close attention paid to *An Phoblacht* was only a warning shot and within a few short years, anti-IRA legislation was back with a vengeance. The government soon came to the realisation that a robust Special Branch was not such a bad idea after all.

Chapter 6

BLUESHIRTS AND HARRIERS, 1933–1937

Without a large number of well-armed men, no republic will ever be able to grow or, if it does so, to maintain itself.

Machiavelli

By late-1933, the emergence of the quasi-fascist Blueshirt organisation presented a serious new challenge for the Garda Síochána and led to the controversial injection of manpower into the Special Branch who now found themselves fighting a war on two fronts. After ten years in power, the Cumann na nGaedhael party was now in opposition and the IRA decided to disrupt their political meetings at every opportunity. This led to wholesale disorder with riots, baton charges and general mayhem in Dublin and many towns around the country. It went on for several years. IRA leader Frank Ryan spelled out their policy as, 'no matter what anyone says to the contrary, while we have fists and boots to use, and guns, if necessary, we will not allow free speech to traitors.'[1]

The Blueshirt movement (officially the Army Comrades Association)[2] since July 1933 led by dismissed commissioner Eoin O'Duffy, evolved from a desire to have a force with the ability to confront the rioters and protect speakers at election rallies. Risteárd Mulcahy recalled attending an election meeting with his father at the Parnell Monument in

O'Connell Street in 1933 and saw the serious disruption caused by Fianna Fáil and IRA supporters. He believed that the failure of the police to protect these meetings and control disorder was largely responsible for the creation of the Blueshirts.[3] The wearing of blue shirts served to distinguish friend from foe at political rallies and were a nod to then popular European-style fascism. They also adopted the straight-arm salute. This may sound incredible to modern readers, but one must remember that many at the time (including de Valera) greatly admired Mussolini's successes in Italy until his popularity waned after he threw in his lot with Hitler during World War Two.[4]

In August 1933, O'Duffy announced a commemorative parade to Leinster House for Sunday 13 August, at which he said 20,000 Blueshirts would attend. He added, 'it has been canvassed in government circles that we intend seizing the seat of government and the military barracks in Dublin on this occasion. No serious-minded person will believe this.'[5]

The government was not so sure, however, and feared that O'Duffy would use the occasion to stage a coup, echoes of Mussolini's march on Rome in 1922. The suspicions about his planned coup the previous year was, no doubt, foremost in their minds. On 9 August, the government's concerns were outlined in the Dáil by the new justice minister, P. J. Ruttledge when he said:

> I have, however, been informed, as already reported to the Minister, that certain members of the organisation hold extreme views, and would be prepared to urge the use of force in pursuit of their policy.[6]

Commissioner Broy was summoned to a meeting with de Valera and Ruttledge and asked what the attitude of the gardaí would be if O'Duffy tried to seize power. Broy assured them that they would remain loyal. However, the government, who had already sacked O'Duffy and Special Branch chief David Neligan, and relegated leading Branch men to obscure desk jobs, was taking no chances. They decided that an injection of manpower, with proven loyalty to Fianna Fáil, was required in Special Branch. In the interim, fifty uniformed gardaí armed with revolvers were billeted in the College of Science (now the Taoiseach's Department) near Leinster House. Backed up by plainclothes officers, they took up duty at each gate and patrolled the corridors. For the first time uniformed gardaí could be seen on the streets openly carrying revolvers.[7]

There can be no doubt that the threat of a coup was palpable and there must have been a sense of dread and panic inside the government of the young state. O'Duffy's statement on 8 August that the current British-styled system of government had outlived its usefulness and needed to be replaced with a corporate state, only served to raise tensions regarding his intended parade at government buildings.[8] It is arguable that this dread led de Valera to take the drastic measure of enlisting the assistance of his former comrades in arms in the IRA, albeit under the banner of An Garda Siochána.

Oscar Traynor TD was given the task of organising the new intake of detectives and 200 men, mostly from the Dublin area, were originally selected. The existing recruitment regulations were totally ignored. Some of the new recruits were not the required height, some were over the required age (in their forties), some were married, some had even been dismissed from the force during the Cosgrave administration and some served prison sentences.[9] However, none of that mattered, but, what was important was that they all had been members of the anti-Treaty IRA, had proven loyalty to de Valera and were proficient with guns. The first group was brought to Garda HQ where each was issued with a .45 revolver and 200 rounds of ammunition. They were subsequently brought to Dublin Castle where they were given what may have been the swiftest training course ever known in the history of policing – a ten-minute lecture from Chief Superintendent Thomas Clarke. Afterwards, they were rapidly brought to Government Buildings where they took over protection duty from the armed uniformed men on duty there.[10]

Their arrival in Dublin Castle was greeted by a less than wholehearted welcome by the astonished Branch men looking out their windows. To quote Conor Brady:

> At the Special Detective Unit in Dublin Castle veteran detectives gazed in shocked amazement at their new colleagues dismounting from a lorry which had pulled into the Castle Yard. Almost without exception, they could recognise every face as those of the men whom they had sought out and pursued over the previous ten years. These were the men whom, apart from charging them in open court, they had spied upon, hauled into the Bridewell for long nights of questioning, or knocked from their bicycles with the glancing blow of a patrol car.[11]

By Sunday morning, 2,000 gardaí as well as the new Branch men, who were almost immediately christened Broy Harriers (after a pack of hounds known as the Bray Harriers)[12], were on duty around Leinster House. The IRA, who also feared a Blueshirt coup, stationed units at railway stations and other points in the city to confront them.[13] The government, however, banned the march and O'Duffy cancelled the parade thus averting a potential crisis and serious loss of life.

After the initial intake of Harriers, a further group with impeccable Fianna Fáil credentials was recruited bringing the total up to 367 officers. They benefited from a little more training – three days. Concern was expressed by the secretary of the Department of Justice, Stephen Roche, about the irregular method of appointing these recruits. No provision was made in the estimates to fund the recruitment. Retrospective legislation was passed in February 1937 with the Garda Síochána Act, 1937 that finally regularised their appointment.[14]

It cannot be over-stressed how steeped in IRA service the Broy Harriers were. They were de Valera loyalists to a man. A typical example of a Harrier recruit was James Crowley [Reg. No. 8590] from Kinneigh, County Cork, who was 40 years of age and married when he joined in

1934. Born in 1894 he had seen service in the Old IRA during the War of Independence and was captain of the 4th Battalion of the Kinneigh Company since its formation in March 1918. After the Treaty, he took the anti-Treaty side and led a flying column that carried out attacks on Free State troops. He was captured on 1 March 1923 and interned. After a hunger strike, he was released on 12 July 1924.

Crowley was always very circumspect in later years about his IRA activities but he confided to his son-in-law (Jim Coakley – a garda inspector) that he led the IRA unit that fired at Michael Collins' convoy at Béal na Bláth on 22 August 1922. They were irritated that Collins proclaimed that his own people in West Cork would not harm him and their intention was to fire a few shots in his direction to shake him up – without meaning to kill him.[15]

One of Crowley's duties was to monitor the movements of IRA men arriving and departing from Glanmire Station (now Kent Station) in Cork, a task he was ideally suited to as he knew most of them from his IRA days. Among them was legendary guerrilla fighter Tom Barry who took the anti-Treaty side and was still a leading member of the Cork IRA. Barry (who was IRA chief of staff for a brief period in 1937), now featured regularly in Crowley's reports, as the following extracts from his diary showed.

> 7 June 1935, 'Tom Barry arrives on the 9.40pm, another work parole'.
> 12 June 1935, 'Glanmire Station. E. O'Neill, Sean O'___ [illegible] and Tom Barry left on the 3.50pm for Dublin.'
> 16 August 1935, 'Tom Barry went on the 3.50pm.'
> 26 September 1935, 'Tom Barry left on the 3.50pm to Dublin.'
> 1 January 1937, 'Tom Barry's father is found dead.' [Was actually his father-in-law Michael Price][16]
> 14 January 1938, 'Tom and Mrs Barry and T. McCurtain (*sic*) left on the 3.58pm train for Dublin and returned on the 3.25pm on the 16.1.38.'[17]

On 9 December 1933, O'Duffy found himself in serious trouble after an intemperate speech in Ballyshannon, County Donegal during which he thundered, 'Mr de Valera and his party had murdered Kevin O'Higgins and Michael Collins because they said in 1922 and 1927 what Fianna Fáil were saying now; [and] he was entitled to the same fate he gave Michael Collins and Kevin O'Higgins.' This was seen as incitement to murder de Valera and he was brought before the military tribunal to face the charge on 2 January 1934. The charges included membership of an unlawful organisation known as the Young Ireland Association, making a seditious speech, and incitement to murder. However, O'Duffy went to the High Court and challenged the authority of the tribunal to try him. In a judgement issued on 21 March, the High Court agreed saying, though the tribunal would have powers to try him for being a member of an unlawful organisation, they had no jurisdiction to issue a summons in the case and that he was entitled to jury trial for these in the ordinary courts.[18]

He was in trouble again on 17 December 1933, when he entered Westport in County Mayo dressed in a blue shirt to address a large crowd of supporters. Gardaí were instructed not to admit anyone to the town wearing blue shirts and a strong force of gardaí was on duty. Superintendents Joseph Murray and Gerald Flynn arrested O'Duffy and brought him to Westport Station where he was detained under Article 2A of the Constitution (which was reintroduced in August 1933 following violent clashes between Blueshirts and the IRA) on suspicion that he was a member of an unlawful organisation. Once again, O'Duffy went to the High Court. He complained that Sergeant Cox had forcibly removed him from the platform and unlawfully imprisoned him in Westport Station from the 17 to 19 December and subsequently in Arbour Hill Barracks until 21 December. Mr Justice O'Byrne held that while the superintendents might have had suspicions that O'Duffy was a member of an unlawful organisation, he was satisfied that the reason for the arrest was that O'Duffy persisted in entering the town and addressed a meeting while wearing a blue shirt. He said it was a case meriting substantial damages as he was a man who had held a responsible position as Garda Commissioner though he agreed the gardaí were attempting honestly to carry out their instructions. He awarded him £200 damages with costs.[19]

The existence of two paramilitary or quasi-military factions in Ireland in late-1933 posed unique challenges to the Special Branch. In the autumn and winter of 1933, the IRA carried out several violent attacks on Blueshirts in County Cork. In a particularly vicious incident on 29 October, masked men broke into the home of Hugh O'Reilly (34) in Innishannon, dragged him a short distance away and gave him a severe beating. His father, John O'Reilly, an RIC pensioner, found him a short distance from his home covered in blood. His son managed to tell him, 'they gave me a cruel doing.' Despite the best efforts of doctors, he died on 28 December. Another youth, Denis O'Leary was severely beaten and shot in leg that same night but survived. He also received a broken nose, lacerated lip and jaw, along with severe head wounds and numerous other bruises.[20] On Christmas Eve, another Blueshirt, Cornelius Daly, a Dunmanway publican, was returning from midnight Mass when unknown men assaulted him and left him lying on the ground with a fractured skull. He died eleven days later without regaining consciousness.[21]

Chief Superintendent Matt Fitzgerald of Bandon had an IRA informant who was close to Tom Barry, then OC of the No. 1 Cork Brigade. The informant told Fitzgerald that the O'Reilly killing and the O'Leary attack was an unofficial IRA action carried out by local IRA men as a reprisal for an alleged assault on one of their number, Denis O'Connor of Innishannon, by O'Reilly, O'Leary and others. The informant insisted that Barry did not sanction the assault. Fitzgerald was sceptical of this latter claim and was of the view that Barry did, in fact, authorise it if not actually take part in it himself.[22]

Despite the IRA's brutal attacks on the Blueshirts, the focus of the Special Branch was also firmly on O'Duffy's fascists. The most serious confrontation between the Harriers and Blueshirts took place when a riot broke out at a cattle sale in Marsh's Yard in Cork City on 13 August

1934 during which the Harriers recklessly opened fire killing a 22-year-old man. Cattle were seized for non-payment of land annuities from the farm of Michael Corkery of Poulavone, Carrigrohane, Cork on 9 August amid violent scenes. The Sheriff and his staff were backed up by thirty uniformed gardaí and twelve Special Branch officers (Harriers). With their arrival the church bell was rung, and a hostile crowd gathered, including Father Ahern CC, who was aggressive towards the gardaí. The Sheriff seized seven dairy cattle and brought them to Marsh's Yard for sale. They then went to the farm of John Coveney of Bishopstown, some two miles from the Corkery farm. Here, Coveney and others confronted them with hayforks and dispersed the cattle while threatening the Sheriff and his men. Four men were arrested and brought to Union Quay Station. The Sheriff and his men secured six cattle and loaded them onto a lorry. They drove off and a short distance away they found broken bottles on the road ahead. When the lorry stopped, stones were thrown toward them, breaking the windscreen. The detectives chased the culprits across fields firing shots over their heads.[23]

The auction was set for noon on 13 August and it was expected that large numbers of Blueshirts would turn up to protest. Serious trouble was anticipated. As tensions were high, Chief Superintendent Michael Fitzgerald placed huge numbers of gardaí and detectives on duty to police the event. It included 330 uniformed gardaí of various ranks, two detective sergeants and thirty-three detectives. He provided a special escort of seven detectives (Harriers) armed with rifles to protect the cattle buyer 'Mr O'Neill'[24] who was the target of the crowd's fury. 3,000 Blueshirts assembled for the protest and fifteen of them armed with batons drove a lorry, protected by metal plates, through the police cordon followed by others on foot. Several gardaí jumped on the running board and tried to divert it by turning the steering wheel but the men inside the lorry beat them off with batons. The gate crashed open, knocking down the chief superintendent and injuring his foot. The Harriers immediately opened fire with rifles and revolvers killing 22-year-old Michael Patrick Lynch and wounding seven others, all of whom were on the lorry. The injured were brought to hospital while eleven others on the lorry were arrested. Gardaí baton charged the crowd and dozens of people were injured including several gardaí.[25]

Lynch's funeral, on 15 August, was attended by a massive crowd including thousands of Blueshirts led by Eoin O'Duffy, former President William T. Cosgrave along with many other TDs. On arrival at Dunbullogue cemetery in Carrignavar, several bands playing solemn music escorted the cortege along with a guard of honour of uniformed Blueshirts, consisting of about 200 men and 100 women. After the burial and the playing of the Last Post, O'Duffy gave an oration at the graveside during which he thundered, 'there is associated with the Garda Síochána, a murder gang – the so-called Harrier Force.' This was greeted by applause from the crowd but O'Duffy rebuked them saying it was not an occasion for applause. He continued, 'I would advise the government – even now it is not too late. I would ask them here at this open grave to disband the force – the so-called Harrier force – which they have built up, and not to break up forever our Garda Síochána.'[26]

At the inquest on 31 August, the coroner's jury heard evidence from Detective Garda John F. Rogers (one of O'Neill's escort) that he fired three shots in the air and then three shots into the crowd. Garda T. J. O'Rourke said he saw Lynch, who was still alive, lying on the ground and he asked the guard to get a priest. A priest came and anointed him and as he lay dying Lynch said to his mother, 'I forgive them; they hurt me.'[27]

The lorry driver, William Crowley of Upton, County Cork, one of those injured during the shooting, was charged in Cork Circuit Court with unlawful assembly and resisting and obstructing the County Sheriff in the execution of duty and damaging the gate of the sale yard. Detective Garda O'Meara, another of the cattle buyer's bodyguards, told the court that when the firing stopped, he assisted Crowley, who was wounded, from the driver's seat. He sat him on the ground and told the detective his name and confirmed he had been driving. When asked why he did such 'a mad act', Crowley replied, 'I had to do it. I was threatened with a gun.' The jury convicted him of unlawful assembly and malicious damage to the gates. They also added a rider, to the effect, 'we are of the unanimous opinion that the local and district garda acted with commendable discretion. On the other hand, we disapprove of inexperienced armed detectives operating without being directly under some local superior officer's control. We strongly recommend the accused man to his lordships mercy.' He was sentenced to twelve months imprisonment.[28]

The government refused to hold an inquiry into the affair but Lynch's father, Daniel Lynch of Lyre, Carrignavar, County Cork, took a civil action against three of the Harriers, named Owen Moore (8322), John Kennedy (8505) and John F. Rogers (8282)[29]. The defence made the case that the detectives believed that the lives of both O'Neill and the gardaí were in imminent danger and that if they fired at civilians, it was in the belief that the shooting was necessary to protect life, property and public order.[30]

However, Judge Hanna held against them and in his judgement was particularly scathing of the Harriers. He held that Moore started the fusillade. Moore had called on his colleagues to fire and had himself emptied his revolver at the lorry and then got a rifle and fired several more shots. He rejected the defence submission that they fired to protect their lives. He was not impressed that Moore and Condon were promoted to sergeant shortly after this event. He said that an ordinary guard takes years of hard service to attain the rank of sergeant, but these two men were given the rank about a year after joining the force. He added the withering sentence, 'these 'S' men are not real Civic Guards. They are an excrescence upon that reputable body.' He said the evidence disclosed a prima facie case of manslaughter and it was his duty to direct the attention of the Attorney General to the evidence. He awarded the plaintiff £300 against the detectives. They appealed this to the Supreme Court and their appeal was dismissed.[31] This case, and Judge Hanna's remarks confirmed the public perception that the Harriers was a dangerous, undisciplined section of the force. No doubt the government had no illusions about them but regardless of their shortcomings, recognised their effectiveness in dealing with both Blueshirts and the IRA.

The Broy Harriers were hastily recruited and largely untrained and that, in certain instances, was a recipe for ill-discipline and corruption. Detective Sergeant Moore, now stationed in Dublin, got into a further disciplinary scrape in November 1935 following an incident in Dundalk in a dispute between a cattle dealer, Edward Haughey and Thomas Morgan (i.e., the cattle buyer 'Mr O'Neill'). Haughey bought six cattle from Morgan for £15 but apparently later removed them without first handing over the cash, allegedly with Moore's assistance. Both parties originated from north of the border and Moore, a native of Armagh, knew them both.[32]

Garda management was not impressed with Moore's antics, and he was later disciplined for saying to cattle dealer, Michael J. McGee, 'listen here, if you want to know where these cattle are, they are at my place in Ravensdale' before adding, 'I shot a man before and it would not give me any trouble to shoot another.' This was an obvious reference to the Marsh's Yard shooting. He was convicted and received a formal written caution and warned that in the event of a similar complaint, the Commissioner 'may be obliged to take a more serious view of the matter'.[33]

A bitter Detective Moore resigned from the force on 29 March 1938, and in a four-page diatribe to Justice Minister Patrick J. Ruttledge complained that there were rumours circulating in the force that he was a confidential informant for the IRA and was using a garda vehicle to transport arms and ammunition. He blamed Detective Sergeant John R. Cruise[34] for being behind these rumours, describing him as 'an unscrupulous blackguard, a discredited sergeant of the Special Branch devoid of any semblance of honour, principle or self-respect.' He went on to describe the hours of work he had put in to deal with the 'No Annuity Campaign' and the sale of seized stock and complained that his home in Ravensdale had been picketed. He felt it was impossible to continue in the Force in these circumstances, though he did offer to continue his work in handling seized stock in a civilian capacity.[35] Five years later he was killed in an accident while felling a tree near his home at Ravensdale Park in Dundalk.[36]

There were extraordinary scenes in Fermoy, County Cork on 3 May 1935 following another seizure of animals from a number of farmers for non-payment of land annuities. The gardaí had intense security measures in place to ensure the event passed peacefully, no doubt with the memory of the Marsh's Yard shooting the previous August still fresh in their minds. To ensure tight security, the military barracks was selected as the venue for the auction. Prior to the auction, groups of farmers began to arrive in Pearse Square in cars and pony traps. At 10.15 a.m., two busloads of gardaí arrived from Cork City and took up positions around the army base. Astonished onlookers watched as two uniformed gardaí carrying rifles and wearing bandoliers of ammunition took up duty at each entrance to the barracks. The cattle buyer then arrived, accompanied by a large escort of Special Branch men, two of whom were carrying Thompson sub-machine guns. The auction proceeded without incident and once again, the only bidder was Mr O'Neill who bought all the cattle, sheep and lambs on offer. The animals were later moved by goods train to Dublin under heavy Special Branch escort.[37]

At 2.30 a.m. on 5 June 1935, Blueshirt gunmen opened fire with rifles on Kildorrery Garda Station in County Cork shattering the window of the dayroom, where a garda was on duty, and the window of a bedroom where a second officer was asleep. There were no injuries. There was intense police activity in the following days and several individuals were arrested but most were quickly released.[38]

Phone lines were cut in the area to delay the arrival of assistance. It was suspected that Blueshirts carried out the attack in retaliation for the recent arrest of one of their number, James Cronin of Kildorrery. Some of the suspects involved in the wire-cutting admitted their part and told gardaí that they received their instructions from John Sheehan. They detained Sheehan, along with Patrick Sheehan, and Michael Dwane all from Kildorrery. Later gardaí placed John Sheehan along with one of the cooperating suspects, William McCarthy, in cells opposite each other so they could whisper to each other at night. They primed McCarthy on what to say and listened from a concealed position unknown to Sheehan.[39]

Among things Sheehan was heard saying over two days on 11 and 12 June 1935 was, 'I told them nothing, I denied everything. There was a young fellow [Joseph Creed – another cooperating suspect] down there in the room today and he gave me away, the young bastard.' When asked by McCarthy if he (Sheehan) told Creed to cut the wires he replied, 'I did, the bastard, and I'll get three years for the wires, but when they don't get the guns for the other [*sic*] I'll not be doing badly. Have a big parade for me when I come out.' In a later overheard conversation Sheehan said, 'I'll plug all round me when I get out and we have plenty of stuff [guns]. I'll have another crack at the barracks too.' Patrick Sheehan made a statement admitting his part in the shooting to Detective Sergeant Michael Wymes (7845 - later Garda Commissioner). Michael Dwane made similar admissions to Superintendent Con Brady and said it was he who fired the rifle. Despite his bravado in the cell, John Sheehan also admitted giving instructions to have the wires cut knowing of the pending attack on the barracks. He also admitted involvement in earlier unrelated armed incidents.[40] On 19 December 1935, the military tribunal sentenced Dwane and Patrick Sheehan to five years imprisonment while John Sheehan received a three-year sentence. A number of others received lesser sentences. When sentences were passed John Sheehan gave the order, 'Attention, salute' and the men then raised their arms in the fascist style salute and shouted, 'Up the Blueshirts.'[41]

However, the Blueshirts soon broke up in rancour with internal splits and quarrelling. By 1936, they faded completely from the Irish political landscape. According to Manning, 'the whole Blueshirt phenomenon can be seen as a final instalment of the Civil War saga. The demise of the Blueshirts was to coincide with the establishment of something approaching normal relations between government and opposition.'[42] Their downfall was no doubt assisted by O'Duffy's erratic and volatile leadership, his final adventure being the ill-fated crusade to Spain to fight for General Franco.

Following Judge Hanna's less than complimentary remarks about the Harriers, they were dogged by ongoing controversies. A government decision in 1934 to use the Harriers to provide protection for former president William T. Cosgrave TD and General Richard Mulcahy TD (both now on the opposition benches) was bitterly resisted by both men. Up to then, the army provided security. Cosgrave, who had a home at Beechpark, Templeogue wrote a strident letter to the secretary of the Department of Justice on 26 March noting 'that no police guard or other guard unknown to my household be allowed to enter Beechpark.'[43]

Mulcahy, who lived at Lissenfield House in Rathmines, was similarly incensed. He did not think gardaí were suitable for this type of work and worried that being seen 'accompanied by big men who by their presence would merely bring me under notice.' He said that none of the protection party would be allowed to enter his house except under a search warrant. Like it or not, detectives were appointed to protect him and this prompted him to write several further complaints.[44]

In one incident, he complained that he was at a performance in the Abbey Theatre with his wife and afterwards he went to the café. He noticed Detective McGuire [D/Garda Michael McGuire, 8546 – a 'Harrier'] 'walking insolently around the vestibule.' McGuire asked a young man nearby to get him cigarettes as 'we're escorting this fucker.' Mulcahy wrote, 'this is not the language of protection and I want to draw your attention to the contents of my letter of the 10th April and to say again that I will not tolerate a continuance of the present police circumstances which surround my home and my movements.' Following the many complaints made by both TDs, Chief Superintendent Woods recommended that the special escort be withdrawn, just leaving protection on their respective homes. This was overruled by the Minister for Justice who directed that the escorts be retained. However, the protection was finally removed from Mulcahy in November 1937.[45]

On 25 April 1934, Mulcahy made another complaint about the Harriers. This related to how they had treated John Murray of 109

Dillon's Cross, Cork. He quoted from an affidavit in which Murray outlined how he was under police protection after giving evidence against six men at the military tribunal for attacks on his house. Three of them were convicted in February and sentenced to terms of imprisonment.

In his affidavit, Murray complained that on 7 April there were two uniformed gardaí and two members of Special Branch (Harriers) on duty outside his home. At 1.45 a.m., he could hear his front door opening and two detectives started coming up the stairs. They were arguing with each other, and he could hear one of them whom he named as Lalor[46] saying, 'I'll go up and shoot him.' His colleague Detective Sullivan was trying to restrain him. Murray peered out and could see Sullivan struggling with Lalor, who had a revolver in his hand, and saying, 'I'll shoot him and put an end to him and you can give evidence against me then.' Finally, Sullivan persuaded Lalor to desist and he put the revolver back in his pocket saying, 'if I go down without shooting him it will break my heart.' The detectives left and Murray got up, slipped out the back door, and later complained about the matter in McCurtain Street Barracks.[47]

The matter was again raised in the Dáil the following August when former justice minister, Fitzgerald-Kenney, spoke of how other gardaí had the greatest difficulty in restraining one of their number from shooting the man they were there to protect and that, 'he had to flee from his house from an armed guard who declared that it would break his heart if he did not shoot him.; He asked if that man was still in the force. In his reply, Minister Ruttledge said, '...that man was not allowed to remain 24 hours in the Force.'[48] Lalor was, in fact, dismissed on 15 May 1934.

On the night of 7 January 1937, a drunken Harrier, Thomas Carass (8252)[49], opened fire on one of his colleagues at Dolphin's Barn in Dublin. Detective Gardaí Patrick Kirwan (12309) and James Kelly (8279 – also a Harrier) were making enquiries around Dolphins Barn in Dublin about a local suspect named James Foran. They went into Leech's pub and quizzed the bar staff but they were unable to help. As they were talking, two officers from the local station in Crumlin, Gardaí Power and McKee, came in and had a conversation about Foran. At about 8.30 p.m., Carass entered the pub in a drunken belligerent condition. Addressing Kirwan, he said, 'I'll give you a drink, but I hate you.'

Kirwan was not aware of any reason for his hostility and said, 'I don't want a drink and I never did anything on you to hate me.'

Shouting at the top of his voice Carass said, 'You CID bastard, you rat, you murderer, you raided a house in Kimmage; you tore the place asunder and threatened to murder the people in the house.'[50]

Realising there was no point in arguing with a drunk, Kirwan, Kelly and the two Crumlin gardaí slipped out of the pub and began to walk away. Carass followed and drew his revolver, firing several shots at Kirwan who fled down the road and took shelter in a doorway. There were three bullet holes in his overcoat, but he was not injured. Detective Garda Kelly and Garda Power pursued Carass who threw his now empty gun away saying, 'there's the damned gun for you.' Kelly picked up the gun and meantime Garda Power caught up with him and knocked him unconscious with a punch. Carass was brought to Dublin Castle where Detective Inspector Mansfield confined him to barracks and arranged to have him suspended the following day. He also seized Carass' revolver and remaining ammunition.[51]

Carass was charged with shooting at detectives Kirwan and Kelly with intent to murder them or cause them grievous bodily harm. At his trial in March 1937, J.A. McCarthy SC, prosecuting, told the court that Carass 'behaved like a drunken rowdy' on the night. In his own defence, Carass told the court he was a member of the IRA between 1917 and 1925. He said he had consumed a considerable amount of drink on the day in question and claimed that it was Kirwan and Kelly who were needling him in the pub. He said he thought Kirwan was going to draw his gun and shoot him, so he took out his own gun and fired six shots but that he did not fire at any individual. The jury retired for two hours and returned with a verdict of guilty of shooting at the detectives with intent to do grievous bodily harm, but not guilty of attempted murder. Justice

O'Byrne sentenced him to eighteen months imprisonment with hard labour.[52]

In his report to the Department of Justice on 11 January 1937, Assistant Commissioner Woods said of Carass:

> He is a native of Dublin and was one of those members specially recruited in 1933 [i.e., a Broy Harrier]. He is the father of a large family of some seven children. It is known that he was never a good husband and was generally a type altogether unsuited for a police force. Previous to this incident disciplinary action was taken against him for neglect of duty on the 19/12/36.[53]

There was further controversy in June 1937 when another Harrier, Detective Garda John Brocklebank (8268), shot dead a young IRA man in Clanbrassil Street in Dublin. On the evening of 15 June, three Special Branch detectives (all Harriers), Detective Sergeants Wilfred Dowd (8259) and John Moroney (8369), as well as Brocklebank, were searching for suspects in relation to the theft of a car. A garage proprietor, James Paton, who ran a motor business in Denzille Lane near Merrion Square, earlier reported that he unwillingly lent a car to two unknown men on 13 May after they produced revolvers and said they were from the IRA. They promised to return the vehicle in an hour-and-a-half but failed to do so. Gardaí found the vehicle abandoned on Merrion Square the following day with the engine still warm. They were sceptical of Paton's story and suspected that he knew the men and had voluntarily given them the car, but later got worried when it was not returned, fearing he would be implicated in their activity.[54]

Brocklebank watched 48 Lower Clanbrassil Street in an attempt to catch up with 22-year-old Samuel Wheelock, who was suspected of involvement. At 5 p.m. on 15 June he spotted Wheelock entering his home while three 'minders' waited on the opposite side of the street. From time-to-time, Wheelock emerged and talked to the minders before returning inside. Brocklebank asked a uniformed garda on traffic duty at Leonard's Corner nearby to contact Dublin Castle for assistance. A

Special Branch car arrived with Detective Sergeants Moroney and Dowd and he acquainted them with the situation.

On spotting the detectives, one of the minders, 20-year-old Henry Dale, ran towards the house with Brocklebank in pursuit. They intercepted Dale before he reached Wheelock's room. Dowd restrained him while Brocklebank ran upstairs to Wheelock's flat and arrested him.[55]

Brocklebank and Dowd put their two prisoners in the back seat of the patrol car. As Dowd was closing the door, Peter McCarthy (20) from 207 Clonard Road, Crumlin, approached the car brandishing a revolver and shouted, 'stick them up'. A quick-thinking Brocklebank in the back seat quietly took a .32 calibre pistol out of his pocket and fired at McCarthy. He jumped out of the car and took a gun from McCarthy, who was lying motionless on the footpath. It was a short .455 Webley revolver loaded in two chambers. He pursued a second youth named Eamon Fagan (19), who fled from the scene. He arrested him nearby. One of the prisoners asked to see McCarthy's revolver and on being shown it he pointed out that the two loaded chambers would be the last to fire and that McCarthy was not a man who would have actually fired.[56]

McCarthy's funeral in Mount Jerome Cemetery on 18 June was attended by about 3,000 people. The hearse was accompanied by an escort of various republican organisations including Sinn Féin, Cumann na mBan, and Fianna Éireann. A firing party discharged three volleys of revolver shots over his grave.[57]

At the opening of the inquest on 29 June, solicitor (and IRA member) Con Lehane told the coroner, Dr. D.A. MacErlean, 'it is my case – I will be perfectly frank about it – that Peter McCarthy, an unarmed boy, was shot down, callously, and without reason or provocation, by the gentleman described as Detective Guard Brocklebank.'

Martin Maguire SC, for the state, argued:

> The evidence at this inquest, on behalf of the Attorney General, will be that Peter McCarthy attempted to rescue the other two prisoners, and

> that, in the course of doing so, he had in his hand at the door of the car a deadly weapon – I think a Webley revolver – loaded in two chambers, which he presented to the chest of Detective Sergeant Dowd. There will be the clearest evidence that this unfortunate boy had this weapon, that he had it presented at Detective Sergeant Dowd, that he tried to force open the door of the car, and that, at the time, he shouted, 'Hands up,' or 'Stick them up,' in an attempt to hold up the police officers in the course of their duty.'[58]

Interestingly the other two prisoners did not disagree unduly with the police version of events. Wheelock's only quibble was that McCarthy 'was only in the act of drawing a gun'.[59]

The inquest, which lasted three days, concluded on 22 July 1938. McCarthy's mother was present along with Maud Gonne MacBride while her son, barrister Seán MacBride, represented the family along with A.E. Wood SC. The curious aspect of the case was that Brocklebank shot McCarthy with an unofficial gun – a .32 semi-automatic pistol of a type not issued to the force. He frankly admitted as much at the adjourned hearing on 20 July. When asked by Mr Sean MacBride, 'Was not the gun you took off McCarthy an official gun?', Brocklebank replied, 'no.' The reason for this question was that the court previously heard evidence from weapons expert Superintendent D. Stapleton that McCarthy's gun was a short Webley of RIC pattern but was not on the official list of RIC weapons handed over to the Garda Síochána.[60] MacBride continued, 'You were not charged under the Firearms Act for having in your possession an unofficial revolver?' to which Brocklebank replied, 'Why should I be charged?'

Addressing the jury, Mr Wood said; 'It was inherently improbable that a young man like McCarthy would try to 'hold up' a squad car in which there were three detectives.' He also referred to the unofficial gun used by Brocklebank and wondered why he was not charged in relation to that. He added, 'the position revealed in this case, appears to be that in this city, when an incident like this takes place, there is no investigation, no disciplinary action of any kind by the garda authorities. Is not that a paralysing state of affairs.'[61]

The jury found that Peter McCarthy died of gunshot wounds after an affray in Lower Clanbrassil Street on 15 Jun 1937 and added:

> But we cannot agree on the following points: -
> (1) that Peter McCarthy was armed;
> (2) that Detective Officer Brocklebank could not have inflicted the wounds from the position in which McCarthy was standing.[62]

Charges were brought against Dale, Wheelock and Fagan but all were acquitted. Detectives believed all three along with the deceased were members of the Dublin Brigade, IRA.[63]

At that time, it was a common practice among Special Branch men (mostly ex-IRA men) to hold on to favourite weapons they had since the War of Independence and/or the subsequent civil war. Brocklebank, who was in the anti-Treaty IRA, described himself as 'Late O/C H Coy, 4 Batt, Dublin Brigade' in a reference letter he wrote in 1938 for a Cumann na mBan applicant for a military service pension.[64] Clearly, garda management turned a blind eye to the practice though they later clamped down on the practice.[65]

In the early years, relations between the Harriers and veteran detectives were fraught, and on occasion they refused to take orders from 'Free State' officers.[66] They even elected their own sergeants, and their decisions were upheld when reported to Garda HQ. In time, a few drifted away, some were dismissed while others who were not suited to regular police work were allocated duties involving cash escorts and protection duties that they were happy to carry out. The remainder blended in well and became competent detectives. As former IRA men they were well-placed to combat the movement as they knew many of them personally and were aware of their haunts and hideouts. They would go on to become formidable opponents of their former associates and some would pay with their lives.

Chapter 7

MISPLACED PATIENCE, 1934–1936

We have been very patient during the last three years....our hopes, apparently have been misplaced.
Eamon de Valera, 31 March 1935

Apart from the unwelcome diversion of having to confront the Blueshirt violence in the early-1930s, the main task of the Special Branch was the ongoing battle with the IRA who continued with low-level violence, intimidation and an occasional murder. As F.S.L. Lyons pointed out, the IRA was a different proposition, not only because they were an underground organisation, but also because they had ties to the ruling party which made it difficult for de Valera to bring the full force of the law against them, only doing so after other methods failed.[1]

For their part, the IRA was also in a period of transition. Seán Russell, Quartermaster General, was developing his plans for a bombing campaign in British cities.[2] But de Valera was moving inexorably towards a new constitution and the new state did not require a second army. Despite 1935 overtures between Russell and de Valera[3], and the latter's efforts to transition personnel from the IRA into the legitimate forces of the state through the formation of the Volunteer Force, and to pension them off using the Military Pensions Act, 1934[4], the IRA was never going to be a legitimate part of a constitutional Ireland. In any event, those extreme elements of the movement would most certainly not give up their cause. The government had no option but to defend the state and that role fell to the Special Branch.

On the night of 11 February 1934, the IRA carried out a revenge attack at the home of Joseph McGrory at 8 Annaville Terrace, Chapel St in Dundalk, County Louth. McGrory gave evidence at the Military Tribunal against two members of the IRA who were charged with assault and robbery, and imprisoned. Two men approached McGrory's home and one of them broke the front window while the second threw a bomb inside which exploded shortly afterwards. It demolished the house and injured the only occupant, Joseph's mother Mrs Frances McGrory. She was removed to hospital and discharged on 3 March, having only apparently received slight injuries but died on 18 March at her new home at 36 O'Hanlon Park. The inquest found she died from heart failure which was aggravated by the shock caused by the explosion.[5]

On 10 May 1935, five Dundalk IRA men were charged with murdering Mrs McGrory. They were Thomas Walsh, James Finnegan, Bernard Murphy, Eamon Coffey and Richard Goss. On being charged Murphy replied, 'as a soldier of the Irish Republican Army I will not recognise any court set up under the Imperial British Junta.' On searching Finnegan's home gardaí found a Thompson sub-machine gun along with six handguns and a quantity of ammunition.[6]

The state, however, had a star witness who possessed first-hand detail on what happened. Former IRA man Matthew McCrystal from County Tyrone was present when the bomb was being prepared and when it was thrown. Afterwards, he became disillusioned with the IRA and approached detectives with information, including details on the arms found in Finnegan's house. On 10 November, at the request of Detective Headquarters, McCrystal was recruited into the Garda Síochána as a 'Harrier' and given the garda registered number 8591.

McCrystal told the court he was present in the Sinn Féin rooms in Market Square in Dundalk where he saw Walsh, assisted by Murphy and Goss, putting sticks of gelignite and detonators into a petrol can. Finnegan had a Thompson machine-gun under his coat while Goss, Walsh and Murphy had revolvers. Outside they saw Eamon Coffey who told them, 'the coast is clear if you go by Crowe Street.' Finnegan was in charge and told Walsh and Murphy to throw in the bomb. Walsh lit the fuse and Murphy threw it in before they ran off in different directions.[7]

The case hinged on McCrystal's evidence. In court, Murphy denied the charge and alleged that the gardaí carried out the bombing. On 18 July 1935, the tribunal found all five men not guilty. The president of the tribunal noted that the suggestion that the gardaí were responsible was 'beneath contempt' but added, 'we are not however, satisfied that guilt has been sufficiently brought home to the accused in this case and consequently give them the benefit of the doubt and accordingly we acquit the five accused.'[8]

The department of justice was not consulted about McCrystal's irregular appointment and, in a memo to the commissioner, pointed out he was disqualified by virtue of Section 31 of Article 2A, and instructed he was to be discharged. Commissioner Broy appealed against this saying he had the makings of a good guard and he was now a marked man whose life would be in danger if discharged. However, McCrystal voluntarily resigned on 25 May 1935 but moved into the depot as a civilian state witness in need of protection.[9]

In May 1934, the military tribunal convicted Cork IRA commander Tom Barry of possession of a Thompson sub-machine gun along with 384 rounds of .45 ammunition. He refused to answer when asked his name and declined to plead. He complained loudly about prejudicial articles in the *Irish Press* and *Irish Independent*, quoting the Bishop of Galway's remarks saying:

> I am charged here with having IRA arms, and the Bishop of Galway, in a published statement that the IRA were a lot of gangsters and that the arms in these men's hands were not used for any high national purpose but for

> intimidation, private revenge and armed robbery. If that is not prejudicing my case, I would like to hear what would.

The tribunal dismissed his concerns and went on to hear the case. Detective Sergeant John Collins (2262) of Carrigtwohill revealed that he and other detectives searched Barry's home at Bellevue Terrace in Cork. The only occupant was Barry's father-in-law Michael Price, and detectives found the cartons of ammunition in the pantry under the stairs. Detective Garda Maurice Kennedy (8496 - a Harrier) gave evidence of finding a Thompson sub-machine gun in three parts while the stock was found elsewhere in the house.[10] Barry told the court, 'any arms I ever had under my control were the arms of the IRA.' He added, 'it was not only the right of Volunteers to have arms, but it was their bounden duty to arm themselves and those under their control until this country was free.' He was sentenced to twelve months imprisonment.[11]

As we have seen, the IRA was very active, especially in County Clare during the 1920s and 1930s. However, local detectives had a very good handle on their actions and the level of intelligence they were getting about their activities was staggering. They clearly had some well-placed sources inside the IRA in that county. Between February and August 1934, they submitted almost weekly reports with the most precise details shown in the following examples:

- Full details of an IRA convention of the East Clare Battalion at the home of Cornelius McMahon of Clooney, Ennis on 14 February 1934 with names and ranks of all who were present.
- Details of a North Clare Battalion meeting at the home of Michael Madigan in Church Street, Ennistymon on 15 February 1934, with names and ranks of all who were present.
- Details of a 'Battalion Council Meeting' of the West Clare Battalion on 12 August 1934 concerning the selection of a delegate for the General Army Convention then being planned. It was presided over by T.J.

> Ryan and the meeting decided to put a number of matters forward for discussion at the Army Convention. These included a proposal to assist Fianna Fáil and Labour at the next general election, and that all members attending the Communist Congress in Athlone be dismissed from the Army.[12]

In late-1934, a dispute arose in Edgeworthstown, County Longford between landlord Gerald More-O'Ferrall and his tenants. The tenants refused to pay their rent and demanded a 50 per cent reduction. As tensions rose, the IRA pledged their support to the tenants 'in their fight against landlordism.' A meeting in Edgeworthstown on Sunday 2 December 1934 heard several fiery speeches from IRA speakers including a man named as Peadar O'Rourke who was introduced as being from IRA headquarters. This was probably an alias as detectives could not establish his identity. O'Rourke told the crowd that the IRA 'would support any fight against landlordism, capitalism and imperialism.' He urged the tenants to resist the bailiffs and 'if the bailiffs were accompanied by Guards or Broy Harriers they must be beaten.' He was sure 'there were plenty pitchforks and boughs of trees around Edgeworthstown, if required.' Another IRA speaker, Michael J. Kelly, urged the tenants if they were evicted, they were to go back to their homes and break down the doors and if the gardaí and Broy Harriers used sticks and batons, they must use sticks and batons. 'If the Guards used rifles and revolvers, they must use rifles and revolvers', he suggested.[13]

At 9 p.m. on 9 February 1935, a team of IRA men wearing garda uniforms entered More-O'Ferrall's home just after the family had dinner. All the intruders had revolvers and one asked O'Ferrall to come outside. O'Ferrall responded, 'I'm damned if I'm going outside. Who are you?' The men tried to drag him out but his 21-year-old son Richard intervened and pulled one of the attackers from his father and hit him in the face. The gunmen beat both men, and one shot Richard in the back and he fell to the floor in agony. He told his sister Marjorie that his 'legs were gone.' Garda Breen from Edgeworthstown arrived in the house at 9.40

p.m. and found Richard lying on his right side with arms outstretched. He was still alive and moaning in pain but on 20 February he died in hospital from his wounds. Gerald More-O'Ferrall was lying nearby with his face covered in blood. He handed the garda a fully loaded revolver while Miss More-O'Ferrall handed him a garda-type cap. This was one of a selection of old garda caps donated to a band in Longford and stolen earlier from their room.[14]

On 1 April, four men appeared in a special court in Longford before District Justice J.H. Rice, charged with the murder. They were John 'Nipper' Shanley from Dromod, County Leitrim, James J. Reynolds and his twin brother John, also from Dromod, and William Mulligan from Ward's Terrace, Longford. As Superintendent P.J. Finnegan began to give evidence, James Reynolds stood up and said, 'you assaulted me half an hour ago, why is he not charged with it?' The justice told him to sit down and after being restrained by detectives, he resumed his seat. When the superintendent gave evidence of arrest Shanley said, 'it is a trumped-up charge, and that man – (pointing to Superintendent Sean Liddy of Longford) – knows it. We never murdered anyone, Mr Rice.' Garda HQ earlier received a tip off from inside the IRA that the Longford Battalion decided to take 'drastic action' against Superintendent Liddy because of the vigour with which he was pursuing the killers of More-O'Ferrall. They arranged for two armed detectives to escort Liddy for some time afterwards.[15]

At an identification parade in Mullingar on 3 April, Geraldine More-O'Ferrall, wife of Gerald and mother of Richard, identified John Reynolds as the 'red-haired man who shot my son' while her daughter Marjory identified all four of the raiders. She identified John Reynolds[16] as the man who shot her brother, while James Joseph Reynolds, John Shanley and William Mulligan were identified as the other three men who were present. The ten-day trial ended with a hung jury when the foreman told the judge, 'there is no possibility whatsoever of an agreement'. The verdict was met with cheering and shouts of 'Up the Republic' as the prisoners were returned to Mountjoy Jail.[17]

The re-trial commenced in December, and after hearing seven days of evidence the jury brought in verdicts of not guilty and all the accused were discharged.[18] They were welcomed home at a meeting in Mullingar at which Maurice Twomey (then IRA chief of staff) addressed the crowd. He said the recent trial resulted from Republicans striking at landlordism – the chief imperialist institution of the country. The IRA was the only force which could smash imperialism. Later a crowd of 300 people, led by a band, greeted them in Edgwardstown.[19]

During the O'Ferrall investigation, an IRA intelligence officer was busy gathering information on the local gardaí. Detectives got their hands on a document written by the IO (Intelligence Officer) of the Leitrim Battalion (most likely from a source inside the local IRA) giving a rundown on the gardaí in Dromod Station in County Leitrim.[20] It read in part as follows:

> (a) Sergt. Kelly; native Bohola, County Mayo; stationed Kiltyclogher previously; very diligent; the main spring of the case; [meaning the More-O'Ferrall case] no good.
> (b) Guard Sinnott; very dutiful; came from Leix or Offaly to Dromod.[21]
> (c) Guard Sullivan; native of Kerry; not considered too dutiful.
> (d) Guard Lindsay came into the force since the Fianna Fáil Government came into office; very dangerous; native place unknown.[22]
> (e) Guard Morgan; seems to be quiet; native place unknown.
> (f) Broy D/O Preston; native of Tipperary; came from Drumshambo to Dromod; very dangerous man; very clever.[23]
> (g) Broy D/O Daly; native of County Kerry; very dangerous; also came from Drumshambo to Dromod.

A bitter strike by Dublin tram and bus workers commenced on 2 March 1935 following the dismissal of a tram driver. The strike lasted seventy-six days and feelings were running high. On 15 March, an anonymous telephone caller rang the Special Branch office in Dublin Castle and said that the Communist Party were going to 'do in the industry and

Commerce Minister, Seán Lemass, and William O'Brien, who was then General Secretary of the ITGWU, 'if they attempted to run the buses.' The caller refused to give his name but said he was a former member of the Communist Party.[24] At the time, the Communist Party was holding numerous public meetings in Cathal Brugha Street, supporting the workers and denouncing the Tramway Company. At a meeting on 19 June 1935, Comrade Prender waxed lyrical about the delights of living in the workers Utopia of communist Russia where there was full employment, 'workers only worked seven hours a day, got a month's leave each year with pay' and that the great problem there was the shortage of workers.[25] Comrade Prender must have been unaware of Stalin's Great Terror which was then underway.

On 20 March, the government sent in army lorries to assist the hard-pressed citizenry get to and from work. The IRA issued a statement condemning strike-breaking by the army. As soon as army lorries appeared on the streets, gunmen began sniping at their tyres. On 26 March, on government instructions, there followed a mass roundup of IRA suspects when forty-three men were arrested and lodged in the Curragh. Those arrested included Peadar O'Donnell, Mick Price, and Roddy Connolly though a number of others, who were anticipating the raids, were not home when detectives called. They included Seán MacBride, Maurice Twomey and Seán Russell.[26]

At 12.05 a m on 24 March 1935, Sergeant Victor Lockhart (DMP No. 12221) and Garda Humphrey Leary (3390) were patrolling Grafton Street when three men on bicycles rode up and almost immediately opened fire on them with revolvers. Both gardaí fell to the ground wounded, and the attackers rode off. Lockhart was shot in the left knee while Leary was struck by two bullets, one in the right knee and the other on the thigh. A passing taxi driver drove them to Mercer's Hospital nearby. Detective Inspector McGloin and Detective Garda Frederick Lalor (8328) of the Special Branch (a Harrier) went to the scene and found five bullet holes in the shutter of 95 Grafton Street. A few minutes later, Garda Thomas Daly was on duty near the *Irish Press* office on Burgh Quay when he was approached by four men on bicycles who opened fire on him without warning. He threw himself on the ground and escaped injury though he later found three bullet holes in his great coat. [27]

In the hospital, Sergeant Lockhart named his assailants as two striking bus drivers, Mick Byrne and Herbert Earnshaw. Investigators first theorised that the shooting had nothing to do with the bus strike but related to rancour between Lockhart and bus drivers on the Killester route (where Lockhart lived). Lockhart was charged before a sworn disciplinary enquiry in the Bridewell in September 1934 when Byrne, Earnshaw and other bus employees gave evidence against him. They hypothesised that the bus workers were aggrieved that Lockhart was not dismissed or reduced in rank and decided to administer their own justice. They suspected that the shots fired at Garda Daly on Burgh Quay were a distraction to give the impression it was an IRA operation connected with the strike. By 3.45 a.m., Special Branch detectives led by Detective Sergeant Cruise arrived at Pearse Street Station with both Byrne and Earnshaw in custody. Lockhart picked out both men in an identification parade organised in the hospital. They made statements strongly denying their involvement.

Chief Superintendent Woods was not convinced by Lockhart's identification and was impressed by the alibi statements taken on behalf of the two men. He felt it was far-fetched that both shootings were carried out by the same men. As bus drivers they would be well-known to gardaí in the city centre and would have taken a great risk of identification or capture. Byrne's alibi was supported by five witnesses including a Garda Clarke from Fitzgibbon Street who said Byrne was in his company at the time of the shooting and could not have been involved. Both men were released without charge.[28]

After three years in office, de Valera's patience with the IRA was fading fast. He had tried to woo them with wholesale prison releases, a purge of the Special Branch, repealing the sweeping powers under Article 2A of the Constitution (though he reintroduced it in August 1933 in the face of Blueshirt/IRA violence), and lifting the ban on *An Phoblacht*. He even went so far as to meet IRA chief of staff Seán Russell in April 1935 where he urged that the movement disband and hand over their arms. Russell, however, would only offer that they would agree to cooperate with Fianna Fáil for five years provided he would then declare an Irish Republic which de Valera rejected and the meeting ended.[29]

In a speech to the quarterly meeting of the national executive of Fianna Fáil on 31 March 1935, his frustration was apparent when he said:

> We have been very patient during the last three years. We have used the powers we possess sparingly. Realising the need of the country for harmony, and anxious to put an end to the disastrous divisions that have existed among us, we have put up with things which no other government in the world would tolerate. We have hoped all along that common sense and patriotic instincts would at last assert themselves. Our hopes have, apparently, been misplaced.'[30]

The IRA was about to learn that de Valera had an even more ruthless streak than Cosgrave.

De Valera's concerns were probably heightened when detectives discovered a sheaf of IRA documents in Kilkenny City. One of the documents dated 31 August 1934 and signed by Maurice Twomey, Chief of Staff, announced that the General Army Convention had decided that 'at least within twelve months the Army be trained, equipped and fit to take to the field.' It continued:

> The primary responsibility of the Army Council and General Headquarters Staff will be:
> (a) The drawing up of plans for the seizure and consolidation of power
> (b) Allotting of initial military tasks to Units
> (c) Providing of equipment
> (d) Giving of directions on training and on preparation of plans by Units.

It went on to say that they would have to have the 'right material' and that this would involve 'the complete elimination of a number of unsuitable volunteers from the Army.'[31] To the government this clearly sounded like plans for an attempted coup, especially the reference to 'the seizure and consolidation of power.' However, Special Branch chief Thomas Woods was probably correct when he expressed the view that 'the IRA will never be a serious menace to the government' and that the 'ready to take the field' instruction was 'an effort to put a bold face on a situation and is an effort at self-preservation more than anything else.'[32] The government was not convinced, however, and the Special Branch swung into action and began a major round-up of IRA men.

Thirty-one men were apprehended and held in the Bridewell in Dublin, nine in the Curragh and one in Cork. They included some of the top IRA members in the country, including chief of staff Maurice Twomey (author of the August 1934 directive), Roddy Connolly, son of the executed 1916 leader, and Tom Barry. Searches continued for Seán Russell and Seán MacBride.[33] Some were released quickly and twenty-five were detained in the Curragh pending trial before the military tribunal, where sentences ranging from one to six months were handed down for offences such as refusing to answer questions and membership of an unlawful association. Tom Barry got six months for membership and refusing to give an account of his movements.[34]

Solicitor and IRA man Con Lehane, who for a time was OC of the Dublin Brigade[35] was charged with sedition for a speech at Cabra on 7 March 1935 in which he urged those present to join the IRA, 'if not then and there, owing to the presence of police thugs in the audience, then during the week, from 7 to 8 o'clock each evening.' The 'thugs' he referred to were Detective Gardaí Thomas Keelan (12506), along with Detective Gardaí Sullivan, Lannigan, O'Leary and McGowan of the Special Branch, who noted who was present and the content of the speeches. Lehane added that, 'they would not rest until they had driven the last British soldier and Free State soldier out of the country; and that they had the arms and ammunition necessary to do so.' Before the meeting, about eighty men formed up and responded to military words of command. On 24 April, the military tribunal sentenced him to eighteen months imprisonment while five others, including *An Phoblacht* editor Donal O'Donoghue, were each sentenced to six months.[36]

The heightened tension between the IRA and the Garda Síochána resulted in certain uniformed gardaí being issued with revolvers. At around midnight on 12 May 1935, 24-year-old Garda Joseph Egan (8532) of Lad Lane Station (a native of Kilcormac, County Offaly) approached four young men he saw painting a slogan which read 'Join the IRA' on the footpath at the junction of Lower Leeson Street and St Stephen's Green. He quizzed them on what they were doing and on receiving an insolent response, arrested one of the men. The others ordered him to release the captive and when he refused, they produced guns and fired several shots, wounding him in the right arm and left leg. The gunmen must have been startled when Garda Egan produced his own revolver and fired back. He gamely held on to his prisoner, shouted for assistance and blew a piercing blast on his whistle, which seemed to unnerve the attackers. They fled the scene. A passing motorist assisted the garda, by putting the prisoner in the back and driving them to Lad Lane. The injured officer was taken to Baggot Street Hospital and later to St Bricin's Military Hospital. His wounds were not too serious, though he lost a lot of blood. He was visited in hospital by Commissioner Broy. The arrested man was Thomas Murphy, a bus conductor, of 5 Londonbridge Road, Sandymount.[37]

At Murphy's trial on 7 June, W. Black, S.C. for the state, told the tribunal that he would take off his hat to Sergeant Egan (he had been swiftly promoted to sergeant in the meantime) if he met him on the street:

> He took his prisoner to Lad Lane and no soldier better deserves to be called the bravest of the brave than this young man. If the country can produce from its humble ranks men like this, it may hold up its head among the nations no matter how domestic traitors may stab it in the back. These men claim to belong to the IRA, but the fighting IRA that we

> all knew fought armoured cars and lorries loaded with riflemen. It must be very galling to the members of a fine body to find men like these going around painting the IRA letters on the footpath, flaunting its name and mouthing its principles – and bringing both into the deepest disgrace.

Murphy was sentenced to two years imprisonment for membership of an unlawful association, and with assaulting Sergeant Egan.[38]

Two other men were arrested later, John Fitzsimons of McGuinness Square, Dublin and Thomas McGrattan of Kenny's Cottages off James' Street. On appearing before the military tribunal, they refused to plead saying that as soldiers of the IRA they did not recognise the court. On 11 June, Fitzsimons was sentenced to ten years imprisonment for shooting at Garda Egan and possession of grenades and other ordnance. Egan identified him in court as the man who shot him. Having served less than three years, he was released by government order on 4 May 1938.[39] McGrattan received six months imprisonment for refusing to account for his movements. The prosecution brought Murphy to court to give evidence against his comrades, but he refused saying, 'as a member of the Irish Republican Army I refuse to give evidence against these men.' On 11 June 1935, he was sentenced to two years and three months along with a further consecutive six-month sentence for contempt of court. He was released three months later on 10 September. As he was led from the court, the other prisoners clapped, one of them shouting, 'they tried to make an informer out of you and couldn't. That is the stuff to give them.' Evidence was given that McGrattan's thumb print was found on the mudguard of a bicycle abandoned near the scene of the shooting.[40]

Egan was awarded the Scott Gold Medal for bravery by Commissioner Broy at a ceremony in Garda HQ on 8 November 1937. That same month, his colleagues also presented him with a gold wristwatch at a ceremony in Lad Lane Station in appreciation of his courageous conduct.[41]

A Sinn Féin public meeting was held at Cathal Brugha Street on the evening of 11 June, the same day as Fitzsimons was sentenced to ten years.

One of the speakers, Councillor Laurence Raul, a member of the Sinn Féin *Ard Chomhairle* (Executive), gave the following insightful analysis:

> A young man has been sentenced to ten years for shooting a policeman, but as long as the police carried guns concealed about them, they would be shot at. This policeman fired on boys that were painting something on the footway, and they fired in defence. He was promoted for his brave deed. The difference between a dead IRA man and a dead policeman was that the IRA man would be rewarded for fighting for his country, while the dead policeman would go to hell for eternal damnation.

The speech was greeted by applause from a section of the audience.[42]

On Sunday morning 14 July 1935, a large team of Special Branch detectives accompanied by uniformed gardaí raided an IRA training camp at Giles Quay on the south side of the Cooley peninsula about six miles from Dundalk. They arrested twelve IRA men from Belfast including their OC, Charlie Leddy (son of an RUC inspector), and Harry White. The men were brought to Dundalk Garda Station. Leddy told the superintendent that he was in charge. The gardaí seized five Lee-Enfield rifles, one Colt revolver, two hand grenades and 179 rounds of .303 rifle ammunition. Detective Sergeant William J. Hinphy,[43] Detective Heffernan, along with other detectives chased a small group of men who fled the scene, one of whom turned and pointed a rifle at them. Hinphy fired shots over their heads, at which time they stopped and were taken into custody. A second group of Belfast men were at a training camp in Omeath some miles to the north. On hearing of their colleagues arrest, they and their supporters descended upon Dundalk that evening and held a noisy demonstration outside the station. This lead to a baton charge and one arrest. The following day the prisoners were removed to the basement cells in Mountjoy Prison where they could hear a prison officer humming the rebel song *Kevin Barry* as he paced up and down outside – no doubt for the benefit of his listeners.[44]

All twelve later appeared before the military court. The men refused to answer when their names were called. They were named as Charles Leddy, Sean Mac Con Uladh, William Mulholland, Brian Burns, John O'Hara, George Broderick, William Rice, Peter Doherty, Patrick O'Hara, James Hardy, Liam O'Connor and John Brown,[45] Superintendent P.J. Carroll of Drogheda gave evidence that thirty-four gardaí raided the camp, where he saw a large number of men drawn up in line formation. They were each sentenced to two years imprisonment and taken to Arbour Hill prison.[46]

Superintendent F. O'Driscoll was in charge of Cobh district between 1934 and 1936 and incurred the wrath of some local criminal types with IRA connections owing to his vigour in pursuing them. Ex IRA man, John Hartnett of Carrigtwohill, was particularly aggrieved at having lost his job in Carrigtwohill Post Office for causing malicious damage and blamed the superintendent for his travails. On 20 December 1935, Hartnett followed the superintendent into Carrigtwohill Station and complained:

> I have it straight from the horse's mouth that you have made a number of confidential reports about me and, amongst other things, you have alleged that I am the father of three illegitimate children in Carrigtwohill. I don't mind being blamed for criminal acts, but I resent being reported as an immoral character.

O'Driscoll assured him he submitted no such reports, but Hartnett insisted he would not stand for being maligned and left the station muttering under his breath. O'Driscoll was already aware that Hartnett was also part of a criminal gang with access to firearms. He was dismissed from the IRA for carrying out unauthorised armed attacks and robberies. In May 1934, he was sentenced to four years for his involvement in relation to a bomb explosion at the home of a Blueshirt in Carrigtwohill. He was released the following July.[47]

The following March, Sergeant Joseph Curran (859) of Carrigtwohill Station submitted a report that he received reliable information that Hartnett and his associates were planning to shoot Superintendent O'Driscoll. It involved committing an outrage of some description in Carrigtwohill village which would necessitate the presence of the superintendent. Their plan was that Laurence Dunlea from Cork City would keep watch for his car and signal by flashlight on seeing it pass. Hartnett would be waiting for the signal further on and then fire at the car as it approached him. If this failed, a third accomplice, William Conroy from Carrigtwohill, would wait near Carrigtwohill Station and fire on the superintendent as he arrived. However, O'Driscoll was sceptical, believing Hartnett to be too shrewd to involve himself in such a scheme. He was proved correct, and the attack never occurred.[48]

Conroy got into further trouble in September 1936 when he and four other men were found by Detective Garda L. O'Connor at 3 a.m. on 11 September painting a slogan on the road in Cork City centre. O'Connor called on them to stop twice but they ignored him. The detective produced his revolver and fired a shot over their heads and marched them to the garda station. An unfinished slogan on the road read 'Join the ____' while a second slogan read 'Cork welcomes the King's representatives.' All five appeared before the military tribunal on 29 September 1936 charged with membership of an unlawful organisation. When asked if they were professionally represented one of them said, 'I refuse to recognise this Court which murdered Sean Glynn.' Conroy received eight months imprisonment while his four companions got six months each.[49] During World War Two, Conroy was interned from 11 May to 5 November 1940, at which time he was released having signed the undertaking to repudiate any connection with illegal organisations.[50]

The Seán Glynn referred to was an IRA prisoner in Arbour Hill who hailed from Pennywell Road in Limerick. He suffered a breakdown while in prison and took his own life on 13 September 1936. He was found by military guards hanging from a shelf over his bed. Two towels were tied together – one end around his neck and the other tied to the support of a shelf above his head. He had written letters to his mother complaining that he had suffered 'cruel treatment' at the hands of the gardaí in William St [Limerick]. He alleged they had passed all kinds of remarks and told him he was suffering from a terrible disease and would rot in a month.'[51] The jury returned a verdict that the death was self-inflicted, adding a rider that he was not a fit subject for solitary confinement. They also found he was not ill-treated by either the gardaí or by the authorities in Arbour Hill. On hearing the verdict, Glynn's brother turned to the jury and shouted, 'my brother did not commit suicide; he was murdered.'[52] Thousands attended his funeral in Limerick on 15 September 1936, during which an unknown man fired three shots over the grave. During an oration by Seán Keating, who announced himself as 'a member of the Headquarters Staff of the IRA', said, 'I lay the blame for the murder of Seán Glynn in his cell at Arbour Hill on de Valera and his ministers, whose hands are red with blood.'[53]

A Committee of Enquiry was set up to investigate the circumstances of Glynn's death and to determine if there was any neglect of duty on the part of any member of the public service. It was chaired by William O'Brien, chairman of the Revenue Commissioners. Glynn was in Arbour Hill from 10 July 1936 up to his death on 13 September, during which time he was medically examined on no less than six occasions by three different medical officers. None of the medics noted any mental abnormality and they found that the governor and medical staff were entirely unaware of any mental abnormality in the deceased. They were also satisfied that these officers carried out their duties in full compliance with their instructions and with kindness and humanity.[54]

On 18 September 1938, the IRA unveiled a memorial to Glynn at Mount St Laurence Cemetery in Limerick. At the unveiling ceremony, the IRA chief of staff Maurice Twomey delivered an oration during which he referred to:

> ...the sacrifice made by Sean Glynn in laying down his life so that the Republic might live, which should be an inspiration to the youth of

> Ireland who should follow in his footsteps until the country is free and united.[55]

By this time, war clouds were once again gathering in Europe and de Valera was determined that Ireland would avoid any involvement in the coming conflagration. He knew that the biggest threat to Ireland's neutrality was the IRA. His efforts to wean them away from the path of violence had been a spectacular failure. From now on it would be the iron fist.

Chapter 8

CLAMPDOWN, 1936–1939

In waking a tiger, use a long stick.

Mao Tse-Tung

Two appalling IRA murders in 1936 triggered the de Valera government's decision to clamp down hard on the IRA. These were the shootings of Vice-Admiral Henry Boyle Somerville in Cork on 24 March, and IRA man John Egan in Waterford on 26 April. The ban on the IRA was re-imposed on 18 June and three days later the annual IRA ceremony in Bodenstown was also prohibited.[1] Even then, the government made one final effort to coax the IRA away from the path of violence. On 30 June, Attorney General Conor Maguire announced in the Dáil that there would be a general amnesty for all members of the IRA who would sever their connection with that organisation. There is no evidence that anyone availed of the opportunity.[2]

Somerville, who was 72 years of age, was shot and killed at his home in Castletownshend, County Cork on the night of 24 March 1936. His offence, apparently, was his practice of writing references for local youths wishing to join the Royal Navy. His wife Mabel heard footsteps on the gravel outside his home and told her husband someone was coming. He grabbed a small reading lamp and went to the door. She heard a voice asking, 'are you Mr. Somerville?'. He replied, 'I am'. A shot rang out and she heard the crash of the lamp on the ground, followed by several more shots. Mabel rushed out to find her husband lying on the ground and at least two men retreating from the house and down the avenue. A card left with his body read, 'this English Agent sent fifty-two Irish men into the British Army in the last 7 weeks.' The words were cut from newspapers and glued to the card.[3]

The biggest garda investigation in years was launched and on 25 March, detailed instructions were sent from Garda HQ to the chief superintendent in Cork, spelling out in detail the steps that were to be taken. The most experienced members of Special Branch and uniformed gardaí were to be used and they were instructed to check every car in Cork and parts of Kerry, to ensure all were accounted for on the night of the murder. Any car movements noted by garda patrols were to be tabulated and checked and a daily report on all vehicles checked to be submitted. All potential suspects in Cork and Kerry were to be checked on and files prepared on each one ensuring that no prominent member of the IRA escaped attention.

Detectives quickly established that a car, vaguely described as a 'Baby Ford' type with three men on board, was seen in the area before the shooting and again afterwards, travelling at high speed in the opposite direction through the village of Castletownshend. Where normally there would be many people hanging around the village, on the night of the murder the streets were deserted as a travelling picture and variety show was running in the village hall and most of the locals attended. This was a rare enough occurrence, and detectives believed the murderers chose this night to minimise the number of potential witnesses.[4]

Cork IRA commander Tom Barry had, in fact, ordered the murder. At the exact time of the shooting Barry and a friend approached a garda in Cork City and asked him the time, ensuring he had a cast-iron alibi.[5] Investigators knew that Barry rarely acknowledged gardaí on the street and thought it significant that he went out of his way to talk to one at the time of the murder. When interviewed by detectives, he declined to make a written statement but said he was at home between 7 p.m. and 9 p.m. and met Eugene Powell, an insurance agent, about increasing his policy from £300 to £500. Powell later confirmed this. Barry told the detectives that, 'Powell does not belong to us', meaning he was not in the IRA. However, in 1933 Powell was charged with stealing a rifle from a Free State soldier in Cork. When he appeared in the District Court in Cork charged with this offence, he gave the classic IRA response, 'as a soldier of the Irish Republic I refuse to recognise the court.'[6]

Detectives were satisfied that Powell was, in fact, involved in the murder, that he drove his own car to the scene, and was accompanied by Thomas Kelleher from Upton and Patrick Joseph Collins, who was OC of the Dunmanway unit of the IRA. The detectives described Kelleher as being 'one of the most notorious gunmen in the South of Ireland' and believed he carried out the shooting. While being interrogated he boasted to detectives of his involvement in the killing of Colonel Peacock in Innishannon during the War of Independence in 1921. He gleefully described how he knocked Peacock with his first shot and then ran up and fired three more rounds into his victim as he lay on the ground.[7] Detectives thought it was significant that several leading members of the IRA in Cork, gave a full account of their movements including detailed written statements (apart from Barry who gave a verbal account), something they never did before. Meanwhile, 'lesser luminaries' refused point blank to speak. The authorities were satisfied that the accounts were carefully constructed to give each other alibis for the night of the murder. An IRA informant told detectives that there was concern at the level of recruitment to British forces but the matter was taken out of their hands. The killing was organised at a higher level in the IRA in Cork City with no local involvement in case of 'leakage.'[8] The fact that the killers asked Somerville to confirm his identity reveals they did not know him by sight.

Though detectives were quite satisfied Powell, Kelleher and Collins were the killers, they had no hard evidence and no one was ever charged. All three were later arrested in a general roundup of IRA men and the Military Tribunal sentenced Powell to three months for failing to account for his movements at the time of the murder. Kelleher and Collins each received twelve months for being members of an unlawful organisation and possessing incriminating documents. In January 1937, Collins, Kelleher and a third prisoner, Michael Hogan, were released and greeted by a crowd of supporters at Glanmire (now Kent) Station in Cork. A pipers' band led a parade to Patrick Street where a public meeting was attended by Maud Gonne MacBride and others. Collins made a speech calling on all young men to join the IRA. The rally was attended by about 200 people and described by Detective Sergeant Moore as 'a very tame affair.'[9]

On 15 August 1936, the *New York Daily News* published an interview with 'General' Seán Russell, described as 'Quartermaster General of Ireland's secret Republican army'. In it, he claimed that Admiral Somerville was 'executed' by a Republican order.'[10]

On 26 April 1936, IRA man John Egan (24) was shot dead in Mitchell Street, Dungarvan, County Waterford, after an IRA court martial. He was suspected of giving information to the police.[11] Two men masquerading as detectives called to his home at 11 p.m. looking for Egan. His father told them John was out but would not be long. The men told him that 'Superintendent Quinn of Cappoquin wanted to see him.' One of them was wearing a trench coat, and, after a short conversation they drove away in a large saloon car with two other men. Egan and his wife became concerned, and left the house to search for their son. A few minutes later they heard a scream, followed by several shots. The couple ran to the scene to discover their son dying on the ground. Evidence at the inquest showed he was shot twice in the head, once in the chest, and once in the leg.[12] On 30 July 1935, Egan and five others appeared before the military tribunal charged with membership of an unlawful organisation and possession of ammunition. The cases against Egan and two others were not proceeded with while two of the remaining three were sentenced to three months imprisonment.[13]

On 30 April 1936, Cork gardaí launched a major roundup of leading IRA men in the city and county in response to the Somerville and Egan murders. By day's end, thirty-four men were arrested, thirty-one of whom were detained in Arbour Hill Prison. They also tried to take in Tom Barry, but he was missing from his home when they called.[14] The train carrying the prisoners arrived in Kingsbridge Station (now Heuston) in Dublin where a small force of gardaí and detectives armed with rifles and a Thompson sub-machine gun was waiting. The boisterous prisoners sang and shouted slogans such as 'Up Tom Barry' and 'Up the Republic.' Some struggled violently with gardaí and detectives as they were led to waiting lorries and taken to Arbour Hill.[15]

Between 27 and 29 May 1936, the military tribunal sentenced twenty-five men to between three and twelve months imprisonment. Five others were acquitted or had their charges dropped. On 27 April, Sergeant Michael Murphy accompanied by Detectives Hanlon and Hogan, who were investigating the Egan murder, went to a garage in Clonmel, County Tipperary, where IRA man Michael Conway worked. Murphy asked him to account for his movements at the time of the murder and Conway refused. They left but on 12 May, went to his home at 23 Mary Street, Clonmel with a search warrant. They found nothing incriminating but arrested Conway and brought him to Waterford Garda Station. When interviewed by Superintendent Michael Walsh under Article 2A of the Constitution (which made it an offence not to answer questions) Conway simply said, 'I refuse to answer' or gave flippant answers to most of the questions. He did, however, proudly admit to being a member of the IRA which he described as 'the only lawful military organisation in this country.'

When the written record of the interview was read over to him, he refused to sign. When asked to give his fingerprints he again refused, but they were forcibly taken. Sergeant H. McNamara later identified a finger mark lifted from the door of the car used by the killers as being from Conway's right middle finger. The car was stolen the night of the murder from District Justice John S. Troy when four gunmen called to his home and demanded the keys. Two men drove off with his car while two others stayed near the house overnight to ensure the family did not raise the alarm.[16]

Conway was charged with murder and appeared before the military tribunal on 15 July 1936. He refused to have a solicitor or counsel present to defend him. When the charge was read over to him, he said, 'I refuse to recognise the authority of this Court, composed as it is of traitors to the Republic, to try me on this charge or any other. I might say I had neither hand act nor part in the murder of John Egan.' Having heard the case, the tribunal asked Conway if he wished to testify but he replied that he would be prepared to give evidence before a jury but did not recognise this court. He complained that a government minister, Seán MacEntee, was quoted in the *Irish Press* of 22 June as saying in reference to Egan's murder, 'you will get the proof in the next few days and it will be a sorry day for those responsible for the crime. It will be their last shooting.' He said he had already 'been sentenced to death by the Fianna Fáil cabinet and now it only remains for you to carry out the instructions of your masters.' The tribunal denied that McEntee's remarks had any influence on them.[17] On 21 July 1936, he was sentenced to death and the execution date was fixed for 12 August. However, on 25 July the government commuted the sentence to life imprisonment, and he was released on 4 May 1938 after serving less than two years. He was greeted in Clonmel by a large crowd and, after welcoming speeches, was escorted to his uncle's home in a procession led by a band.[18]

There was great sympathy for the Egan family in Waterford and a vigorous local campaign was organised to provide some form of compensation for them as they were in straitened circumstances. Mrs Egan wrote a pitiful letter to President de Valera saying:

> Pardon me for taking such liberty on myself on writing to you but I know you will excuse me. I am in a terrible state, myself my husband and my children, my husband idle with past 5 years and our only hopes to be murdered poor John Egan [*sic*]. You know how hard it is on a mother and father after rearing a son for 24 years, poor and miserable living now on the dole. Could you do something for us and God will reward you.'

A reply from the department informed her that 'this is not a case in which compensation can be paid out of public funds.'[19]

Despite Conway's close brush with the gallows, he did not learn his lesson and on 12 July 1940 he was spotted by a Special Branch sergeant cycling on Harold's Cross Road. The sergeant called on him to halt. Conway brushed past him on his bicycle and in the struggle that followed, the sergeant shot him in the leg. He grabbed the revolver and continued to struggle until the sergeant struck him on the head with it. Two civilians came to the policeman's assistance and helped him bring the prisoner to Terenure Garda Station. A search of Conway yielded twelve rounds of revolver ammunition and IRA documents. He was later sentenced to two years' imprisonment for possession of ammunition without a certificate, assault with intent to resist arrest, membership of an unlawful organisation and possession of incriminating documents.[20] He later left the IRA and took to the religious life in 1951 when he became a brother with the Cistercian community in Collon, County Meath.[21]

At 11.30 a.m. on Thursday 21 May 1936, Special Branch men arrested IRA chief of staff Maurice Twomey as he walked from Mass at Corpus Christi Church on Home Farm Road in Drumcondra. He was detained in the Bridewell and two days later sent to Arbour Hill Prison. The arresting officer was Detective Garda Michael Cunningham who was accompanied by Detective Gardaí John J. O'Sullivan and Thomas McDermott.[22] They searched his home at Mobhi Road and seized a large number of documents. At noon the same day, another team of detectives searched Maud Gonne MacBride's home in Roebuck House, Clonskeagh but found nothing incriminating. She told the *Irish Independent* that she was 'outraged' but had no complaint with the manner in which the detectives carried out their duties.[23] At 12.30 p.m. solicitor Con Lehane was arrested and taken to the Bridewell. On 18 June 1936, the government declared the IRA to be an unlawful organisation under Article 2A of the Constitution. De Valera remarked, 'the Old IRA had been an army of the nation…of the whole people but had now become a group of instigators of sectional strife.'[24]

Twomey's trial was held on 19 June before the military tribunal. He was not legally represented and repeatedly challenged the jurisdiction of the tribunal by claiming, 'it was not a lawfully constituted assembly of the Irish nation.' Detective Garda T. Doyle said he and other detectives searched Twomey's home where they found documents headed 'Department of Intelligence', including a map of Arbour Hill Prison. Detective Sergeant John R. Cruise asked him his name and Twomey replied, 'read all the questions you want to ask me and I'll see about answering them.' Cruise asked him, 'do you know the chief of staff of the Irish Republican Army?' Twomey replied, 'the same comment.' He gave the same answer to a series of questions about his knowledge of the Somerville and Egan murders, and whether the army council sanctioned them. Cruise obviously knew quite well that Twomey was IRA chief of staff and would have sanctioned these killings but that his refusal to answer questions earned him a prison sentence from the military tribunal.

After hearing evidence, the president of the tribunal sentenced Twomey to three years for being a member of an unlawful organisation and refusing to give an account of his movements.[25] Twomey was released along with fifty-four other prisoners in a general amnesty announced in April 1938.[26] On 3 June 1940, he was re-arrested and interned under the Emergency Powers Acts but released on 20 June following a medical report which listed a number of medical problems. In November 1941, Chief Superintendent Sean Gantly of the Special Branch reported that they still suspected Twomey of being 'the power behind the scenes in IRA activity.'[27]

The relentless anti-IRA measures being taken by the Special Branch clearly had an effect, as is apparent from an IRA document intercepted by detectives and dated 22 May 1936. It warned that the 'Police Forces' were given 'the greatest latitude in proceeding against Volunteers' and that the recent raids on parades in Dublin indicated 'that Volunteers are liable to be arrested if found drilling.' It gave instructions on measures that were to be taken during drilling sessions to guard against raids. They were to ensure they were not surprised by 'enemy forces' while drilling or holding meetings and that adequate measures were taken to ensure arms or documents were not seized. Sentries were to be posted during training to warn of the approach of the 'enemy' to allow time to take arms safely away and the 'officers' were warned against carrying documents unnecessarily.[28]

The garda authorities issued their own instructions to the force on how the campaign against the IRA should be conducted. On 25 June 1936, Chief Superintendent Thomas Woods of Special Branch HQ issued a directive to each chief superintendent in the country instructing them to arrest speakers forthwith when they encouraged the use of arms or invited persons to join the IRA. Similarly, anyone seen holding collections on behalf of the IRA was to be arrested on the spot. At political meetings, specially nominated gardaí or detectives were to be detailed to take written notes of any seditious utterances by speakers with a view to a prosecution later.[29]

In May 1937, the IRA announced that there would be a 'monster demonstration to repudiate the Coronation of an English King [George VI] as King of Ireland, and to demand the immediate restoration of the Republic.' The parade was to take place on the evening of 11 May and the various organisations were asked to assemble at St Stephen's Green and march to College Green. Minister for Justice Patrick Ruttledge issued a proclamation banning the event. Large numbers of uniformed gardaí and Special Branch detectives were detailed for duty to frustrate any attempt to hold the parade. Branch men learned that the organisers changed their plans and intended to hold the meeting in O'Connell Street at 9 p.m. As a result, a considerable number of gardaí were diverted from St Stephen's Green to O'Connell Street.[30]

At 8.30 p.m., about 150 men and thirty women formed up at Liberty Hall intending to march to O'Connell Street but were prevented from doing so by a strong force of gardaí under Inspector Doody. The marchers drew sticks and attacked the gardaí and Inspector Doody ordered a baton charge which quickly scattered the crowd. Two men crouched down near Eden Quay and opened fire on the gardaí with revolvers but there were no injuries, though a bullet did pass through Inspector Doody's raincoat. There were other skirmishes and baton charges in the city centre area and several windows were broken. Seven gardaí received minor injuries and were treated in Jervis Street Hospital.

The following night, 12 May, a crowd of men marched in formation four deep and held another meeting in O'Connell Street. Many wore bandages on their heads from the previous night's skirmishes. Speakers called for the release of republican prisoners and condemned de Valera's proposed new constitution. They complained they were prevented from holding a meeting the previous night by brute force. Tom Barry appeared on the platform, also with a bandaged head, and said that he 'was not in a fit state to speak for long owing to the batonings by Civic Guards on the previous night.' The meeting broke up without incident.[31] Detectives were anxious to arrest Barry, but he only stayed on the platform for a few minutes before disappearing into the crowd accompanied by four or five armed bodyguards. The waiting detectives were instructed not to approach him if there was any danger of gunfire as the garda authorities were anxious to avoid a repeat of the Marsh's Yard shooting. On 24 July 1937, Barry was arrested by detectives who spotted him in Oliver Plunkett Street in Cork City shortly after he left a wedding ceremony, but he was released without charge on 27 July.[32]

An IRA informant tipped off detectives about the identities of the Eden Quay shooters and on the morning of 19 May Detective Sergeant John R. Cruise (8247) and a party of detectives arrested Daniel Joseph Guilfoyle of 8 Marlborough Place, Dublin. They described him as 'a member of the Dublin Brigade, IRA' along with James Coade of 6 Palmerstown, County Dublin. However, Inspector Doody told investigators that neither he nor any of his men could identify the gunmen and both were released without charge.[33]

Early in the morning of 13 May 1937, a bomb explosion destroyed the statue of King George II on horseback in St Stephen's Green in Dublin. Owing to the recent anti-coronation disturbances, Garda James Armstrong (Reg. No. 7373 – a native of County Monaghan) was detailed to patrol the park with a night watchman. During the night they encountered four young men in the park, two of whom were carrying revolvers. Armstrong later said he believed they were members of Special Branch but on enquiring discovered that no Branch men were sent there. He searched the area with the night watchmen, but the men disappeared through the trees in the darkness. On checking the statue, they noticed something attached to the horse's foot with wires protruding. Suspecting a bomb, the garda notified his station in Lad Lane who reported it to Garda HQ. The army was notified but before they got to the scene the bomb exploded, blowing horse and rider clean off the pedestal.[34]

The incident was viewed 'with the gravest concern' by the government. A minute written by J.J. McElligott, secretary of the Department of Finance, stated that the story, 'when reduced to essentials, shows ineptitude, cowardice, and inefficiency that puts the public service to shame.' He said Garda Armstrong's explanation that he thought the armed men were Special Branch men 'is too far-fetched to be believed unless members of the Detective Division are accustomed to prowling round the Green in the early hours of the morning brandishing revolvers and ignoring other members of the Garda Force.'[35] One can only agree with McElligot on that point. It would be normal practice for detectives to identify themselves to a uniformed garda in that situation. It is puzzling why he did not at least try to talk to the individuals concerned to check their bona fides but being unarmed and outnumbered, he may well have been afraid to challenge them. His story about thinking they were detectives is not credible. While we do not know what his instructions were, he probably should have stayed in the vicinity of the statue though it probably would have made no difference as an unarmed garda more than likely would have been held at gunpoint while the bomb was being planted.

An unsworn enquiry into the night's events was carried out by Assistant Commissioners Murphy and Cullen. In a twenty-eight-page report, they recommended disciplinary action against Garda Armstrong who was criticised for doing a general patrol of the St Stephen's Green area without confining himself to the statue. The report also pointed to the inability of the military authorities to have a party of engineers dispatched to the scene before the bomb exploded at around 8 a.m. Disciplinary proceedings were instituted against Garda Armstrong but this was stopped by Commissioner Broy who felt Armstrong was 'a victim of circumstances' and the 'undesirable publicity that might attach to such a formal process of investigation.'[36]

Another bomb exploded in Exchange Court, beside the City Hall in Dublin, at 6.05 a.m. on 11 November 1937. It blew the Royal Coat of Arms (a plaster cast with the lion and unicorn), off the wall of a building called the Royal Escutcheon, leaving a hole in the wall. The building housed the Engineering Branch of the Post Office and was once home of the G Division of the Dublin Metropolitan Police. It was the scene of the controversial killing of three IRA men 'trying to escape' during the War of Independence. The force of the blast shattered hundreds of windows in other buildings over a wide area including Exchange Court, City Hall, Parliament Street, and Dame Street. The first Special Branch men on the scene were Detective Sergeant Denis O'Brien (8288) and Detective Garda Richard Hyland (8333), both of whom would be killed by the IRA in separate incidents within a few years.[37] The IRA obviously believed that these symbols of British imperialism had no place in Ireland's capital city. Despite intensive investigations, nobody was ever arrested or charged in connection with these attacks.[38]

At 6 p.m. on 28 October 1938, Detective Garda Thomas P. Sweeney was attacked and severely beaten by eight IRA men armed with sticks and revolvers at the townland of Carrigrohanebeg in Ballincollig, County

Cork. He had just escorted a man to his home in nearby Coolatanavalley and was cycling back to his station. There was a plasterer's strike in Cork at the time and measures were put in place to protect the non-striking plasterers. Sweeney tried to draw his .45 revolver but was struck a vicious blow with a stick on the wrist. The gun and five rounds of ammunition were seized. The leader of the gang, whom he recognised as leading Cork IRA man Tomás MacCurtain said, 'will we shoot you now?' They escaped in a car they commandeered at the scene 'in the name of the IRA.' There were four calves in the back of the car which they released on the road first and they then drove off towards Cork city. They told the owner, 'we will leave your car outside the city' and it was later found abandoned at St Luke's.[39]

Sweeney struggled to his feet and a woman in a nearby house wiped the blood from his face with a towel. He managed to stop a passing motorist who took him to Ballincollig Garda Station and later to the Mercy Hospital where he was detained for five weeks. He was treated for twenty-one injuries all over his body. The men in the commandeered car also recognised some of the others and named them to investigating gardaí. As a result, arrests swiftly followed and detectives rounded up Tomás MacCurtain of 1 Grosvenor Place, Roger Ryan of 128 Blarney Street, Denis McDonnell of Burton Place and Denis Griffin of 38 Leitrim Street. All were well known Cork IRA men. Detectives searched their homes without finding anything incriminating, though a bloodstained shirt was found in Ryan's home which he refused to account for. The search party at MacCurtain's home included Detective Garda John Roche who had a fatal encounter with MacCurtain in 1940. (See chapter 9)

The three men whose car was commandeered were later visited by IRA men and threatened with serious consequences if they gave evidence. In court, the prisoners were offered bail but MacCurtain said he refused to recognise the court and did not accept bail saying, 'there is no necessity to fix bail as I don't intend to give any. It is obvious this is another trumped up case by the police to finish me because I am a soldier of the Republic.' Showing remarkable courage, the witnesses did in fact give evidence in court but told gardaí in advance that they would not identify anyone but would give a general description of the raiders. MacCurtain was the only one of the defendants sent forward for trial in Cork Circuit Court. His sister, Siobhan Ní Curtáin BL, a practising barrister, busily made notes in court and passed them to her brother for the purpose of examining witnesses. He was found not guilty by a jury before Judge J. K. O'Connor on 11 January 1939. The jury did not even retire to consider a verdict. It was greeted by cheers and shouts of, 'Good man, MacCurtain' and 'We'll meet you again Sweeney' to the annoyance of the judge who asked, 'who is keeping order in this court? Is there any police force in this court to keep order? I don't see any member of the guards making the smallest attempt to suppress this.'[40]

A garda report to the Department of Justice expressed irritation at the way the judge conducted the trial. They felt he was partial towards MacCurtain and complained about how in his charge to the jury he referred to the defendant as 'poor MacCurtain' who was called to account whenever 'an offence was committed of a political smack'. It was alleged this gave the jury the impression that he had great sympathy for him. The judge did not express any sympathy to the injured detective, nor did he condemn the attack he suffered. During his summing up, he stated there was a great deal of evidence tendered which in no way connected MacCurtain with the crime. Further, he did not wish to take up their time with it, adding that they could at that stage acquit the accused if they so desired. He paused for about a minute but when there was no response from the jury, he continued the summing up. The minister later sent the file to the Attorney General who returned it with a brief note, 'the Attorney General directs me to return the attached file which he has read and noted.'[41] Despite the blatantly partial manner in which the trial was conducted, there was nothing the AG could do owing to the independence of the judiciary.

It is not clear why such a leading IRA man was not tried before the military tribunal. The fact that he was the son of a republican icon who was shot and killed by the Black and Tans during the War of Independence could well have had a bearing. It is possible that a government consisting of many of his father's former IRA colleagues intervened to ensure he was tried in the normal courts before a sympathetic judge in the hope that he would be acquitted.

Gardaí believed that the attack on Detective Sweeney had nothing to do with the plasterer's strike and was in fact a reprisal for being the principal witness against IRA man Jeremiah Cronin, who was charged with possession of firearms earlier that month. Cronin was found not guilty by a jury. It followed an incident where shots were fired over the grave of a pre-Truce IRA man Richard O'Mahony in Carrigrohane graveyard the previous June. Sweeney was present and recognised Cronin as being one of the shooters but deemed it prudent not to take action at the time. He waited until 2 a.m. the following morning when he, along with a squad of gardaí and detectives went to his home and arrested him.[42]

At 6.05 p.m. on 15 August 1939, gardaí and detectives under Inspector Patrick McNamara (269), raided an IRA training class in progress in a loft at the rear of the home of Patrick Muldoon in Clara, County Offaly and arrested seven men. The raiding party included Detective Gardaí McCarthy and Ring and Garda Cuskelly of Naas, Garda Spain of Tullamore and Garda O'Rourke of Kilcormack. They found six men in an outhouse seated on a bench, and a seventh standing apparently giving instruction. A blackboard was set up in front of the group on which a diagram of a clock mine was drawn with chalk. They seized articles including an alarm clock, detonators, toy balloons, pepper, sugar, chalk, a white powder, gelignite and books on military subjects. All were charged with offences under the Explosive Substances Act before the military court in Collins Barracks, Dublin. A man giving the name Harry Anderson from Belfast took responsibility for the material found and was given two years imprisonment. Patrick Muldoon (the house holder) got twelve months as did Richard Pender and Joseph Duffy, both from Tullamore and Matthew Conroy from Kilcormac. Conroy was an elderly bachelor with World War One experience, who was given a rifle and sent up a tree to watch out for gardaí. In a farcical twist, when he was called down for his tea, he left the rifle behind, and it was then that the raid occurred.[43]

Harry Anderson was in fact Harry White, later IRA chief of staff, who recounts the episode in his biography. It is not clear if the authorities discovered his true identity on that occasion. A garda report at the time said he was 'not definitely identified, and it was quite possible this was a fictitious name.'[44] White also claimed that a garda who was courting Patrick Muldoon's sister warned him some days earlier that he was about to be arrested.[45] There clearly were some individuals in the force sympathetic to the IRA, as will be seen in the next chapter.

White was released from Arbour Hill prison on 18 February 1941 and, not being familiar with the city, asked a man standing on a corner for directions to O'Connell Street. The man helpfully replied, 'get into the car there; sure, we're going that way ourselves.' The obliging stranger was Detective Sergeant James McDonald (4700) of the Special Branch. Suspecting nothing, White got in and found himself sitting beside Tommy Curran, another prisoner who was released earlier that day. Curran asked him, 'Harry, would you be surprised if I tell you we are going to the Curragh Internment Camp?' Too late he realised he had been duped by the detectives and they drove straight to the Curragh where both were interned.[46]

White wrote a note to the Curragh authorities on 29 May 1942 admitting that his correct name was Henry White of 78 Anderstown Park, Belfast. He asked to be released and gave an undertaking that he wished to sever his connections with the IRA and to return to Belfast and take up employment. Despite objections from Garda HQ (well founded as will be seen), White was released on the directions of justice minister Gerald Boland in an order signed on 15 June 1942.[47]

The war drums were beating in Europe for several years and by September 1939, Europe was again engulfed in war. In time-honoured fashion, the

IRA saw it as another opportunity to strike another blow for Ireland's freedom. England would be preoccupied with the war and, as in the case of the previous war, they could expect German help. The Special Branch was about to face their biggest challenge yet – and the price in death would be high.

Chapter 9

THE WAR YEARS AND BEYOND, 1939–1947

Vengeance is mine saith de Valera.
Harry White, IRA

By 1939, with war imminent in Europe, de Valera announced that Ireland would remain neutral. He was aware of British fears that Ireland could be used by Germany as a back door to an invasion of Britain and was determined not to allow the IRA to upset the diplomatic tightrope on which he found himself.[1] In time-honoured tradition, the IRA saw the approaching conflict as another case of 'England's difficulty is Ireland's opportunity.' To combat this threat, the Special Branch was reorganised and new men put in charge; Chief Superintendents Patrick Carroll, and Michael Wymes along with Superintendent Sean Gantly.[2]

Mayo anti-Treaty republican Tom Maguire was elected to the second Dáil on 19 May 1921, and it was not formally dissolved before the June 1922 election. It planned to meet for the last time on 30 June but, owing to the outbreak of the civil war on 28 June, this meeting never happened. This was the IRA's dubious justification for claiming that, despite the passage of time, they were still the legitimate government of Ireland. They considered the partitionist twenty-six county parliament to be an unlawful entity forced on the country by the wiles of the perfidious

British. In late-1938, Maguire and his colleagues decided to transfer the right to establish a republican government to the IRA army council. After their meeting on 8 December 1938, the council graciously accepted this honour, stating, 'we accept this authority in the name of the Army of the Republic in the spirit in which it is tendered.'[3]

A headline in the *Wolfe Tone Weekly* on 17 December 1938 boldly proclaimed, 'IRA TAKE OVER THE GOVERNMENT OF THE REPUBLIC' and the article opened with the words, 'One of the most memorable events of our time took place in December 8, the anniversary of the Four Martyrs,[4] when the Government of the Republic of Ireland was taken over from the Executive Council of Dáil Éireann by the Council of the Irish Republican Army.'[5] With this bizarre logic the IRA now claimed to be the lawful government of Ireland with the right to wage war in the name of the Republic.

On 12 January 1939, the IRA sent British foreign secretary Lord Halifax a courteously-worded ultimatum warning him to withdraw British forces from all parts of Ireland. It gave him four days to comply, or they would take 'appropriate action without further notice.' There was no response from Lord Halifax and some days later posters appeared around the country announcing, 'We call on the people of all Ireland at home and in exile to assist in the effort we are about to make in God's name to compel that evacuation and to enthrone the Republic of Ireland.' It was signed by Seán Russell (then chief of staff), Stephen Hayes, (who later succeeded Russell as chief of staff), Patrick Fleming of Killarney, Peadar O'Flaherty of Enniscorthy, Larry Grogan of Drogheda and George Plunkett of Dublin.[6] All were members of the IRA Army Council. The ill-fated British bombing campaign followed with bombs exploding in London, Manchester, Birmingham, Coventry and many other places. While on a fund-raising trip in America in May 1939, Russell was interviewed by the *San Francisco Chronicle* regarding the London bombings and said:

> The Irish Republican Army ordered the bombings… the bombings are the military action of military men who are acting in a state of war toward

> England. We declared war on the 12th of last January...We take this action as the only military means possible for us. They will go on until English soldiers are withdrawn from Ireland.[7]

Russell opined that:

> De Valera would be pushed along the national road by our activity. He would not dare interfere with IRA men going out to take part in the campaign or their return for shelter. The British would blame him for such a policy and very soon he would be forced to take his stand with us and the 1920-21 position would be restored. Alternatively, de Valera would interfere with us. The people would rise in anger against him and rally round us and so the 1920-21 position would be restored under IRA leadership.[8]

De Valera would prove Russell disastrously wrong on both counts. The government swiftly introduced two draconian pieces of legislation, the Treason Act 1939 (which provided for the death penalty for treason) and the Offences Against the State Act, 1939. The latter act provided the state and the Garda Síochána with the legal framework necessary for ruthlessly suppressing the IRA. Much of it was similar to Article 2A which lapsed after the passing of the 1937 constitution, though it was not quite as draconian. It included sweeping powers of arrest, detention and search and created a range of new offences including membership of an unlawful organisation, usurping the functions of government, unlawful drilling as well as providing for the setting up of the non-jury Special Criminal Court. It gave senior garda officers the power to close down buildings used by unlawful organisations and even the power to ban public meetings being held by such organisations. By far the most effective powers from the Special Branch point-of-view were under sections 30 and 52 of the Act. Section 30 provided for extensive powers of arrest, not only of persons suspected of an offence under the Act, but also those suspected of having information or possessing documents about such an offence. They could be detained for twenty-four hours, followed by a further twenty-four if authorised by a chief superintendent. While so detained, section 52 provided that a prisoner could be asked to account for his movements during a specified time period, and, on refusing to answer could be sentenced to six months imprisonment. These powers were extended within a year, with two new acts giving military courts the power to impose death sentences and providing for internment without trial. Between 1940 and 1945, over 1,100 IRA men were interned.[9] These measures decimated the IRA during the war years, though the Special Branch paid a heavy price in the process.

War broke out on 1 September 1939, with the German invasion of Poland, followed quickly on 3 September by declarations of war by Britain and France. De Valera's first move to was to replace justice minister Patrick Ruttledge with Gerald Boland, who had a proven pedigree as a justice 'hardman'. He temporarily acted for Ruttledge three years earlier during the latter's illness. He wasted no time and asked the Special Branch to draw up a list of likely troublemakers. Raids were underway by 9 September. The first was at 16 Rathmines Park and was led by Detective Inspector Michael J. Mansfield[10] where most of the IRA Army Council was rounded up. They included some of the signatories of the ultimatum to Lord Halifax, Laurence Grogan, and Peadar O'Flaherty, along with Patrick McGrath and William McGuinness. Grogan tried to flee by jumping over a back wall but was chased and caught by Detective Keyes. Stephen Hayes and Mattie Tuite managed to sneak out the back of the house undetected. Upstairs, detectives found two Smith and Wesson .45 and a Colt automatic .37 pistol and ammunition for which Grogan took responsibility. Detective Sergeant Denis O'Brien also found a photo of Special Branch men.[11]

The prisoners were brought to Dublin District Court on 11 September charged with membership of an unlawful organisation. Grogan, McGuinness and O'Flaherty were also charged with possession of two revolvers and an automatic pistol. Inspector Mansfield told the court that Grogan had a wallet with £23 and 315 US dollars while McGuinness had a wallet with a staggering 7,950 US dollars. They showed the traditional IRA contempt for the courts. One of them interrupted the judge asking, 'is the business of the court over, we did not come here to listen to a dissertation on the law?' A second prisoner added, 'you are quoting British law', to which the judge remarked, 'no sir – you are listening to the law of this land.'[12]

They were sent for trial to the military tribunal in Collins Barracks and on 23 October, Grogan, McGuinness and O'Flaherty were sentenced to eighteen months imprisonment for possession of firearms and other assorted offences. Patrick McGrath was seriously ill after being on hunger strike and was unable to attend the trial. The charges against him were dropped – a decision that would shortly have fatal consequences for two detectives.[13]

Over fifty IRA men were arrested in various parts of the country, including twenty or so in Dublin. They included solicitor Con Lehane, Irish language activist Mairtín Ó Caidhin, Michael Quill (Listowel) and Richard Goss from Dundalk. Seven men were arrested in Tralee, one in Limerick, three in Tipperary, seven in Roscommon, and some others in Leitrim and Galway. Veteran IRA man Joseph Clarke was arrested on 15 September and held in Arbour Hill military detention barracks but released without charge on 28 October.[14]

The government suffered a setback on 28 November when the High Court held that parts of the Offences Against the State Act, 1939 were repugnant to the constitution.[15] This resulted in the release of sixty-four internees. Following a minor amendment to the act the following year, all were re-arrested and re-interned along with several hundred others.

The IRA's most audacious raid ever was carried out on the Magazine Fort in the Phoenix Park on the night of Saturday 23 December 1939. The fort was the army's storage depot for its reserves of weapons and ammunition. After several months planning, the IRA discovered that security at the fort was negligible and its isolated position in the Phoenix Park, which was closed at night, reduced the chances of detection. They correctly guessed that in the days leading to Christmas, the army sentries would be even more relaxed. At 8.35 p.m. that night the bell rang at the Fort and when the military policeman looked out, he saw a man with a bicycle holding a package in his hand. Thinking it was a kindly benefactor with some Christmas spirit for the bored troops, the MP opened the gates and went outside to collect the booty. The cyclist stuck a gun in his ribs and ordered him back inside while the rest of the raiders rushed in and rounded up the other sentries, herding them into one room.

It took an hour for the raiders to load up most of the army's stock of ammunition, 1,084,000 rounds. They drove off with it in thirteen lorries. Those around the country preparing dumps were totally overwhelmed by the amount of material they were asked to store. A simultaneous raid on the army barracks in nearby Islandbridge was also planned but abandoned when a ruse to open the gates failed.[16] The government response was swift and decisive. Two new acts were rushed through the Dáil in January. The Emergency Powers (Amendment) (No. 2) Act, 1940 was passed, permitting military courts to impose death sentences from which there was no appeal. The Offences Against the State (Amendment) Act 1940 provided for internment. All garda and army leave was cancelled, and country-wide checkpoints and searches carried out.

It was a Pyrrhic victory for the IRA. By 1 January, police and army raids recovered 850,000 rounds of ammunition and they eventually recovered more ammunition than had been stolen. Scores of IRA men were rounded up and either charged before the military tribunal or simply interned without trial. Ten men appeared before the tribunal on 11 January 1940. They received sentences ranging from three to six months for refusing to account for their movements between 12 noon on 23 December, and 12 noon on 24 December (the times between which the raid was carried out). One of the men, John Fitzsimons of McGuinness Place, Dublin was sentenced to ten years imprisonment on 11 June 1935 for shooting Garda Egan but was released in May 1938.[17] Military witnesses identified some of the raiders including John Parnell of 20 North Great Georges Street, John Lyons of 4 Berkeley Street, Joseph McDermott of Baldoyle and Thomas Doyle of 36 Comeragh

Road, Drimnagh. Parnell, McDermott and Lyons were later sentenced to twelve years imprisonment.[18]

On 30 December 1939, a team of detectives and uniformed gardaí, backed up by troops, searched the house and farm of James Rooney at Beamore, Drogheda, County Meath. In an outhouse, they found 135 boxes of Thompson machine-gun ammunition, each containing 2,000 rounds. The total haul amounted to 271,900 rounds of the ammunition stolen in the Magazine Fort raid. When questioned, Rooney denied all knowledge but he and three of his workmen were arrested. The workmen agreed they saw the ammunition stored there but knew nothing further. Rooney and two of the workmen, Joseph Farrelly of Beamore and Patrick Gregory of Duleek Street, Drogheda, were charged with possession of ammunition with intent to endanger life. After a trial in the Special Criminal Court in Collins Barracks on 19 February 1940, all three were found not guilty and released. Detectives believed that while Rooney was sympathetic to the IRA, he was not a member, and that Farrelly and Gregory were certainly not members and took no interest in politics. They were all quite forthcoming with answers to garda questions and signed memos of interview. This would have been very unlikely if they were IRA men. It is likely they knew more than they revealed but were too afraid to resist IRA requests to store the ammunition.[19]

In January 1940, the Special Branch suffered the first of three fatalities that year when Detective Garda John Roche (4905) was shot and killed in Cork city. At 9.15 p.m. on 3 January, Roche, along with Detective Sergeant John Collins (2226), and Detective Garda Quinlan, all of Union Quay Station in Cork, drove to Merchant's Quay near the junction with Patrick Street. They were responding to a call for assistance from Detective Garda Denis Teahan (6169) who spotted wanted IRA man Tomás MacCurtain. He pointed out MacCurtain talking to two men outside the Tivoli Restaurant in Patrick Street.[20]

The detectives approached MacCurtain, and Collins told him they wanted him to accompany them to Union Quay. MacCurtain jumped back and drew a revolver and fired, hitting Detective Garda Roche in the abdomen. Roche fell to the ground and cried, 'oh, God, I'm shot.' A vicious struggle followed during which Collins kicked MacCurtain's stomach and forced him to the ground. As their prisoner was led to the squad car Collins said, 'it was a cowardly act to shoot an Irishman as you have shot Garda Roche' to which MacCurtain retorted, 'I don't know why you think it was cowardly. Wasn't it three armed men against one armed man?' When Collins went on to say, 'but we did not draw guns' MacCurtain replied, 'I am surprised at you that you did not say that 'we are armed' and that 'we are going to use them'.' One can only agree with MacCurtain on that point. It was very foolhardy of the detectives to approach such a well-known gunman without at least one of them first drawing a revolver as a precautionary measure and calling out that they were armed gardaí. Roche was taken to hospital and died at 2.30 a.m. the following day. He was a 35-year-old married man and a native of Abbeyfeale, County Limerick.[21]

On examining MacCurtain's gun at Union Quay, officers found it was a Colt .45 with five live rounds and one spent round under the striker. Tragically, Roche left his own revolver behind in his locker at the station.[22] MacCurtain had many previous brushes with the law and Chief Superintendent Hannigan previously reported (somewhat naively) that, 'it is believed the term of imprisonment which he underwent put a good deal of sense into him, and with the exception of the incidents as referred to hereon he has not otherwise come under notice.' The incidents referred to included MacCurtain's attendance at IRA parades as well as threats he made to staff at the *Irish Times* office in Cook Street in Cork to remove coronation photos from their window. The office window was subsequently smashed with bricks and gardaí had no doubt MacCurtain was behind the vandalism.[23] In 1935, he also carried out a nasty assault on the 15-year-old son of Detective Inspector Jeremiah Sullivan, calling him a 'dirty peeler's spawn, you son of a murderer.'[24]

Wholesale arrests of IRA suspects in Cork City and county followed and within forty-eight hours, twenty-four men were in custody. Five of those were quickly released while nineteen others appeared before the District Court charged with IRA membership and with failing to account for their movements, with most receiving three to six months imprisonment. Seven were re-arrested on their release and interned in the Curragh.[25]

MacCurtain's trial opened in the Special Criminal Court in Collins Barracks on 11 June. He was not professionally represented and said he did not recognise the court. At the conclusion of the state case, MacCurtain made a statement saying that he was fired at on two occasions and assaulted at other times by unidentified assailants. He said that on the night of the shooting he was rushed by several men, one of whom said, 'we want you MacCurtain.' As the street lights were dimmed owing to wartime restrictions, he quickly reacted, bearing in mind the previous attacks on him. He continued, 'it all happened in a fraction of a second. I leave it to the Court to decide whether murder was committed or not.'[26]

On 13 June 1940, the court convicted MacCurtain and sentenced him to death, fixing the execution date for 5 July.[27] There was great interest in the case. MacCurtain, who was 22 years of age, was the son of the former Lord Mayor of the same name and a hero of the War of Independence who was shot by the Black and Tans at his home in Cork City in 1920. There was intense lobbying of the government to commute the sentence including by Cardinal MacRory of Armagh, who appealed directly to de Valera. Lawyer Seán MacBride made a last-minute appeal to the High Court, minutes before the courts rose at 4.00 p.m. on the eve of the execution date, knowing well it would be refused. He correctly calculated that the Supreme Court would not have time to consider an appeal that evening and thus delay the execution. He went to Mountjoy to convey the good news to MacCurtain but to his astonishment, MacCurtain berated him saying he had already said goodbye to his family and made his peace with God. Now he would have to go through the same process again in two or three weeks' time. As it happened, the Supreme Court rejected the appeal, but the government commuted the sentence to life imprisonment on 10 July 1940.[28]

De Valera had yielded to impassioned pleas for clemency, including one asking him to make allowances for the fact that MacCurtain only had, 'hysterical and unbalanced advice available from early childhood; unbalanced by female relations' adulation; ghouls glorified the tragedy of his father's death until he became elated; complete absence of balanced male control and advice; heredity; proved insanity on both sides; and the misfortunes of his birth.' It was a decision de Valera would come to bitterly regret.[29]

Veteran IRA man Dan Keating claimed that several Fianna Fáil TDs led by Martin Corry of Cork (another veteran IRA man) approached de Valera and threatened to resign their seats and run as independents if MacCurtain were executed. He said that de Valera had no choice but to agree as he only had a two-seat majority in the Dáil at the time.[30] There is no corroboration of Keating's claim, but he was certainly wrong about the Dáil arithmetic at the time. In the general election of 17 June 1938, Fianna Fáil won seventy-seven seats against a combined opposition of sixty-one seats – a clear sixteen seat majority. He may have confused it with the July 1937 election after which Fianna Fáil led a minority government, having won sixty-nine seats against a combined opposition of sixty-nine. A more likely scenario was that de Valera yielded to pressure from Cardinal McRory whom he knew well since his days as a lecturer in mathematics in St Patrick's College in Maynooth in 1912 when McRory was also on the staff.[31] The justice minister told the Dáil that 'there were exceptional circumstances in that there was a special background to the MacCurtain family.'[32]

On 9 October 1941, the arresting officers, Detective Sergeant John Collins and Detective Garda Denis Teahan, were awarded Scott Gold Medals for heroism at a ceremony in Garda HQ by Justice Minister Gerald Boland. Collins was a native of Abbeyfeale, County Limerick, and was among the first recruits to join the force in 1922. He was subsequently promoted through the ranks and was a chief superintendent by

1963. He retired in 1968 and died on 14 December 1990. Teahan was from Waterville, County Kerry and joined the force in 1924. He remained in Union Quay Station in Cork throughout his service before retiring in 1966. He died on 20 August 1970.[33]

At 4.30 p.m. on Saturday 17 February 1940, a young man called to the Meath Hotel at 40 Parnell Square West and booked a room so he and some friends could 'have tea' later that evening. In the event, sixteen men turned up and went to the room. However, alert Special Branch men on duty at bus and railway stations noted the arrival of leading IRA men in the city. At 9 p.m. a large force of gardaí and detectives backed up by 150 troops sealed off Parnell Square West. Two machine guns were placed at the front of the hotel and three more in a lane at the rear. Special Branch detectives led by Detective Sergeant Denis O'Brien (8288) along with Detective Gardaí Patrick Downey (6663), William Ahesy (8320), William O'Leary (8283) and Frank Cooper (5666), accompanied by a squad of soldiers with fixed bayonets, entered the hotel and arrested all sixteen 'tea drinkers' and transported them to the Bridewell. They seized a document relating to IRA activities, and £100 in cash.

On Monday 19 February, all sixteen were charged in the Dublin District Court with being members of an unlawful organisation and some had additional charges of refusing to account for their movements. Follow-up searches were carried out on the men's home addresses in various parts of the country. A detective sergeant later told the military court that Daniel Barry from Cork carried twenty-five sheets of notepaper headed 'Óglaigh na hÉireann' and the inscription 'Headquarters, Cork No 1 Brigade'. When asked to account for this, Barry claimed he got the materials from a man 'to mind for him' and forgot to return them. Barry told the court he was no longer a member of an unlawful organisation and was given the benefit of the doubt and discharged. Most of the remainder were sentenced to various terms of imprisonment for membership of an unlawful organisation and refusing to account for their movements.[34]

At 10 p.m. on 12 April 1940, three IRA men, two of whom were armed with revolvers, entered the Cork Broadcasting Station (then housed in the disused Cork City Gaol) at Convent Avenue in Sundays Well. They held up two staff members at gunpoint and ordered them to the studio on the second floor. One of them produced a sheet of paper from his pocket and began transmitting a message on air. The announcer said the broadcast was from the 'Government of the Republic of Ireland'. Detectives later got a summary of what he said, and it included the following:

> This is the 48th day of the hunger strike of soldiers of the Irish Republican Army as a protest against the refusal of their demands for treatment as political prisoners. They are… [Here he named seven or eight men on hunger strike] and some of them are now at death's door. Plunkett is the son of Count Plunkett whom you all know well. He played a gallant part in that glorious insurrection of Easter, 1916, for which he was sentenced to death, which sentence was later reduced to ten years penal servitude. Tomás MacCurtain, only son of the late Brigade Commandant Tomás MacCurtain, Lord Mayor of Cork, who was murdered by the Royal Irish Constabulary, is accused of shooting a policeman in resisting arrest or maybe even worse. Tomás Óg has been for many years the victim of police thuggery. Should any of these men die, we of the Irish Republican Army will see to it that their sacrifice will not be in vain. Just as Maxwell's methods failed, as Cosgrave's failed, so also will Judas de Valera fail. In conclusion I appeal to all men of age to join the army of the Republic and break the connection with England. Long live the Republic.

The lengthy broadcast justified their recent 'war' in England, adding some anti-Semitic remarks about Mr Hore-Belisha, 'the Jewish War Minister' (Leslie Hore-Belisha, then British Secretary of State for War) who in his Christmas message said, 'we are fighting for all that Christmas means.' The speaker added, 'one wonders what Christmas could mean to this wealthy Jew, except profits.'[35]

One of the raiders fired a shot from his revolver before they all left the building. Detectives led by Detective Sergeant Michael Riordan were quickly on the scene and found the spent .45 bullet in the studio. It was not clear if the bullet was discharged accidentally or deliberately fired so the noise of the shot could be heard over the air at the end of the broadcast.[36] It was strongly suspected that two of the raiders were Thomas Griffin of 38 Leitrim Street, and Denis Joseph O'Sullivan of 1 Coburg Street and detectives searched both of their homes the following morning at 8 a.m. They found and arrested Griffin at home but there was no sign of O'Sullivan. Griffin was later put on an identification parade, but the radio station witnesses did not identify him, though detectives were certain he was one of the raiders.[37]

An informant inside the Cork IRA later gave detectives a detailed account on all involved and their individual roles. He named eleven individuals and said the man who read the message was Patrick Whorley of Friar's Walk while the 'announcer' was Thomas Canty of Thomas Davis Street. He revealed that the man who fired the shot was Denis J. O'Sullivan and another man in the studio was Thomas Griffin (the latter two already suspected of involvement). He named two other raiders who were armed with revolvers as John Kennefick of Roches Buildings, while Patrick Kelly of Ashburton guarded the gate. Five other gunmen were posted at vantage points outside in case of a raid by gardaí. The garda report said there was little prospect of convicting any of the men but most were later interned in a general roundup of IRA suspects in Cork.[38] Cork IRA man Jim Savage later claimed that the reader of the message was in fact Denis J. ('Jobie') O'Sullivan and that the shot was discharged accidentally.[39]

While Special Branch had many agents inside the IRA in 1940, the IRA also had at least one agent in the Special Branch. He was a Harrier and IRA sympathiser named James Crofton (8341), a native of Seaview Avenue, in Wexford Town. He provided information and helped compile a photographic file of Branch men. The IRA planned to place a bomb in the communication room at Special Branch HQ in Dublin Castle to destroy their radio equipment. This was intended as a retaliation for the deaths of Tony D'Arcy and Jack McNeela, two IRA men who died on hunger strike in early-April 1940. Crofton used wire clippers to cut a fence to ease the entry of the bombers. He made sure he was away with a good alibi when the two bombers, 'Black' Dan O'Toole from Belfast and Joe Atkinson, entered to plant the bomb on 25 April 1940.

As it happened, the bungling bombers placed their device in the wrong place – at the wall of a caretaker's house – where it exploded at 5 a.m. Miraculously no one was killed though five detectives and a female housekeeper received slight injuries and were taken to hospital. Detective Sergeant Patrick McKeown was night sergeant in charge of the day room. He went to the sleeping quarters upstairs where he found Detective Garda William Ahesy (8320) was injured by flying glass and suffering from shock. The other four detectives who were uninjured apart from shock, were Edward Cox (8595), William Faherty (8388), John Nolan (12381) and Robert Hayes (8218). All were treated in the Depot Hospital at Garda HQ. A ten-foot square hole was blown in the wall and many windows were broken, including irreplaceable stained-glass windows in the nearby Chapel Royal and Bermingham Tower.[40]

Crofton was arrested by Branch men on 26 February 1941 and questioned by Chief Superintendent Patrick Carroll in the Bridewell about the source of the £50 he used as a deposit for a motorboat named *Ventura* in County Kerry [41]. Crofton replied, 'I refuse to give any information about it. I won't answer any more questions. Take me back to my cell.' On 12 March 1941, he was sentenced to five years imprisonment by the Special Criminal Court for refusing to reveal the source of the cash. He resigned from the force a month before his conviction, telling colleagues he was 'about to engage in work of national importance.'[42] According to Bowyer Bell, the boat in question was to be used to bring German spy Hermann Görtz back to occupied France so he could return to Germany. It was also intended to bring home Frank Ryan, who was then in Germany seeking German arms for the IRA.[43] Crofton was sent to Portlaoise prison where he refused to put on prison clothes and spent two-and-a-half years dressed in blankets. He was refused any contacts or visits from his wife and children, one of whom died while he was in custody. On his release in 1946, he moved to London with his wife and family.[44]

At 9 a.m. on 7 May 1940, IRA men shot and seriously injured two Special Branch men at Holles Street in Dublin. Detective Gardaí William Shanahan (12016) and James McSweeney (12543) were escorting state mails from Pearse Street post office in a motorcycle and sidecar. At Holles Street a car with four men on board pulled across in front of them, forcing them to the kerb. Two Thompson sub-machine guns were thrust through the windows and opened fire. Shanahan took five bullets in the chest and dragged himself out of the sidecar in great pain but managed to fire two or three shots at the gunmen. McSweeney was struck by one bullet but was able to draw his revolver and fire a shot hitting one gunman as he was emerging from his car. The injured gunman was assisted back to the vehicle by his accomplices before driving away. A woman who arrived on the scene found Shanahan clinging to a lamp-post asking that a priest be summoned. Reverend James Robinson from Westland Row quickly arrived and administered the last rites. The injured were removed initially to nearby Holles Street hospital and later to Sir Patrick Dun's Hospital and though Shanahan was in a particularly serious condition, doctors were able to save his life. An IRA informer later told detectives that the shot raider was removed to a house in Palmerston Road and died on 10 May. A second raider was wounded.[45]

The informer's version was contradicted in an account years later by IRA man Séamus Ó Mongáin. He revealed that the raiders' car was driven by Seán Ó Broin who was accompanied by Frankie Duffy, 'Black' Dan O'Toole and Joe Atkinson (the latter two were the Dublin Castle bombers). A fifth man, Gearóid Ó Mongáin (brother of Séamus) played the role of an innocent passer-by who gave a signal when he saw the detectives' vehicle approaching. In the exchange of gunfire, O'Toole was shot and dragged back to the car, which they drove away. He was brought to an address in Dorset Street where a sympathetic nurse extracted a .45 bullet from his thigh, and he recovered from his injuries.[46]

In a radio broadcast on the following day, de Valera described it as:

> A dastardly attack on two Irish police officers escorting the government mails. The government, for many years, has shown an extraordinary patience towards these people – I am afraid that I must say, now, an excessive patience. But as regards the men who are now in hiding and planning new crimes, the policy of patience has failed and is over.[47]

He would be as good as his word.

He visited the injured men in hospital and both were instantly promoted to sergeant. A reward of £5,000 was offered for information leading to the apprehension and conviction of any of the gunmen. The reward was never claimed, and no one was convicted of the attack.[48]

At a ceremony in Dublin Castle on 19 July both men received gold watches for bravery from their colleagues. A gold watch was also presented to Dr Maeve Bigger of Sir Patrick Dun's Hospital in appreciation of the work done by the medical staff.[49] On 9 October 1941, the men were awarded gold Scott Medals for heroism by justice minister Gerald Boland at a ceremony at Garda HQ.[50] William Shanahan was a native of Thurles, Co Tipperary, and fought with the IRA during the War of Independence. After the Truce he joined the Free State Army up to 1923 when he joined the DMP. An accomplished athlete, he represented Ireland at the Paris Olympics in 1924 and won numerous GAA medals at inter-county level. He died in service on 29 May 1954. James McSweeney was from Fitzroy Avenue in Drumcondra, Dublin, and was also an IRA veteran who joined the DMP in 1924. He retired after thirty years' service in February 1955 and died on 5 May 1971.[51]

The beefed-up Special Branch under Chief Superintendent Seán Gantly, along with Military Intelligence (G2) under Colonel Dan Bryan, proved particularly effective in combating German infiltration from the outset of the war. They were aware of IRA attempts to get German aid and that German agents were being parachuted into the country to liaise on the matter. In May 1940, detectives raided 245 Templeogue Road, Dublin, searching for a German spy named Hermann Görtz, who parachuted into County Meath early in the month. They missed Görtz but found a powerful radio transmitter, a used parachute and 20,000 US dollars in cash. They also found documents with details regarding Irish harbours, aerodromes, bridges, and landing grounds along with the disposition of defence forces.

They arrested the house owner, Stephen Carroll-Held, and charged him under the Emergency Powers Act before the military court in Collins Barracks with having possession of a code or cipher, as well as other offences.[52] Also charged was Mrs Iseult Stuart (nee MacBride), wife of Nazi sympathiser Francis Stuart, daughter of Maud Gonne MacBride and sister of former IRA chief of staff Seán. The charges related to her assisting a person with intent to hinder or prevent his apprehension, but she was found not guilty by the Special Criminal Court on 2 July 1940 and discharged.[53]

Görtz remained free for another eighteen months until he was arrested in Dublin in November 1941 along with IRA chief of staff Pearse Kelly. Both were interned for the remainder of the War.[54] Görtz befriended one of his military guards, whom he was bribing, and began sending secret messages to Germany with the help of the soldier who in turn brought back the replies – or so he thought. It was in fact a clever stunt dreamt up by G2 officers who were trying to glean information on his contacts with the IRA or other German agents. The messages were decoded by cryptologist Dr Richard Hayes, director of the National Library, who spoke several languages including fluent German. Then a suitable 'reply' was prepared in German, encoded by Hayes and delivered to Görtz by the soldier. One of the fake replies included the news that he was being 'promoted' to major by his delighted superiors, news which caused him to weep for joy.[55]

Görtz was released on 26 August 1946 and served with a deportation order. On 12 April 1947, he was arrested and sent to Mountjoy Prison pending his appeal against the deportation order but on 5 May the Supreme Court ruled against him.[56] He was released on parole but a visit to the Aliens Office on 23 May he took a cyanide pill and died almost instantly.[57] His views on the IRA were far from flattering. He told one IRA man, 'you know how to die for Ireland, but how to fight for her you have not got the slightest idea.'[58] On another occasion he referred to them as 'the most incompetent lot I ever met.'[59] 'After the war, Major-General Lahousen, who was Sabotage Chief of the German Intelligence Service, revealed that the Germans intended to work with the IRA and use Ireland as a base for sabotage operations against British targets. They would prepare the political groundwork for an uprising in Ireland to coincide with a German invasion of Britain.[60]

At 4 p.m. on Saturday 3 August 1940, detectives surprised a party of men digging a tunnel near Cork Jail in Rathmore Road. When challenged, the men fled and detectives opened fire, killing one and wounding another. The dead man was John Joseph Kavanagh (23) of St Declan's Road, Gurranbraher, and the injured man was Roger Ryan (28), a labourer from 128 Blarney Street, who was shot in the left lung. Two other men, Denis J. O'Sullivan of Coburg Street and Cornelius Byrd of Gurranabraher, were taken into custody. The detectives found a tunnel of about six feet in length, shielded by shrubbery. Cork Jail was being used to hold IRA internees and the tunnel was obviously intended for an escape attempt.[61] On 19 August, Byrd and O'Sullivan were charged in Cork District Court with obstructing officers of the state by force of arms or other violent means.[62] On 2 October, the military court sentenced O'Sullivan to four years while Byrd and the now recovered Roger Ryan received two years each.[63]

The inquest into Kavanagh's death was adjourned several times and on 17 September 1940 the coroner told the court that he received an order from the Minister for Justice, Gerald Boland, under Article 3 of the *Emergency Powers (47) Order, 1940*, directing that the remainder of the inquest be held without a jury and that no further evidence should be taken, other than that relating to identification and the date and cause of death. A lawyer for the family asked for a further adjournment as he intended to challenge the order, but the coroner refused and returned a verdict that 'death was caused from shock and haemorrhage the result of multiple wounds inflicted by a bullet as established by the medical evidence.'[64]

O'Sullivan later escaped from Mountjoy but at about 9 a.m. on 27 September 1941, he was spotted by Detective Garda John Corcoran, who was cycling from Glanmire towards Cork City. Corcoran dismounted and said to Sullivan, 'come on Joby, I want you.' [O'Sullivan was known by the nickname 'Joby']. O'Sullivan drew a gun and pointing it at the detective said, 'keep going or I'll let you have it.' As the detective approached him, O'Sullivan fired two shots that missed. He then fled up Grattan Hill and disappeared. A short time later he was cornered in a laneway by pursuing gardaí and immediately put up his hands and told them, 'Don't you know I did not attempt to kill him. I fired over his head. I thought I would scare him off and get away.' Detectives found a .455 Colt automatic pistol in his pocket. He later appeared before the Special Criminal Court charged with attempted murder and possession of a firearm. He was found not guilty of attempting to murder the detective but was sentenced to fourteen years on the firearms charge. O'Sullivan had psychiatric difficulties while in prison and spent several periods in Grangegorman and Dundrum mental hospitals. He escaped, was recaptured several times and was finally arrested in December 1945, certified sane and returned to Mountjoy Prison. In view of his mental state and as there were no garda objections, the government remitted the unexpired portion of his sentence, and he was released on 14 December 1945.[65]

On 16 August 1940, two Special Branch detectives were shot and killed while a third was seriously injured in Rathgar, Dublin. At 8 a.m.

that morning, a team of detectives led by Detective Sergeant Patrick McKeown (DMP No. 11919)[66], called to 98a Rathgar Road in Dublin to carry out a search under the Offences Against the State Act 1939. With him were four detectives (all Harriers), Detective Gardaí Richard Hyland (8333), Michael Brady (8301), Robert Mullally (8269) and Richard Wilmot (8336). Mullally and Wilmot went to the rear of the building while the other three detectives knocked on the front door.[67]

After some delay the door was opened by a boy of 15 or 16 years of age who asked them what they wanted, and the suspicious detectives felt he was playing for time. Hyland showed his identification card and the three detectives walked in the door. They were suddenly hit by a withering burst of machine-gun and revolver fire hitting Hyland, McKeown and Brady. Hyland, was struck by seven bullets but managed to fire one shot before collapsing on the ground where he died quickly. McKeown and Brady were seriously injured, and Brady managed to crawl out the door to the pathway outside. McKeown was struck by one bullet penetrating the intestine and stomach and died of his wounds the following day.[68]

Three men rushed out the door past the wounded detectives. One was carrying a Thompson sub-machine gun and the other two had revolvers. They ran down Rathgar Road and onto Wesley Road, firing as they went. Mullaly and Wilmot pursued them, firing their guns in reply. The gunmen ran through a walkway onto Rathgar Avenue, disposing of a Thompson sub-machine gun in a hedge as they turned the corner. Two ran into a residence on Rathgar Avenue and out the rear, where they climbed a fence into an alleyway. The third man was younger and made his escape towards the city. Mullaly cornered two of the gunmen in the alley and bluffed them into surrendering by brandishing his now empty gun. He and Wilmot disarmed the men, one of whom had a bullet wound in the leg.

On the way to the Bridewell one of the prisoners said, 'I suppose you men don't know who I am. I am Patrick McGrath. You got the spoils this morning. I am surprised at you men coming to a house where there are republican soldiers, knowing that they are armed.' The other prisoner was Thomas Harte (alias Thomas Green) who was injured by police fire. Detectives later found the sub-machine gun in a garden in Rathgar Avenue after Harte told them where it was located. The bullets that killed Hyland were from Harte's Thompson while the one that killed McKeown came from McGrath's revolver.[69].

On searching 98a Rathgar Road, detectives found that it was being used as Training Headquarters by the IRA. A secret room was constructed under the stairs in which they found circulars and manuscripts relating to the training of members of the IRA along with textbooks on different types of machine-gun and small arms. They also found microphones and information on documents indicating they had plans to set up a wireless transmitter.

On the same day as the shooting, the government passed the *Emergency Powers (No. 41) Order, 1940* which provided for trial by military courts for certain scheduled offences, from which there would be no appeal.[70] The new court sitting in Collins Barracks lost no time in getting down to business and on Saturday 17 August, the prisoners appeared before them charged with the murder of the two detectives. Owing to Harte's injuries, they were brought to court by ambulance.[71] When charged McGrath responded, 'as a soldier of the Irish Republican Army I protest against this charge of murder' while Harte simply said, 'I do not plead.' The court then moved to the Meath Hospital at 3 p.m. to hear the evidence of the injured Detective Garda Brady before returning to Collins Barracks at 3.45 p.m. to continue the hearing.

On Tuesday 20 August, both men were convicted of the murders and sentenced to death by firing squad. On Monday 2 September, the Supreme Court rejected an appeal against the refusal of the High Court to grant an order of *habeas corpus* and both men were executed by a military firing squad in Mountjoy Prison at 6.30 a.m. on Friday 6 September 1940.[72] A Sinn Féin bulletin referred to McGrath as 'Major General' Patrick McGrath[73] while a second document referred to Harte as 'Commandant' Thomas Harte and described both men as having been 'murdered in Mountjoy this morning, 6th Sept. 1940.'[74] IRA hardliners wanted retaliatory action for these executions, including the shooting of a prominent Special Branch man such as D/Sergeant Michael Gill or Sir John Maffey, British Representative in Ireland. However, the plan was abandoned as being 'unwise.'[75]

On the morning he was shot, Detective Garda Hyland was due to give evidence at the trial of a man he arrested when he recovered a lorry load of ammunition that was taken in the Magazine Fort raid the previous December. The trial was adjourned owing to the murder of Detective Garda Hyland.[76] Richard Hyland is likely to have had the premises at Rathgar Road under surveillance for several weeks[77] and by all accounts, was a remarkably competent policeman. He was a member of de Valera's personal bodyguard during the Battle of Dublin in 1922 and was instrumental in securing de Valera's escape from the Hammam Hotel.[78]

On 9 October 1941, Detective Garda Robert Mullally was presented with a gold Scott Medal, while Detective Garda Richard Wilmot was awarded a silver Scott Medal by justice minister Gerald Boland at a ceremony in Garda HQ. This was to honour their exceptional courage and bravery in pursuing and capturing the gunmen who shot their colleagues.[79]

At a ceremony in Dublin Castle on 25 August 2021, Detective Garda Hyland's daughter, Marie Hyland, along with Orla McKeown, grand-niece of Detective Sergeant McKeown and Frank Brady, son of the wounded Detective Garda Brady, were presented with posthumous gold Scott Medals by Garda Commissioner Drew Harris and Minister for Justice, Heather Humphreys TD.[80]

On 25 September 1940, a 23-year-old IRA man, Michael Devereaux (described as 'O.C. Wexford Battalion, IRA') went missing from his home at Maudlinstown, County Carlow. Almost exactly a year later, on 23 September 1941, his badly decayed body was found on Slievenamon

Mountain in County Tipperary. He was shot in the head and his body was hidden under a pile of stones.

He was working as a lorry driver for a petrol company which was useful for the IRA as he could travel all over the country without coming under suspicion. On 24 August 1940, he called to 22 Landsdowne Road in Dublin, apparently delivering a dispatch for the IRA. On his way out he was arrested by Special Branch men and held for three days until his release three days later. Afterwards there was intensive police activity in Tipperary, Waterford and Wexford resulting in the discovery of an arms dump in County Wexford, Devereaux's home county. The IRA suspected Devereaux of having given helpful information to the detectives and this was apparently the motive for his murder.

It was also possible that detectives were aware of the Wexford dump months beforehand and only raided it after the Devereaux arrest to sow suspicion and paranoia amongst the ranks of the IRA. However, rightly or wrongly the IRA decided that Devereaux was guilty and chief of staff Stephen Hayes signed the order condemning him to death. This was done without the usual formality of a 'court martial' at which there would be a 'trial' and Devereaux would have been given a chance to defend himself. Later many IRA members were convinced that the informer was actually Stephen Hayes himself, and that he ordered the summary execution of Devereaux to divert attention from that fact.[81]

The location of the body was pointed out by another IRA man, Patrick Davern, who was arrested on suspicion of involvement. On 11 November 1941, George Plant from Fethard, County Tipperary was charged with murder. Joseph O'Connor of Brosna, County Kerry, was charged with counselling, procuring and commanding Plant to commit the murder. Unusually for an IRA man, Plant was a Protestant who fought in the War of Independence and took the anti-Treaty side in the Civil War.

At their trial on 10 December the two key state witnesses Michael Walsh of Kilmacow, County Kilkenny, and Patrick Davern of Ninemilehouse refused to take the oath or testify. They claimed they were beaten and forced into signing the incriminating statements.

Simon Murphy of Abbey Street, Wexford, did take the oath but when questioned by state counsel Murnaghan, he refused to answer and was sentenced to six months imprisonment for contempt. O'Connor was discharged and Michael Walsh was then arrested and charged with Devereaux's murder. Patrick Davern (who pointed out the body's location) was also charged with the murder. The case against Plant collapsed on 11 December when the state entered a *Nolle Prosequi* and he too was discharged.[82]

The witnesses' reluctance to testify was no doubt prompted by a notice circulated in the locality at the time headed, 'COMPETENT MILITARY AUTHORITY, SOUTH TIPPERARY BRIGADE, IRA' and read as follows:[83]

> WHEREAS it has come to our knowledge that enemy forces have learned of the movements of Republican Troops within this area; WE hereby issue this WARNING that anyone; man or woman, found guilty of giving information to the enemy, or in any way helping or trying to help the enemy, WILL BE SHOT. Furthermore, WE WARN loyal citizens to make absolutely no reference to Republican Army movements, and idle gossip is as dangerous to military success as enemy spying and will in future be treated as such. Any in public or private gatherings of any kind discussing IRA movements does so at his or her own peril.
>
> BY ORDER

The government now changed tack and on 31 December 1941 made an order under the *Emergency Powers (No. 41F) Order 1941*, directing that Plant, O'Connor, Davern and Walsh be charged before the military court with the murder. Legal actions in the High Court by the defence team claimed that this move was unlawful, failed, and the trial in the Military Court began on 12 February 1942. J.A. McCarthy SC for the state told the court he intended to use the provision of Emergency Powers Order No. 139 should the need arise. This allowed for the reading of witnesses' statements into evidence if they refused to give evidence in court. As expected, Simon Murphy again refused to give evidence and a garda witness recounted to the court how Murphy told them he knew Devereux was to be 'court-martialled' by the IRA for revealing the location of arms dumps to gardaí. He had said he was afraid of the IRA as 'they might do the same with me as they have done with Devereux.' In his statement read to the court, Murphy said he met Devereux and got him to come with his car to a field near Bishopswater, Wexford where they met George Plant and Michael Walsh. All three drove off in Devereux's car. He never saw Devereux or his car again.[84]

Barra O'Briain, SC (for Davern) accused Detective Sergeant J. B. Reynolds of ill-treating other prisoners in the past. He put it to Reynolds that while stationed in West Cork, he arrested Rory O'Connor and took him to Rossmore Hill (near Inchigeela), told him to make an Act of Contrition and threatened to shoot him. Reynolds denied this, claiming it was the first he heard of it. O'Briain put it to him that he arrested a blacksmith called Cornelius Creedon and took him to Ballyvourney Garda Station where he beat him with a revolver to try and force him to make a statement. Reynolds replied that it was not true but agreed that Creedon later took a successful civil action against him in the Circuit Court in Cork where damages were awarded, but he insisted that he did not assault him.[85] Returning to the Davern case, O'Briain then put it to him that he took Davern up the road to Clonmel and assaulted him with a revolver, telling him he would be shot if he did not make a statement about Devereaux's disappearance. Again, Reynolds denied it.

Peace Commissioner Richard Stapleton told the court that Davern made a statement to Chief Superintendent E. A. Reynolds and Superintendent John Kelly in his presence at Clonmel barracks on 26 September. Davern, who was illiterate, did his best to point out the location of Devereaux's body on a map. Disguised in a garda waterproof coat and dark glasses he agreed to go with gardaí to Slievenamon Mountain where, after a two-hour search, they located the body. He gave full details of how Devereaux was lured away to the mountain by both

Plant and himself. When they arrived at a prepared hole in the ground, Plant accused Devereaux of betraying information. A no doubt terrified Devereaux denied this but Plant shot him in the head and they buried him in the hole, covering the site over with stones.[86]

Davern entered the witness box on 19 February and claimed that when he was arrested on 19 September, Detective Sergeant Reynolds took him up a boreen, jabbed him with a gun in the back, hit him on the head, and threatened to shoot him if he did not make a statement. As he was frightened, he agreed to make any statement the police wanted. When asked by prosecuting counsel McCarthy why he did not complain about the treatment he replied that, 'the superintendent and the others were not better than the detective sergeant.' He was placed lying on the day-room floor on a mattress with 'drunken men walking on me all night. The barrack was like a brewery with drunken men when the superintendent had gone home. What position would I be in that night if I had complained?' He said he was taken to Cashel Station on 23 September where detectives entered his cell telling him he was going to be 'bumped off'. He alleged they threatened they would make a better job of him than he made of Devereux and that his body would never be found. Later back in Clonmel Barracks he spent two or three hours alone with a detective sergeant who coached him on what to say. He said he would not have made a statement were it not for the threats.

Michael Walsh entered the witness box and made similar allegations. He claimed that a gun was put to his ribs and he was told he was for the firing squad. He made a statement which started in daylight and ended about midnight but refused to sign until two men entered his darkened cell during the night and woke him. One man pointed a gun at him saying, 'if you don't sign the statement, we will take you for a ride.' He told garda superintendents he would give evidence against Plant and O'Connor, but really had no intention of doing so.

On 23 February, the court admitted the statements made by Davern and Walsh. In Walsh's statement read to the court he described himself as a 'Divisional Training Officer' in the IRA and his area included County

Wexford. He said that he and Plant arranged to go to Wexford to contact Devereux and that O'Connor gave each of them a revolver and some ammunition. To entice Devereux, he was told that a dump had to be moved. He claimed he was a reluctant participant and hoped that IRA HQ would reconsider the matter but Plant told him they 'would have to go through with it.[87]

Davern's statement was read to the court by Chief Superintendent Reynolds. It described how he accompanied Devereux and Plant up the mountain to where a hole awaited. Plant said something to Devereux about giving information which Devereux denied. He was then shot by Plant and they covered up his body with stones. He said he didn't know Devereux was to be shot until they reached the hole.[88]

On 26 February 1942, the court found Joseph O'Connor not guilty, and he was discharged, but immediately arrested as he left court. George Plant, Patrick Davern and Michael Walsh were all convicted of murder and sentenced to be shot by firing squad. Submissions made on behalf of Plant pointed out the dangers of convicting in a capital case based on unsworn evidence and referred to allegations made on oath in court that the statements were 'extracted by improper methods.' The court rejected the submissions and Plant was executed by a military firing squad in Portlaoise Prison at 7.45 a.m. on 5 March 1942. The death sentences on Davern and Walsh were commuted to life imprisonment. Plant was described in the *United Irishmen* of October 1948 as 'General' George Plant.[89]

On 5 May 1941, the Northern Bank in Oldcastle, County Meath was held up by four armed IRA men from the Dundalk area who escaped with £704:14s. On 9 June the same gang raided the Hibernian Bank in Castlepollard, this time getting away with £636:7:9d. After a tip-off, a team of detectives led by Superintendent Denis Connolly and Detective Sergeant Carty surrounded the home of Joseph Casey at Oghill, near Drumlish, County Longford, between 5.30 a.m. and 6 a.m. on 18 July 1941. They were backed up by troops from Longford led by Lieutenant Brendan Houlihan. The gardaí were searching for Richard Goss from Dundalk, suspected of involvement in these and other bank robberies.

He was on the run since the Magazine Fort raid in December 1939. Superintendent Connolly knocked on the door but received no reply. He spotted Goss at the side of the building pointing a revolver at a soldier while gripping his rifle. He called on Goss to surrender but the suspect fired two shots that missed and pointed his gun at the soldier saying, 'I will drop him.' The superintendent shouted at his men to 'Shoot to kill' and after an exchange of shots, Goss and three others surrendered and were taken into custody.[90]

Lieutenant Houlihan suffered a neck wound and Private George Kelly was wounded in the groin. The arrested men were Richard Goss (26) and Joseph Callaghan (18) of Dundalk, as well as the householder Joseph Casey (54), and his son Joseph (21).[91] Both Goss and Callaghan had revolvers when captured but while Callaghan's weapon was not fired, all six bullets in Goss' gun were discharged. Taoiseach Eamon de Valera signed an order on 22 July decreeing that Goss and Callaghan be tried before the recently-established military court. Both were charged with shooting at police and troops with intent to resist arrest.[92]

At their trial in August 1941, evidence was given that Goss was picked out at an identification parade as being one of the men involved in the Northern Bank robbery in Oldcastle. Goss told the court that on the morning of his arrest he heard a noise and upon going outside, he met a soldier armed with a rifle. He was trying to move the bolt. He instinctively grabbed the rifle barrel as he was afraid the soldier would shoot him and drew his own gun. He heard the order 'Shoot to kill' and fired several shots in a general direction but did not fire at anyone, but just over their heads so they would not come any nearer. He added that detectives previously threatened to 'get' him and insisted he had no intention of killing anyone.

On 1 August 1941, he was convicted of shooting at gardaí and military. He was sentenced to be shot by firing squad. His defence team made a strong plea to government to commute the sentence, noting there was no execution since the civil war in cases where loss of life was not involved. Despite numerous pleas for clemency, the government refused to commute the sentence and he was executed at Portlaoise Prison at 5.45 a.m. on Saturday 9 August 1941. Joseph O'Callaghan was acquitted, and the state later dropped the charges against Joseph Casey Senior. His son Joseph Junior was sentenced to eighteen months imprisonment on 9 October for his part in a robbery at Dundalk Post Office.[93] The Goss execution marked a new hardening in government policy, and they were in no mood for leniency after the murder of the two detectives in Rathgar. It was the first post-civil war execution for a crime that did not involve loss of life.

On 8 September 1941, at Rathmines Garda Station in Dublin, a young garda Dan Kelleher watched in amazement as a man, who was manacled hand and foot while holding a revolver, hobbled into the building and asked for garda protection.[94] The man was former IRA chief of staff Stephen Hayes, who had just escaped from his former associates who were detaining him in a house in nearby Castlewood Park on suspicion of being a police informant.

On 30 June 1941, Hayes was detained by his IRA colleagues whom he later described as 'six-county men'. They were named in Harry White's biography as Seán McCaughey, Liam Rice and Charlie McGlade all of the 'Northern Command staff'.[95] He was held at various locations including the Cooley Mountains, Clontarf, Glencree and finally in Castlewood Park in Rathmines. They gave him a number of severe beatings and accused him of being in contact with named members of the police force 'political branch' and of betraying men and arms dumps. On one occasion, he was beaten with the handle of a broom to such an extent that the handle broke in his assailant's hand. A 'court martial' was held with McCaughey as prosecutor. It went on late into the night and Hayes was found guilty and sentenced to death.[96]

According to his own account, Hayes decided to make a false confession as this was the only way to play for time and maybe save his life. He calculated that by making a series of outlandish admissions to his captors, other friends in the IRA would realise they were nonsense and thus delay his expected execution as much as possible. Among these 'admissions' was that he was responsible for the Special Branch raid on 16 Rathmines Park on 9 September 1939 when most of the IRA Army Council was rounded up. Another was that he had betrayed Seán Russell to the British, who removed him from a steamer in Gibraltar and murdered him. He finally escaped on 8 September 1941 when one of his captors got careless and left his revolver behind as he answered a knock from the landlady who was looking for her rent. Hayes grabbed the revolver, and, with hands and feet manacled, managed to escape through the window and hobble to the safety of Rathmines Garda Station nearby.[97]

On hearing of his escape, the Special Branch led by Detective Inspector Michael Gill rushed to Castlewood Park and challenged two men near the house. One of them, Liam Rice from Belfast, fired two shots which missed. He ran but was shot and seriously injured by return fire. According to Harry White's biography he was shot by Detective Sergeant Denis O'Brien.[98] The detectives recovered Rice's gun, a Webley Mark 6, and found that it had two discharged rounds and three other live rounds. He was taken to hospital where a bullet was later removed from his shoulder.

Five other men were arrested in follow-up operations, including Seán McCaughey from Belfast (one of the Hayes kidnappers), described during his trial as 'Adjutant-General of the IRA'. Hayes made a full statement of his ordeal to Chief Superintendent Patrick Carroll and Superintendent Seán Gantly in which he named names and later gave evidence against McCaughey in the Military Court.[99] On 18 September 1941, McCaughey was found guilty and sentenced to death by shooting but this was later commuted to life imprisonment following numerous pleas for clemency. Many telegrams and letters were sent from his native Belfast including one from Bishop Daniel Mageean of Down and Connor. In prison, McCaughey refused to wear prison clothes and spent five years naked except for a blanket.

He embarked on a hunger strike in Portlaoise Prison on 19 April 1946 from which he died on 11 May. His death provoked an avalanche of letters of complaint to de Valera, mostly from Irish Americans. A letter from the Chicago Chapter of the Green Cross Organisation thundered:

> ...we rejoice in the fact, that the cause of Ireland is safe so long as she has men who are willing to suffer and die, rather than submit to be branded as criminals of a Military Tribunal set up by the first quislings of the Irish Republic in 1922 that put to death seventy-seven (77) of Ireland's bravest and best, and which still functions with the blessings of the apostate President of the once glorious Republic...

The letter continued in a similar vein. On 8 April 1942, the now-recovered Rice was sentenced to twenty years imprisonment in the Special Criminal Court for possession of firearms with intent to endanger life and shooting at a detective sergeant with intent to murder him.[100]

The hunger strike was a fearsome weapon in the republican arsenal dating from the death of Terence McSweeney in Brixton Prison in October 1920, which galvanised support for the IRA. However, republican prisoners who played 'chicken' with their lives during the 1940s found to their cost that de Valera was made of sterner stuff. He released Patrick McGrath after he went on hunger strike related to his arrest at Rathmines Park a year earlier. As a 1916 and War of Independence veteran, McGrath was held in high esteem and de Valera was persuaded to drop charges against him rather than have him die on hunger strike. McNeela and D'Arcy later went on hunger strike, probably in expectation of the same outcome but the government allowed them to perish. McGrath murdered Detective Sergeant McKeown and Detective Garda Hyland, and was himself put to death along with Harte. In response to barracking from opposition deputies in the Dáil in 1943, de Valera said that the decision to release McGrath was ...

> ...one of the great regrets of my whole life, and will be until my death, that I allowed any consideration of any kind to retract me from the

> position I had taken up. It was one of the biggest mistakes that I have made in my life and, as I have said, I will regret it until my death, because, had it not been for my action, there would have been only one death, whereas, in the event, there were four deaths and two – six deaths in all.[101]

Though Hayes gave evidence against his kidnappers before the Special Criminal Court, he was sentenced to five years' penal servitude by the same court on 3 June 1942, for 'acting as Chief of staff of an armed force styling itself the Irish Republican Army.' A memorandum to government from the Department of Justice listed his 'long history of anti-State activities' and that during his leadership the IRA had,

> ...intensified its activities and its members committed numerous crimes including the following:
>
> (1) Armed raid on Magazine Fort, December 1939
> (2) Use of explosives in detective quarters, Dublin Castle, April 1940
> (3) Attempted murder and serious wounding of police at Holles Street, Dublin, May 1940.
> (4) Murder of police officers at Rathgar Road, August 1940.
> (5) Murder of Michael Devereux, September, 1940.
> (6) Armed raid on Dundalk Post office, larceny of £940 and wounding of a civilian, April 1941.
> (7) Armed raid on Northern Bank, Oldcastle, larceny of £700, May, 1941.
> (8) Armed raid on Hibernian Bank, Castlepollard, larceny of £636, June, 1941.[102]

In view of his lengthy record of subversion, he served his full sentence and was released on 19 March 1946. After his release, he resumed his clerical position with Wexford County Council and his pension entitlements were restored from 9 September 1948.[103]

On Easter Sunday 5 April 1942, shots were fired at detectives at an IRA ceremony at Glasnevin Cemetery in Dublin. Detective Gardaí Martin Hanrahan (8313 - a Harrier) and Patrick Kirwan saw Andrew Nathan of St Jarlath's Road, Cabra in the crowd at the Republican Plot. They spotted someone handing Nathan a revolver and they followed him and Laz (Lasarian) Mangan of Blackhorse Lane, out of the cemetery down the Finglas Road. The detectives grabbed Andrew Nathan while Mangan pulled a gun and pointed it at them. A certain (probably inebriated) 19-year-old Brendan Behan from Kildare Road, Crumlin, shouted, 'use it, use it, give it to me and I'll shoot the bastards.' Mangan threw the revolver to Behan who fired two shots at the detectives but missed. They chased Behan down de Courcy Square and he turned and fired another shot as he fled, before managing to escape over a garden wall.

Behan's own description of the events was somewhat more colourful, 'I looked round and saw the squad cars and inside them sets of fugh-faced [*sic*] bastards intent on nothing less than grievous bodily harm'.[104] As regarding the firing of shots he wrote, 'as I snatched the revolver out of the officer's hand [meaning Mangan], the police opened fire. I didn't, and not until they opened fire, did I fire back at them…'[105]

Some days later detectives spotted Behan in Parnell Street in the city centre. He fled down a laneway and pointed a revolver at them. As there were children in the laneway, the detectives did not fire and Behan escaped again. On 10 April, he was finally apprehended in a house in Blessington Street and arrested. Behan's account of his escape and capture was that on fleeing from the detectives at Glasnevin, both he and his friend Joseph Cafferty found shelter in a sympathiser's house nearby. He claimed that both were to be shot on sight by the Special Branch, on the orders of 'Chief Superintendent Gantly, a whore's melt of a man, and another ex-Free State Army guttersnipe, neither of whom were ever in the Irish Republican Army, at least as active members.'[106]

Behan's fanciful account was that he was arrested in the home of Jack Corr at 15 Blessington Street when:

> The door flew open as if the devil himself was behind it, and a lot of mean-faced bastards grabbed me as I made for the window. I was treated to a piece of verbal abuse by Gantly and his minions, but I was not physically assaulted as I had been in Liverpool when I was last arrested. One of the detective officers slipped me a packet of cigarettes and a box of matches, some would say for to soften me up to give information, but I am always prepared to look upon these things as manifestations of human charity.[107]

What actually happened was more mundane. At around 7 p.m. on 10 April, Detective Garda Doran was in Blessington Street waiting for his colleague Detective Garda Donegan. Doran spotted Behan coming along the street and he retreated back into a doorway to let him pass. He then grabbed Behan from behind and on searching him found he had no gun. He did not resist and was brought to the Bridewell without incident.[108]

On 24 April 1942, Behan was sentenced to fourteen years penal servitude in the Special Criminal Court for shooting at Detectives Hanrahan and Kirwan, and seven years for possession of a revolver, with sentences to run concurrently. Somebody said to Behan afterwards, 'any man who shoots at a policeman at fourteen yards and misses him deserves a year for every yard he missed him by'.[109] He was fortunate not to be facing a firing squad. Less than a year previously, Richard Goss was executed for shooting at detectives and military though no one was killed. Mangan was sentenced to three years for possession of firearms and membership of an illegal body.[110] Nathan got seven years penal servitude for possession of a fully-loaded Webley revolver, membership of an unlawful organisation and possession of incriminating documents. He was released on 17 December 1946.[111] Behan was released on 18 December 1946 as part of a general government amnesty.[112]

In the autumn of 1942, three more Special Branch detectives were killed by the IRA, one in September and two in October. On 9 September, Detective Sergeant Denis O'Brien (a Broy Harrier) was shot and killed as he left his home at Ballyboden near Rathfarnham in Dublin. This was the first time since the murder of Superintendent Curtin in Tipperary in 1931 that the IRA deliberately targeted a member of the force. O'Brien was driving down the avenue leading from his home when he was fired at by a man with a Thompson sub-machine gun from an adjoining field. O'Brien got out of his car, took cover behind a wall, and fired three shots at his assailants. Two or three other men also fired at him, one of them with a sub-machine gun. O'Brien was shot in the head and died instantly. The attackers arrived on bicycles and left the scene the same way, though one of them abandoned his bicycle and fled on foot. O'Brien's wife heard the shots and ran out of the house shouting, 'Dinny, Dinny!' and found him dead at the gate with his revolver in his hand.[113]

Coincidentally, an off-duty detective was cycling to the mountains to cut turf and was about 200 yards away when he heard the shooting. He met two cyclists wearing light coats and caps coming toward him and telephoned their description to Rathfarnham Station. The fleeing gunmen passed through a crowd of some thirty to forty persons though none subsequently came forward to identify them.[114] O'Brien took part in the 1916 Rising and was part of the Marrowbone Lane garrison. He joined the force as one of de Valera's Broy Harriers in 1933 and became a hate figure for his former colleagues in the IRA due to his enthusiasm for bringing his erstwhile friends to justice.

Interestingly, there was information two years previously that the IRA was planning such an attack. An anonymous caller telephoned the Department of Justice on 23 April 1940 asking to speak to the minister (Gerald Boland) but would not give his name. On being told he could not speak to him unless he gave his name and stated his business, he agreed to speak to Boland's private secretary, Peter Berry. The caller told Berry of an IRA meeting in Dublin on 20 April 1940 at which action against Detective Sergeant O'Brien was discussed. The stated reason for this action was O'Brien's involvement in the arrest of Jack McNeela (who died on hunger strike a short time earlier) and other members of the IRA.

In a follow-up telephone call on 1 May the caller said a decision had been taken to have O'Brien shot. The caller added that Minister for Justice Gerald Boland was also to be shot by being machine-gunned from a passing car. This time the caller said that O'Brien's involvement in the arrest of sixteen IRA men in Parnell Square – the Meath Hotel arrests – resulted in a decision that 'he must go'. An IRA active service unit consisting of '[Michael] Conway and four Belfast men' was formed to carry out these killings.[115]

The government immediately offered a £5,000 reward for information leading to the arrest and conviction of those involved in the murder.[116] Notices were placed on garda station windows throughout the country listing the names of those wanted for interview. The names were also published in a garda notice in the *Irish Press*, *Irish Independent* and *Cork Examiner* on 10 October and included three Kerrymen, Michael Quill from Listowel along with Charles Kerins and Timothy Drummond, both from Tralee, Liam Burke, Henry White and Francis Joseph Duffy, all from Belfast; Hugh McAteer from Derry and Thomas Kealy from Celbridge, County Kildare.[117]

On 4 January 1943, Michael J. Quill (25), of Listowel, appeared before the military court in Collins Barracks, Dublin, charged with the murder. The military officers presiding were Colonel J.V. Joyce, President, Colonel Felix Devlin and Major C. Whelan.[118] Quill was arrested earlier by the RUC and brought handcuffed to the border at Carrickarnon, County Louth on 9 October where he was handed over. At the trial, the garda cyclist, who was near the scene at the time of the shooting, identified Quill as one of the cyclists he met seconds after the shooting at an identification parade in the Bridewell.

Quill gave evidence on his own behalf on 15 January. He denied being involved in O'Brien's murder and said he was in Belfast when it happened. He was not in Dublin again until he was handed over to the twenty-six county authorities by the RUC. He was served with an exclusion order and driven to the border, where the police told him to 'start walking'. His alibi was backed up by the perjured evidence of three girls from Belfast who were coached on what to say beforehand in solicitor Con Lehane's office. They were named in Harry White's biography as Sara Malone, her daughter Maureen and Mary McGuigan. All three swore that Quill was in Belfast on 9 September and for several days before and after.[119] He was found not guilty by the military court on 20 January. The President of the court said, 'as there is a doubt in the minds of the Court as to his guilt, the Court has decided to give him the benefit of the doubt.' On leaving the court he was immediately re-arrested and interned.[120]

Detectives finally ran Charlie Kerins to earth on 16 June 1944 when a squad led by Detective Sergeant P.J. O'Connell raided the home of Dr Kathleen Farrell at 50 Upper Rathmines Road at 4 a.m. and found Kerins asleep in bed. In a search of the bedroom, they found a machine-gun, three revolvers, detonators, eighteen hand grenades and over 1,000 rounds of ammunition, along with a loaded Colt pistol with a round in the breech within easy reach. They also found clothing and a clerical collar of a type worn by Christian Brothers.[121]

On 3 September 1944, Kerins was charged with O'Brien's murder. State counsel described the shooting as 'a reprisal by members of an illegal organisation for his efforts for many years to bring members of that organisation to justice.' When told by the judge that he was entitled to counsel he said, 'I consider it an insult to my intelligence to be expected to recognise this as a court of justice or the men here as supreme judges.' Evidence was given by a chief superintendent of a document seized in the room where he was arrested. It was addressed to Kerins as 'Deputy Chief of Staff' and bore the words 'A Chathaill a chara' (Charlie, my friend) and signed by 'Aodh, Chief of Staff' (a reference to Hugh McAteer, who was briefly IRA Chief of Staff in 1942 before being replaced by Kerins).[122]

Kerins' fingerprints were found on the abandoned bicycle. He was sentenced to death on 9 October and when asked if he had anything to say replied:

> All I can say is that if the Free State authorities are satisfied that I got a fair trial here, I hope their consciences are clear on that point. If this is an example of de Valera's justice, freedom and democracy, then I would like to know what dictatorship and militarism are. That's about all I have to say.

Numerous pleas for clemency were made by letter and telegram, including a letter in Irish from Seamus O Muireadhaigh (Seamus Murray) of 50 Dillon Street, Dublin who pointed out he fought at Boland's Mills (where de Valera was Commandant) during Easter Week in 1916. Thousands more from all over the country signed petition forms that streamed into government buildings. The appeals were in vain and on 1 December 1944 Kerins was hanged in Mountjoy Prison by British executioner Tom Pierrepoint.[123] It is not clear why he was not executed by firing squad as had been the case with earlier executions of IRA men but it is suspected that de Valera simply wanted to portray him as a common criminal.

According to an article in the *Sunday Press* in 1985, O'Brien's murder was organised by Archie Doyle (one of Kevin O'Higgins' killers). It was claimed that he was present at the scene with three others when O'Brien was shot but that it was not clear if he took part in the actual shooting. It also claimed that Kerins, as IRA chief of staff, sanctioned the murder and that he was actually present at the shooting and fired the first burst from a Thompson sub-machine gun.[124] This is contradicted in Harry White's biography where he claimed that, while Kerins used the bike on which his fingerprints were found previously, he was not one of those who carried out the shooting.[125] White's account is probably more credible as it was hardly necessary for the chief of staff to carry out the shooting himself though he could well have been present.

In an interview in the Republican Sinn Fein newspaper *Saoirse* (Freedom) in October 2006, veteran IRA man Dan Keating claimed the O'Brien shooting was in revenge for a previous Special Branch killing of IRA man Jackie Griffith in Mount Street. He said Griffith was shot on a Sunday morning on his way to Mass when the detectives drove up behind him 'and Dinny O'Brien took out his gun and blasted him on the street'. Keating said O'Brien was the bitterest opponent of the IRA in all Ireland and that after the Griffith shooting 'it was decided then and there that O'Brien would have to go.' Not for the first time, the elderly Keating's recollection was badly mistaken, as O'Brien was already dead when Griffith was shot. O'Brien was shot on 9 September 1942 while the Griffith shooting was on 4 July 1943.[126]

What happened was that as Griffith, a wanted man, was spotted by Branch men cycling near the corner of Lower Mount Street and Merrion Square in Dublin. The Special Branch car was driven by Detective Sergeant Edward (Ned) Fergus,[127] accompanied by Detective Garda Peter Byrne.[128] Griffith drew a revolver and fired at them, shattering the windscreen. Detective Garda Byrne fired two shots from a Thompson sub-machine gun in reply, fatally wounding Griffith. He, along with five other political prisoners, escaped over the wall from Mountjoy Prison on the night of 1 November 1942. He was serving a ten-year sentence imposed by the Special Criminal Court on 13 March 1942 for attempting to shoot at detectives, possession of a revolver and over 200 rounds of ammunition and receiving three revolvers the property of the Minister for Defence, as well as membership of an illegal organisation. He was buying short arms from a rogue soldier at an army camp in Islandbridge. When his home in Ringsend was searched, detectives found an additional twenty-three revolvers.[129]

Following Kerins' arrest, the IRA decided to shoot one of the arresting officers, Detective Sergeant P. J. O'Connell, as a reprisal. According to a newspaper article by Ryle Dwyer, a tip-off from Tralee IRA man Timothy Drummond (who was also listed as wanted for the murder) led to O'Connell moving into accommodation in Dublin Castle. He put his furniture in storage and his family temporarily moved to Tralee. Drummond's information was very specific – the killing was to be carried out on Christmas Eve at his home in Sandford Avenue, Dublin. Sure enough, on the night of 24 December 1941, four men carrying Thompson sub-machine guns called to O'Connell's home at 28 Sandford Avenue in Dublin looking for him. They briefly held up one of his neighbours, mistaking him for O'Connell. They returned the following day in a second fruitless attempt to kill him. The quid pro quo agreed with Drummond was that the Special Branch would not attempt to arrest IRA gunmen involved. O'Connell and his family would remain in the Dublin Castle accommodation up to his retirement in the 1960s.[130]

Just three weeks after O'Brien's death another Special Branch man, Detective Garda Michael Walsh, was shot by the IRA, this time in County Cavan. On 30 September 1942, IRA man Harry White from Belfast and Paddy Dermody (described in White's biography as 'OC Eastern Command') from Castlepollard, cycled from Dundalk to Ballyjamesduff to attend the wedding of Dermody's sister Jane to Michael Tuite.[131] Both White and Dermody were wanted men at the time as it was known they were active in the recent resurgence of IRA activity. Gardaí wanted to question Dermody about a bank robbery at the Hibernian Bank in Castlepollard on 9 June 1941.[132]

Night was falling when they were about five miles from Ballyjamesduff and dismounted to climb a steep hill. On a bend on the road in the darkness they saw a woman in white seated on a ditch and the two men called out, 'good night' and walked on. The woman made no reply and as the men were confused by this, they decided to go back for a second look. Using flash lamps, they searched up and down but could not find her so they decided they must have seen a ghost. Shortly afterwards, they stopped for a cup of tea at an IRA 'safe house' in Mount Nugent, the home of an old lady, Mrs Monaghan, who was known to Dermody. After some chit-chat White related the story of the lady in white to her. There was a long silence and she said fervently, 'someone will die tonight. That's a sign. But it depends on you. If you don't go to the wedding, Paddy will not go.' Dermody laughed off the woman's concerns and though White had no particular desire to go, he decided to attend. Again, Mrs Monaghan appealed to Dermody, 'you had a sign tonight son, and someone is going to die.'[133]

They cautiously approached the Tuite house at Lismacanican, Ballyjamesduff, to satisfy themselves that there was no police surveillance. Their efforts were not too thorough as they did not spot the detectives and troops already watching from concealed positions. Dermody's sister was married that day and detectives expected that he would turn up either at the church or the wedding party later. The two men entered the house and joined the festivities and several minutes later, at around 1.30 a.m. a party of armed detectives led by Superintendent Bernard O'Boyle of Ballyjamesduff, piled in the door while others cordoned off the surrounding area. The house was crowded with people happily dancing to the music of a fiddle and accordion. Detective Sergeant Thomas C. Delaney (6739) from Monaghan shouted, 'police officers; no panic; stop the music.' Dermody appeared at the door of a room off the kitchen and as the superintendent approached him, Dermody drew a gun and fired at him and O'Boyle fired a shot in reply. Harry White also drew his Parabellum and opened fire on the detectives.[134]

At this there was pandemonium, with screaming wedding guests running to escape from the house. Dermody retreated to the room from which he came and further shots were heard. On entering the room, detectives found Dermody lying dead on the floor. Another guest and two detectives were wounded. Detective Garda Walsh came to the kitchen door holding his side saying, 'I'm shot sergeant'. He dropped his gun by his side and it was picked up by a colleague. He was taken to Cavan Hospital in a serious condition but managed to make a statement about what happened. He told colleagues that Dermody fired at him and that he fired two shots in reply and thought he hit him. He died later the same day.

Detective Sergeant Delaney was also shot and wounded in the left thigh but his condition was not serious. In the confusion, Harry White escaped out a window and ran as detectives fired after him. He had two bullet wounds in his leg but managed to flee across fields, where he laid low for two days. There was a massive follow-up search, but a sympathetic soldier found him, brought him food, and helped him to escape through the cordon. Detectives understood it was White who got away. He was sentenced to two years imprisonment by the Special Criminal Court on 19 October 1939 and on his release was interned. He was released on 15 June 1942 on giving an undertaking not to be involved in IRA activities. Detective Garda Walsh's widow Susan was awarded £2,727:18:0 in compensation in July 1945.[135]

At 10 p.m. on Saturday 24 October 1942, Detective Garda George Mordaunt (6712) was shot and killed during a Special Branch raid on a house at 14 Holly Road, Donnycarney in Dublin.[136] The search party was led by Chief Superintendent Seán Gantly, head of the Special Branch, along with Detective Inspector Michael Gill and accompanied by Detective Gardaí Martin Lanigan, Daniel Connor, Patrick Downey, Henry Gillespie, William Donegan, and Joseph Foley. They were searching for two wanted men, 25-year-old Maurice O'Neill from Cahirciveen, County Kerry and Henry 'Harry' White from Belfast, who escaped after the Walsh shooting in Cavan a month earlier.

As detectives entered the front door the two suspects fled out the back, where they were confronted by other detectives who called on them to halt. The men opened their weapons on the detectives who returned fire. O'Neill retreated to the house, threw down his revolver and was arrested. When searched he was found to have twelve live rounds of .45 revolver ammunition. When asked why he was carrying a revolver he replied, 'to protect myself' and when asked from whom he added, 'from ye.' Meanwhile, Mordaunt and other detectives pursued White through back gardens on Oak Road, firing as they went but he escaped in the darkness. Mordaunt's body was found shortly afterwards in the back garden of 5 Oak Road. He was shot in the head and died instantly.[137]

O'Neill was brought before the military court in Collins Barracks on 2 November 1942, in front of Commandants Tuite and Devlin, and Colonel Joyce. As there was no evidence that O'Neill's bullets caused Mordaunt's death, he was charged with shooting at Detective Gardaí Lanigan, Connor and Downey with intent to resist arrest, then capital offences under the Emergency Powers Acts. During the trial, defence counsel Seán MacBride BL tried to suggest to witnesses that the fatal shot might in fact have been fired by a detective, which they strenuously denied. Evidence was given that the Webley revolver found on O'Neill had five empty shells and one round under the hammer which failed to fire.[138]

On 4 November, O'Neill gave evidence on his own behalf. Replying to questions from MacBride, he said as he and another man were leaving by the back door of the house, he was unaware that it was surrounded or that he was wanted for any criminal charge. While in the lane, somebody started firing at them and he dropped his bicycle and threw himself on the ground. He drew his gun and began firing in the direction of the shots as he did not want to be killed without trying to save his life. Under cross-examination by Mr McCarthy KC, for the state, O'Neill gave non-committal answers or simply said 'I refuse to answer.' He said the gun was for training as he intended 'going to the North.' He did not think it was the gardaí who were firing in the lane.[139]

In his closing arguments, MacBride said it was clear that whoever fired the fatal shot it was not O'Neill. Indeed, if it were not for his own candour there was no evidence that he fired any shots and that he was entitled to an acquittal if he fired to save his own life. On 5 November, O'Neill was convicted of shooting with intent to resist arrest and was sentenced to death.[140] Once again, a massive campaign for clemency was launched and scores of telegrams, letters, and foolscap sheets in addition to twenty-six children's exercise books crammed with the signatures of thousands of people laboriously inscribed. These were sent to the government calling for a reprieve. With the memory of the murders of three detectives in two months fresh in their minds, the government was in no mood for clemency and O'Neill was executed by firing squad at Mountjoy Prison at 8.20 a.m. on 12 November 1942.[141] After Mordaunt's death, it would be twenty-eight years before another member of An Garda Síochána would be murdered.

Harry White remained at large for a further four years but was arrested by the RUC in the early hours of Sunday 20 October 1946 in a shop in the village of Altnahoney, County Derry. The raid was carried out by a large RUC raiding party led by Detective Inspector Corbett. After a detailed search, Corbett found him hiding in what was described as a 'cache' measuring three feet by four feet under the shop counter with a trap-door for ease of entrance. He was ordered out at gunpoint and detained in Crumlin Road Prison in Belfast. The authorities found twelve pistols and revolvers, part of a Thompson sub-machine gun, three hand-grenades and between 2,000 and 5,000 rounds of rifle and revolver ammunition.

On Thursday 24 October, RUC officers escorted him to the border at Tyholland, County Monaghan where Detective Inspector Michael Gill, of the Special Branch, was waiting to arrest him. As White puts it, 'a car containing Detective Inspectors Gill and Weymes [*sic*] and a posse of their gunmen arrived.' He was charged before the Dublin District Court sitting in Green Street later that day with Mordaunt's murder. As he was led from the court, Chief Superintendent Gantly walked over to him and said, 'don't worry, we'll get this over quick and you'll hang, you bastard.'[142]

At the remand hearing on 29 October, Chief Superintendent Gantly, complained to the court that defending solicitor Con Lehane made a false allegation about him to the effect that he was guilty of a criminal conspiracy that planned to have Henry White kidnapped and abducted. He added that White was lawfully arrested on foot of a legal warrant and was before the court in a legal way. Lehane replied that he was acting on his instructions that an illegal act was committed outside the jurisdiction of this state. District Justice O'Grady said he was not concerned with what happened in the north, but only to take depositions.[143]

Lehane said that the manner in which White was brought from Belfast to Tyholland, County Monaghan, was not legal and that he was, in fact, abducted and kidnapped. He said, 'the presence of Special Branch officers in Tyholland to meet Henry White and his kidnappers, fixes

Inspector Gill and his superiors with previous knowledge that Henry White was going to be so kidnapped by Sir Basil Brooke's RUC.' The justice remarked he could hardly deal with the transfer from Belfast to County Monaghan.[144]

In the meantime, lawyers acting for White sought a conditional order of *Habeas Corpus* in the Northern Ireland Divisional Court directing the Northern Ireland Minister of Home Affairs to produce the body of Henry White. In his affidavit, White said that following his arrest on 20 October 1946 he was taken to Victoria Barracks in Derry and interrogated by County Inspector Davidson and Head Constable Fannin. He alleged that Davidson said to him, 'if you tell us the name of the 'line' into Crumlin Road Jail, you will not be handed over the border.' This was an apparent reference to the suspicion that some prison official was conveying messages to and from the prisoners. Fannin added, 'if you are handed over the border, it will be no flowers, by request.' He said he was released from Crumlin Road Jail at 7.30 a.m. on 24 October and that outside the jail he was forced into a car by Inspector Davidson and two other men in plain clothes. He was driven to the border where he was arrested by Inspector Gill and charged with the murder of Detective Garda Mordaunt. The *habeas corpus* application was refused on 29 October. This was appealed to the Northern Court of Appeal which refused it on 18 December on the ground that it had no jurisdiction in the matter.[145]

White's trial commenced in the Special Criminal Court in Dublin on 3 December 1946. Detective Garda Lanigan said while at the back of Oak Road, Donnycarney he fired four shots at Maurice O'Neill, who was firing down the laneway at him. He strenuously denied a suggestion that the man he was firing at was Detective Mordaunt. Detective Garda William Donegan gave evidence that he picked out White at an identification parade in the Bridewell as a man who had fired three shots at him on 24 October 1942 at the house in Donnycarney. Detective Garda J. Coll, a fingerprint expert, said he lifted a fingerprint matching White's from a glass vase in the house.[146]

In cross-examination by Mr Murnaghan for the state, White agreed he had a gun on the night of Mordaunt's death. He said he was acting 'under orders' from his 'superior officers in the Irish Republican Army'. When he went out to the lane with Maurice O'Neill, shots were fired at them from the front but it never occurred to him it was the police. He agreed that he fired several shots at the flashes.[147]

In his closing address, MacBride said that White and O'Neill were leaving by the back and they had no way of knowing that Detective Mordaunt was in the lane. He said that the accused might be guilty of many offences – including possession of firearms, membership of an unlawful organisation and firing at police officers – but the court, he submitted, must be satisfied that it was a bullet fired by the accused that killed Mordaunt. He said that White was the only one in the laneway with a 9mm pistol and the evidence was that Mordaunt was more than likely killed by a .45 calibre bullet (the fatal bullet was never found).

On 12 December, White was found guilty of murder and sentenced to death by hanging. The date of execution was set for 3 January 1947. The president of the court said they were satisfied beyond doubt that the bullet that killed Detective Officer Mordaunt was fired by Henry White from the 9mm automatic pistol, which he carried on the night. On 6 February 1947, the Court of Criminal Appeal quashed the conviction and substituted a conviction for manslaughter, saying that since there was no lawful authority for the intended arrest, it was not murder. He was sentenced to twelve years imprisonment.[148] Harry White gave a newspaper interview in October 1985, in which he claimed that Mordaunt was killed by one of his own men. He alleged that Special Branch detectives made several attempts to kill him in the 1940s and wounded him seriously on a few occasions.[149]

The execution of Charlie Kerins on 1 December 1944 marked the final chapter of the wartime IRA threat. Between 1939 and 1945, the government showed breath-taking ruthlessness to ensure that IRA mischief-making would not impinge on Irish neutrality and give either the Allies or the Germans an excuse to invade the country. Between 1939 and

1946, six IRA men were executed, while three others, Patrick Dermody, Jackie Griffith and John Kavanagh were shot and killed by the Special Branch. Sixty-five IRA prisoners went on hunger strike. Three of them died. During the same period, 463 were convicted and sentenced to imprisonment for offences against the state by military courts, while a further 1,196 were interned without trial. The largest number in custody at any one time was 600.

> Between 1935 and 1945, the IRA was responsible for:
> 10 murders (including six Special Branch detectives)
> 12 attempted murders
> 16 attacks on Defences Forces or its members
> 22 attacks on the Garda Síochána or its members
> 12 attacks on witnesses
> 19 attacks on civilians
> 20 armed robberies
> 30 discoveries of arms dumps
> 6 cases of arson
> 3 cases of kidnapping
> 14 cases of drilling, arms instruction classes, establishing armed camps etc
> 4 cases of association with foreign agents during the war.[150]

In May 1945, a government proclamation revoked Part II of the Offences Against the State (Amendment) Act, 1940 (powers of internment). It added, 'the IRA has disintegrated and the police report that it can no longer be regarded as a serious menace to peace and good order. No crime attributable to members of the organisation, as such, has been committed since July 1943.' This related to the IRA 'fund-raising' hold-up at the Wills factory on the South Circular Road in Dublin on 1 July 1943, which netted £4,500. Internees were gradually released from mid-1944 and by May 1945, just forty men remained in the Curragh along with thirty sentenced prisoners. The final group was released when the inter-party government came to power in 1948. The last of the internees in Crumlin

Road in Belfast were not released until 1950. The IRA was decimated by harsh security measures including executions, shootings, internment on both sides of the border and by agents everywhere ready to tip off the vigilant Special Branch and army intelligence.[151]

The realities of office considerably moderated Gerald Boland's views of the Special Branch. A former staunch IRA man, he was OC of the Dublin Brigade of the IRA in the 1920s before joining Fianna Fáil. As late as 1925, he travelled to Russia with Seán Russell (who later became chief of staff) seeking arms for the IRA.[152] As an opposition TD in March 1929, he told the Dáil, 'the sooner you call off these political CID men, those survivors of the murderers of 1922, the better for everybody.'[153] But in June 1948 he said, 'I want to say that that particular branch of the Garda Síochána was responsible for preventing subversive elements in this country from dragging us into the late war. Had it not been for the service given by that branch this country would have found itself in a very precarious position indeed.'[154]

The Special Branch could now look back on their achievements over two-and-a-half decades with some satisfaction. Since the foundation of the state, they faithfully served democratically elected governments from both sides of the political divide and kept the lid on republican violence, though paying a high price in the process. Of the twenty-two policemen murdered since 1922, sixteen were killed by the IRA including three Oriel House detectives and seven Special Branch men. It would take over twenty years before rioting in Derry in October 1968 would herald the rise of a new generation of republican extremists prepared to challenge the security of the state once more.

ABBREVIATIONS

ADC	Aide-de-Camp
An Phoblacht	The Republic – an IRA/Sinn Fein newspaper
Black and Tans	Nickname for temporary constables recruited to support the RIC. Most were WW1 veterans.
Broy Harriers	Nickname for the over 300 anti-Treaty IRA men recruited into Special Branch by de Valera in 1933.
CDF	Citizens Defence Force
Ceilí	A dance with exclusively Irish dancing.
CID	Criminal Investigation Department – official name for Oriel House men and later (unofficially) for Special Branch men.
Civic Guard	Original title of An Garda Síochána
Clann na Poblachta	The Family of the Republic – a political party founded by Sean MacBride.
Cumann na mBan	Women's Council – female section of IRA.
Cumann na nGael	Society of the Gaels – pro-Treaty political party in power from 1922 to 1932.
Cumann	Political party branch but can also refer to non-political associations.
DMP	Dublin Metropolitan Police
Fianna Eireann	Soldiers of Ireland – IRA Boy Scout movement.

Fógra Tóra	*Hue and Cry* – An internal garda information booklet giving details of crimes, suspects and wanted persons.
FSA	Free State Army
G Division	Detective Branch of the DMP.
GAA	Gaelic Athletic Association – an amateur sporting organisation focused on Gaelic football, hurling, camogie etc.
Habeas Corpus	[Latin – That you have the body]. A legal procedure where a High Court can direct the police or prison authorities to bring a prisoner in their custody before the court to determine if he is in lawful custody.
Harrier	See Broy Harriers
IRA	Irish Republican Army
IRP	Irish Republican Police
Irregulars	Official government term for the anti-Treaty IRA.
LDF	Local Defence Force – army reserve during WW2.
Nolle Prosequi	Latin term meaning 'do not prosecute'.
Óglaigh na hÉireann	Soldiers of Ireland – official name of the Irish Defence Forces. The title is also used by the IRA.
Oriel House	Headquarters of the new CID set up in August 1922
Parabellum	German made Luger P08 pistol
Paxo	IRA nickname for ammonium nitrate mix. [potassium chlorate and paraffin wax]
Peter the Painter	IRA nickname for German made Mauser C96 pistol
Poteen	Moonshine – Illegally distilled Irish whiskey.
QMG	Quartermaster General
RIC	Royal Irish Constabulary

RUC	Royal Ulster Constabulary
Saor Éire	Free Ireland – a left wing breakaway group from the IRA.
SDU	Special Detective Unit – official title of the Special Branch.
Special Branch	Also 'S' Branch – commonly used name for the Special Detective Unit.
TD	*Teachta Dála*, Member of Parliament.

NOTES

Introduction

1 Malcolm, *The Irish Policeman,* p. 123/4.

2 Herlihy, *The Dublin Metropolitan Police*, pp 122-15.1

3 McCracken, Donal P. *Inspector Mallon,* pp 65-12.0

4 https://ifiplayer.ie/granite-and-chalk/

5 Dorney, John. The Civil War in Dublin, p. 1.2

6 Andrews - *Man of No Property* – p. 55/56.

7 An tOglach – January 1929, copy in NAI Jus 8/68.1

8 Behan, *Confessions* p. 30/31.

Chapter 1

1 *Freeman's Journal*, 20 March 1922.

2 The internees included Seán Lemass, then member of anti-Treaty IRA (later Taoiseach) who was interned in the Curragh on 28 November 1922 where he remained for about a year. Evans, *Sean Lemass, Democratic Dictator*, p. 23.

3 Jordan, Anthony. *W.T. Cosgrave – Founder of Modern Ireland*, p.85.

4 McCarthy, *Kevin O'Higgins,* p. 120.

5 Allen, *The Garda Síochána*, p. 91.

6 McCarthy, *The Civic Guard Mutiny,* p. 179/180.

7 McGarry, *Eoin O'Duffy*, p. 123.

8 Herlihy, *The Dublin Metropolitan Police*, p. 187.

9 Allen, *The Garda Síochána*, p. 10.

10 Brady, *Guardians of the Peace,* p. 123.

11 The CDF was a semi-secret group consisting of mostly ex-British soldiers who guarded banks and other buildings and also acted as bodyguards for ministers under threat. They never used names when submitting reports but used a personal number instead.

12 An armed group set up to protect government buildings as well as TDs and Senators or government supporters under threat. [http://irishgenealogyqueries.yuku.com/topic/1148/Citizens-Defence-Force#.WL6sv_nyjIU]

13 NAI S3331

14 He was closely involved with Collins in organising many assassinations of British soldiers, RIC and DMP

men as well as informers inside the IRA. He was appointed Director of Intelligence in September 1922 but removed in November 1922 to become ADC to the new Governor General Tim Healy. Later he was appointed Superintendent of the Houses of Oireachtas.

15 McGrath was an officer in the Irish Volunteers and took part in the 1916 Rising in Marrowbone Lane. He was elected to the 1st Dáil in 1918 and later arrested in connection with the 'German Plot' and interned in Ballykinlar. He later became Minister for Labour in the 2nd Dáil and would go on to found the Irish Hospital Sweepstakes in 1930 [Military Pensions Archive – W24SP10501]

16 Hopkinson, *Green Against Green,* p. 225.

17 This is the origin of the practice in the force even to this day of referring to detective gardaí as 'D.Os' when one would think it should be 'D.Gs'.

18 De Vere White, *Kevin O'Higgins,* p. 106.

19 *Freeman's Journal,* 31 August 1922.

20 *Irish Times*, 19/20 September 1922.

21 O'Malley, *The Singing Flame*, pp. 202-204.

22 *Irish Independent*, 4 October 1922.

23 *Freemans Journal, Irish Independent*, 18 November 1922.

24 *Irish Independent*, 31 October; *Anglo Celt*, 4 November 1922; NAI S1849A

25 *Irish Times,* 1 December 1922, NAI S1884

26 MacEoin, *The IRA in the Twilight Years*, p. 91.

27 NAI H99/114

28 McGarry, *Eoin O'Duffy*, p. 123.

29 NAI H99/109

30 *Ibid*; Allen, *The Garda Síochána,* pp. 226/7.

31 NAI H169/34

32 *Freemans Journal*, Irish Independent, 27 December; *Sunday Independent*, 31 December 1922.

33 NAI H169/34

34 *Irish Independent*, 10 December 1922.

35 NAI FIN 1/1268 & FIN 1/2530

36 NAI H169/3

37 *Irish Independent*, 7/8/9 February 1923.

38 *Irish Independent*, 17 February 1923.

39 NAI S2108

40 *Freemans Journal*, 23/24 February 1923.

41 *Freemans Journal*, 2 July 1923.

42 *Freemans Journal*, 30 July 1923.

43 MacEoin, *Survivors, Memoirs of anti-Treaty IRA activist Maire Comerford*, p. 48; O'Malley, *The Singing Flame*, p. 221.

44 NAI FIN 1/2745 & S3331

45 *Irish Independent*, 23 October, 30 November; *Freemans Journal*, 20 October 1923.

46 John Mooney, DMP No. 11988, born in Dublin 1894. [Herlihy, The DMP, Complete Alphabetical List, p. 177.]

47 Peter Doran, DMP No. 12006, a native of Baltinglass, Co Wicklow.

[Herlihy, The DMP, Complete Alphabetical List, p. 66.]

48 *Sunday Independent*, 21 October 1923.

49 *Freemans Journal*, 30 October 1923.

50 *Irish Independent*, 23 October 1923.

51 *Irish Independent* & *Freemans Journal*, 24 October 1923.

52 *Irish Independent* & *Freemans Journal* 30 October 1923.

53 *Irish Times*, 30 November 1923.

54 *Belfast Newsletter* & *Cork Examiner*, 1 November 1923.

55 O'Connor interview with retired civil servant Sean Caffrey, on 11 November 1985. Caffrey said he was an adjutant in an IRA Active Service Unit during the Civil War and Donnelly reported the shooting to him within an hour of the event. *Irish Independent*, 24 November 2012.

56 Dáil Debates, 8 December 1922.

57 Regan, *The Irish Counter Revolution*, p.122.

58 Mulcahy, p. 194.

59 At the time of writing this he was not to know Collins would be shot just days later, on 22 August.

60 NAI S2817

61 *Freemans Journal*, 31 August; *Anglo Celt*, 2 September 1922.

62 *Meath Chronicle*, 2 September, *Freemans Journal*, 1 September & *Anglo Celt*, 2 September 1922.

63 *Freemans Journal*, 5 September; *Irish Times*, 12 September 1922.

64 NAI S1784

65 *Irish Independent*, 19 August; *Irish Times*, 24 August 1922.

66 http://www.irishmedals.ie/Anti-Treaty-Killed.php

67 *Sunday Independent* 3 September; *Freemans Journal*, 4 & 5 September 1922.

68 *Southern Star*, 30 September 1922.

69 *Sunday Independent*, 8 October; *Irish Independent* & *Freeman's Journal*, 9 October 1922.

70 *Southern Star*, 14 October 1922.

71 *Irish Independent*, 14 & 19 October; *Freemans Journal*, 17 October 1922.

72 *Freemans Journal*, 17 October 1922.

73 O'Halpin, *Defending Ireland*, p. 14.

74 *Irish Times,* 14 February 2015.

75 Military Service Pension File 24SP1153

76 *Freemans Journal* 9 & 10 November; *Irish Independent*, 13 November 1922.

77 *Freemans Journal*, 30 December 1922 & 1 January 1923.

78 *Irish Independent*, 26 March 1923.

79 *Irish Times*, 31 March 1923.

80 Described as a 'Free State murder gang' by C.S. Andrews – *Man of No Property*, p. 24.

81 *Freemans Journal*, 10 April 1923.

82 McKenna, Michael - *Who was Seamus Dwyer?* Irish History Online - 2 September 2013 [https://www.theirishstory.com/2013/09/02/who-was-seamus-dwyer/#.YS-2Xo5KjIU]

83 *Irish Independent*, 5 April 1923.

84 *Southern Star*, 7 April 1923.

85 *Irish Independent*, 23 April 1923.

86 *Freemans Journal* & *Irish Independent*, 24 April 1923.

87 *Irish Independent*, 4 August; *Sunday Independent*, 5 August and *Freemans Journal* 6 August 1923.

88 *Irish Independent*, 18 August 1923.

89 *Freemans Journal*, 15 October 1923.

90 *Freemans Journal*, 23 October 1923.

91 *Sunday Independent*, 14 October1923.

92 *Freemans Journal*, 15 October 1923.

93 *Irish Independent*, 16 October 1923.

94 Later to head the Special Branch.

95 *Irish Independent*, 23 October 1923.

96 *Freemans Journal*, 24 October 1923.

97 *Irish Independent*, 23 June & 24 October 1925. More on Bergin murder in NAI 2007/56/15.

98 Durney, *Civil War in Kildare*, p.168.

99 *Irish Independent*, 19 July 1923.

100 *Freemans Journal*, 23 August 1923.

101 Coogan, *The IRA*, p. 41,

102 *Irish Independent*, 29 May 1923.

103 NAI S3435

104 Brady, *Guardians of the Peace*, p. 101.

105 *Cork Examiner*, 27 December 1923.

106 *Freemans Journal*, 17 July 1924.

107 Andrews, *Dublin Made Me*, pp, 164/165.

108 Andrews, *Dublin Made Me*, p. 269.

109 NAI S3306

110 A Ministry of Home Affairs memo to the Department of Finance on 6 June 1923 confirms that prisoners and detectives received the same food. NAI FIN 1/2748.

111 NAI S1849; 2003/16/6

112 Dáil Debates, 30 May 1923, Vol. 3 No. 19.

113 Dáil Debates, 17 January 1923, Vol. 2 No. 1.8

114 NAI 2007/56/71

115 Coogan, *De Valera*, p.354.

116 Speech by Kevin O'Higgins to Irish Society of Oxford University on 31 October 1924 copy in NAI S10632; Coogan, *The IRA*, p. 32.

117 Dáil Reports, 1 March 1923.

118 Hopkinson, *Green Against Green*, p. 222.

119 O'Halpin, *Defending Ireland, The Irish State and its Enemies*, p.13.

Chapter 2

1 David Neligan, DMP (Reg. No.s 11444 & 11662) born 1899 in Templeglantine, Co Limerick. [He resigned from the DMP on 11 May 1920 but was persuaded by Michael Collins to re-enlist in the G Division to work as a spy for Collins. Neligan, *The Spy in the Castle*, pp 68/74.

2 As told to the Dáil by justice minister Kevin O'Higgins on 8 July 1924. *Freemans Journal*, 9 July 1924.

3 *Freemans Journal*, 24 October 1923.

4 Two months later Ennis featured in the society column of the *Irish Independent* on the occasion of his marriage to Miss Evelyn Keena of 73 Leinster Road, Rathmines. It listed Inspector F. O'Driscoll as his best man. After

the wedding reception at the bride's home the couple departed for their honeymoon to the Italian lakes. [*Irish Independent,* 28 December 1923].

5 *Irish Independent*, 24 & 30 October 1923.

6 NAI FIN 1/3543

7 On 29 September 1929 the eighty members of Detective Division moved from Pearse St to the Lower Castle Yard in Dublin Castle. MacEoin – *The IRA in the Twilight Years*, p. 170.

8 *Sunday Independent*, 28 April 1929; NAI FIN 1/3543.

9 *Irish Independent*, 20 November. *Freemans Journal*, 22 November 1923.

10 *Freemans Journal*, 22 November 1923.

11 NAI S3693 & 2008/117/199; *Saturday Herald*, 22 March 1924.

12 Jefferies, John, *Death on the Pier*, p. 59.

13 MacEoin, Uinseann, *The IRA in the Twilight Years*, p. 101.

14 NAI S3693

15 MacEvilly names the same five men and said that the attack was carried out with the approval of then chief of staff Frank Aiken. MacEvilly, *A SPLENDID RESISTANCE*, p. 132.

16 NAI 2008/117/198, also *Freemans Journal*, 19 May 1924, copy in NAI 2008/117/199.

17 *Freemans Journal*, 29 October 1924.

18 *Irish Independent*, 30 October 1924. NAI 2008/117/198

19 NAI 2008/117/199

20 NAI 2008/117/198

21 NAI 2008/117/198

22 *Cork Examiner* 13 July 1927.

23 *Irish Independent* & *Freemans Journal*, 23 October 1924.

24 *Freemans Journal*, 9 December 1924.

25 Brady, *Guardians of the Peace*, p. 131.

26 Herlihy, Jim, *The Dublin Metropolitan Police*, p.187/188.

27 Ibid p. 153.

28 *Irish Independent*, 2 March 1925.

29 Brady, *Guardians of the Peace*, p. 135.

30 *Ibid* p.138/9

31 *Evening Herald*, 7 August & 6 November 1925; *Cork Examiner*, 28 October 1925

32 *Irish Independent*, 23 October 1926, 18 February 1928, *Anglo Celt*, 30 October, 6 November 1926; *Irish Times*, 3 March 1928.

33 MacEvilly, *A Splendid Resistance*, p. 171.

34 NAI S5983/6

35 *Irish Independent*, 19 November 1926.

36 *Southern Star*, 20 November 1926.

37 NAI 2007/56/59; *Cork Examiner*, 10 February 1927.

38 *Irish Independent*, 7 January 1927.

39 NAI 2007/56/59

40 NAI 2007/56/59; *Irish Independent*, 3 December 1926.

41 *Irish Independent*, 20/22 November. 1926, *Southern Star*, 20 November 1926.

42 Allen, *An Garda Síochána*, p. 70.

43 Brady, *Guardians* pp 145-147.

44 Allen, *An Garda Síochána*, p. 70.

45 NAI 2007/56/154

46 *Irish Independent*, 15 November 1927.

47 *Ibid.*

48 NAI S6296; 2008/117/201; 2007/56/154; *Irish Independent*, 16/17 November 1927.

49 *Sunday Independent*, 28 November 1926.

50 *The Kerryman*, 20 & 27 November 1926.

51 *An Phoblacht*, 19 November 1926, copy in NAI 2007/56/59.

52 NAI S5260 & 2008/117/740

53 *Ibid.*

54 NAI S5260

55 http://www.historyireland.com/20th-century-contemporary-history/poppy-day-in-dublin-in-the-20s-and-30s/

56 Andrews, *Man of No Property*, p. 55/56.

57 George Fennell, DMP No. 11459, born 1897, from St. John's, Limerick City; died 1944. Herlihy, *The Dublin Metropolitan Police, A Complete Alphabetical List.* p. 83.

58 Albert Jackson, DMP No. 12545, born 1896, Trim, Co. Meath. Herlihy, *The Dublin Metropolitan Police, A Complete Alphabetical List.* p. 121.

59 *Irish Independent*, 13, 20 November & 11 December 1926.

60 *Irish Independent*, 30 December 1926.

Chapter 3

1 NAI 2007/56/187

2 *Irish Independent*, 11 July 1927.

3 *Irish Independent*, 26 July 1927.

4 Son of Major John MacBride, executed in 1916. He would later be IRA chief of staff for a brief period in 1936, and later still a noted jurist, founder of Clann na Poblachta, government minister, and winner of the Nobel Prize as well as the Lenin Prize.

5 MacBride, *That Day's Struggle*, p.107.

6 *Connaught Telegraph*, 3 September 1927.

7 *Irish Independent*, 9 September 1927.

8 MacBride *That Day's Struggle*, p. 107

9 Keane, *Sean MacBride*, pp. 50/51.

10 McGarry, *Eoin O'Duffy* p. 177

11 Dáil Debates, 9 May 1929, Vol. 29, No. 14.

12 NAI S5478A & Jus 8/690; *Irish Independent*, 3 February 1981.

13 O'Grady was born in Ballylongford, Co Kerry in 1894.

14 NAI 2007/56/187

15 Doyle was sentenced to ten years penal servitude for armed robbery on behalf of the IRA in Dublin Circuit Court on 6 February 1930. *Irish Independent*, 7 February 1930.

16 McCarthy, *Kevin O'Higgins*, pp. 287-292; *Sunday Press*, 6 October 1985, *The O'Higgins Mystery Solved* - copy in NAI S5478B.

17 From Roger Gannon's account in NAI 999/591.

18 O'Higgins-O'Malley, *From Pardon and Protest*, pp. 16, 18, 202.

19 *Harry White*, p. 106.

20 *Irish Press*, 8 October 1985.

21 Jordan, *John A Costello*, p. 32.

22 Jordan, *W. T. Cosgrave*, p. 87; Mulcahy, *A Family Memoir*, p. 194.

23 De Vere White, *Kevin O'Higgins,* p. 185.

24 *Ibid.*, p. 232.

25 Christopher Jordan, DMP No 11997, born in Dublin City in 1897. [Herlihy, The DMP, Complete Alphabetical List, p. 123.]

26 Thomas Heaphey, Garda Reg No 4964, born Limerick 1895 and joined the Garda Síochána in 1923.

27 *Irish Independent,* 29/31 January & *Sunday Independent,* 30 January 1927; *Leitrim Observer,* 5 February 1927; *Longford Leader,* 5 February 1927.

28 *Leitrim Observer*, 5 February 1927.

29 *Irish Independent,* 26 November, 13 December; *Southern Star,* 1 December 1928; *Limerick Leader*, 2 March 1929.

30 *Irish Independent*, 15 & 29 October 1928.

31 *Irish Independent*, 15 & 29 October, 4 December 1928; *Southern Star,* 8 December 1928.

32 Mark Byrne, DMP No. 11987, born in Dublin in 1898. [Herlihy, The DMP, Complete Alphabetical List, p. 23.]

33 *Irish Independent*, 8 November 1927 & 5 July 1928.

34 The 'I don't recognise the court' policy was dropped by the IRA after the passing of the Criminal Law Act 1976 which increased the penalty for membership of the IRA from three months to a maximum of seven years and the Special Criminal Court began to impose heavy sentences for membership.

35 NAI 2008/117/488

36 Harling was inaccurately referred to as a detective in several newspapers at the time.

37 Brady, *Guardians of the Peace*, p. 150.

38 *Sunday Independent*, 22 April 1928.

39 NAI 93/4/3

40 Redican, *Shadows of Doubt*, pp. 170 & 219.

41 McCracken, Donal P. *Inspector Mallon,* p. 145.

42 NAI 2008/117/740

43 According to Harry White's biography it was IRA man George Gilmore who blew up King William's statue and later kept his head at a dump in the Massey Estate near the Hellfire Club. *Harry White*, p. 106.

44 After the split in the movement in 1970 both sides continued to use the Easter Lily, the only difference being that the Official IRA/Sinn Fein badges had adhesive backs *(leading them to be called 'Stickies') while the Provisional IRA/Sinn Fein had badges which were attached with small pins (leading them being called 'Pinheads').

45 Dáil Reports, 17 April 1929, Vol 29; *Southern Star*, 11 May 1929.

46 *An Phoblacht*, 18 May 1929, copy in NAI S1899

47 *Ibid.*

48 NAI S11564A

49 *Irish Times*, 2 February 1929.

50 *Irish Times*, 11 December 1928.

51 *Irish Independent*, 8 November 1928 & 21/23 February, 12 March 1929.

52 Garda report to Commissioner 'C' dated 25 April 1929, NAI S5862.

53 *Leitrim Observer*, 18 May 1929.

54 *Donegal News*, 7 December 1929.

Chapter 4

1 Abbot, *Police Casualties in Ireland 1919-1922*, p. 123 & 186.

2 O'Sullivan was born in Skibbereen, Co Cork in 1896 and joined the force on 20 March 1925. He previously served with the Irish Volunteers during the War of Independence and later in the National Army in 1922.

3 *Irish Times*, 18 July 1929.

4 *Irish Independent*, 15 June 1929; NAI S5997.

5 *Irish Independent*, 18 July 1929.

6 Brady, *Guardians of the Peace*, p. 154.

7 *Irish Independent*, 1 August 1929; *Nenagh Guardian*, 3 August 1929; Dáil debates, 31 July 1929.

8 NAI 2007/56/154

9 *Limerick Leader*, 19 January 1931; *Connaught Tribune*, 24 January 1931

10 NAI S6640

11 *Irish Independent*, 11 & 21 December 1929, 1 February 1930; *Leitrim Observer*, 28 December 1929.

12 David Tormey, Reg. No. 5787, born 1904 in Co. Leitrim. He joined the force in 1924.

13 *The Kerryman*, 24 October 1931.

14 *Anglo Celt*, 31 October 1931.

15 Dáil Debates, 5 November 1931, Vol. 40 No. 8

16 NAI S5864A; www.historyireland.com/volume-21.

17 *Sunday Independent*, 1 February 1931.

18 *Irish Independent*, 4 February 1931; *Connaught Sentinel*, 3 February 1931; *Leitrim Observer*, 7 February 1931.

19 *The Kerryman*, 28 February 1931.

20 Letter from O'Duffy to Minister for Justice, 11 March 1931, in NAI 2007/56/110.

21 NAI 2007/56/111

22 *Irish Independent* 23 March, & *Sunday Independent*, 22 March 1931.

23 *The Kerryman*, 27 June 1931; *Irish Independent*, 27 May 2010.

24 NAI 2007/56/111

25 Quoted by President Cosgrave in Dáil Debate on 14 October 1931, Vol. 40 No. 1.

26 Brady, *Guardians of the Peace*, p. 156.

27 *Irish Independent*, 21 July 1931; *Munster Express*, 24 July 1931; *Nenagh Guardian*, 25 July 1931.

28 MacEoin, *The IRA in the Twilight Years*, p. 5.

29 *Irish Independent*, 10 July/8 December 1931; *Irish Press*, 8 December 1931.

30 *Irish Independent*, 10 & 23 July 1931.

31 *Irish Press*, 8 December 1931.

32 *Irish Independent*, 9/10 December 1931; NAI S2744

33 MacEvilly, *A Splendid Resistance*, p. 203.

34 NAI S5864A; *Irish Press*, 28 September 1931.

35 MacBride, *That Day's Struggle*, p. 114; *Irish Press*, 14 September 1931.

36 *The Kerryman*, 25 July 1931.

37 *The Kerryman*, 12 December 1931.

38 *Irish Press*, 18 September 1931.

39 *Limerick Leader*, 19 October 1931.

40 Memo to Minister for Justice by S. A. Roche, Assistant Secretary in Department of Justice –NAI S6296 & Jus 8/688.

41 NAI Jus 8/306

42 *Irish Independent*, 21 October 1931.

43 Bowyer Bell, *The IRA*, p. 91.

44 *Irish Press*, 3 November 1931.

45 Numerous examples listed in newspapers in December 1931 and January 1932.

46 *Belfast Newsletter*, 14 January 1932.

47 *Irish Independent*, 11 March 1932.

48 *Irish Press*, 28 December 1931.

49 *Irish Press*, 29 December 1931.

50 NAI 2008/117/76

51 Patrick McGeehan, garda Reg. No. 7794, was born in Fintown, Co Donegal on 11 February 1904. He served in the National Army from 1922 to 1928 and joined the Garda Síochána on 17 May 1928. [https://garda.ie/en/about-us/our-history/roll-of-honour/roll-of-honour-description/mcgeehan-patrick.html]

52 *Irish Independent*, 9 March 1932.

53 Leddy joined the RIC in 1910 and served in Clare and Belfast where he was struck on forehead with a brick, had a baton wrenched from his hand and struck on the head with it which left him short tempered. He resigned from the RIC in 1920 and got married. He got a pension for services rendered to the IRA after he retired from RIC. He said he gave them a revolver and ammunition and instructed young fellows in drill. He had considerable difficulties in getting pension and sought assistance from Mr Reynolds and General MacEoin; *Irish Press*, 10 March 1932.

54 *Irish Independent*, 15/16 February, 9 March 1932.

55 *Irish Press*, 10 March 1932.

56 *Ibid.*

57 *Irish Independent*, 10/11 March 1932.

58 *Donegal Democrat*, 5 May 2010.

59 NAI Jus 8/318

Chapter 5

1 *Irish Independent*, 2 March 1931.

2 *Irish Independent*, 10 February 1932.

3 *Connaught Tribune*, 26 Mar 1932.

4 Evans, *Sean Lemass*, p.78.

5 Bowyer Bell, *Secret Army*, p. 93.

6 Coogan, *IRA*, p.60.

7 Brady, *Guardians of the Peace*, pp. 167/8.

8 McGarry, *Eoin O'Duffy*, p. 189.

9 Manning, *The Blueshirts*, p.153 & 211.

10 McGarry, Fergal, *Eoin O'Duffy*, p. 275.

11 Manning, *The Blueshirts*, p.153 & 211.

12 NAI S2419; *Irish Independent*, 11 March 1932; *Connaught Tribune* 12 & 19 March, 1932; *Meath Chronicle*, 19 March 1932.

13 *Irish Independent*, 28 March 1932.

14 MacEoin, *The IRA in the Twilight Years*, p. 799.

15 Brady, *Guardians of the Peace*, p.169.

16 *Ibid.* p.163.

17 *Ibid.* p.164. The author recalls bitter discussions in garda stations about this incident especially from senior guards up to the 1970s. The adjectives used about de Valera are not printable.

18 *Irish Independent*, 27 July 1932.

19 *Belfast Newsletter*, 15 July 1932.

20 *Irish Independent*, 6 & 27 July 1932.

21 *Irish Independent*, 6/7 September 1932.

22 Myles Muldowney was from Ballinakill, Co Laois, born in 1902 & joined the force in 1924. Michael Carroll, was from Co Galway, born in 1903 and joined the force in 1925.

23 *Irish Independent*, 16 August 1932; *Leitrim Observer*, 27 August 1932.

24 *Irish Independent*, 24 August 1932; NAI S6392A

25 NAI S6292A

26 *Irish Independent*, 30 August 1932.

27 NAI 2006/132/261

28 *Irish Independent*, 8 September 1932.

29 *Irish Independent*, 9 September 1932.

30 *Ibid.*

31 NAI S6292A; *Irish Press*, 2 November 1932.

32 NAI S2874

33 NAI S6292B & 2006/132/178

34 *Irish Independent*, 3 September 1932.

35 NAI 2006/132/178

36 NAI 2396/1, S2396/1B

37 NAI S2396/1

38 *Ibid.*

39 Hennigan, Hal, *The World of Constable John Hennigan*, p. 369.

40 Brady, *Guardians of the Peace*, p. 176.

41 NAI S6485A

42 Dáil Debates, 14 March 1933.

43 Evans, *Sean Lemass*, p.84.

44 *Irish Independent*, 16 March 1933.

45 *Irish Press*, 24 February 1933.

46 *The Kerryman*, 11 March 1933; *Irish Independent*, 16 March 1933.

47 *Irish Press*, 13 May 1933.

48 *Irish Press*, 27 February 1934.

49 Brady, *Guardians of the Peace*, p. 181.

50 *Irish Times*, 28/29/30 March 1933.

51 *Irish Press*, 30 March 1933.

52 *Irish Press*, 31 March 1933.

53 *The Kerryman*, 15 April 1933.

54 NAI 2006/132/178

55 NAI S2396/1B, Allen, *The Garda Síochána*, p. 104.

56 NAI Jus 8/717, *The Kerryman*, 25 November 1933.

57 NAI Jus 8/68

58 *Irish Press*, 4/13/17/18/25 January 1934.

59 NAI Jus 8/67

60 NAI Jus 8/68

61 *Ibid.*

62 NAI 2008/117/488

63 NAI 2008/117/672 & 2008/117/721

64 http://www.decadeofcentenaries.com/launch-of-military-service-1916-1923-pensions-collection-gpo/

65 The second Dáil was never formally dissolved so the IRA would later use this as justification for not recognising the third or any subsequent Dáil.

66 *Cork Examiner,* 19 September 1934; NAI 2008/117/290

67 McCullagh, *De Valera, RULE,* p. 49.

68 MacEoin, *The IRA in the Twilight Years,* p. 283/4.

69 http://www.mayolibrary.ie/en/LocalStudies/MayoPeople/ThomasDerrig/

70 Brady, *Guardians of the Peace,* p. 130.

71 Dáil Debates, 14 March 1929.

72 *Irish Independent,* 16 March 1933.

Chapter 6

1 Jordan, *John A. Costello,* p. 35.

2 One of several name changes – they were later called the National Guard, the Young Ireland Association and the League of Youth but commonly known as the Blueshirts.

3 Mulcahy, *Richard Mulcahy,* p. 235.

4 *Ibid,* p. 237.

5 *Irish Independent,* 1 August 1933.

6 Dáil Debates, 9 August 1933, Vol. 49 No. 13.

7 *Irish Independent,* 7 August 1933.

8 McGarry, *Eoin O'Duffy, A Self-Made Hero,* p. 237.

9 Allen, *The Garda Síochána,* p. 111.

10 Brady, *Guardians of the Peace,* p. 199.

11 *Ibid.* p. 199.

12 The hunt was called the Bray Harriers and were seen at the time as West Brits, wherein lies the slur.

13 Bowyer Bell, *The Secret Army,* p. 107/8.

14 NAI S2205

15 Hanley's book reproduces the IRA report submitted to GHQ after the ambush which indicates that nine men took part without naming them. Hanley, *The IRA,* pp. 48-9.

16 *Irish Independent,* 4 January 1937.

17 Details about James Crowley are from his daughter Mrs Helen Coakley who also kindly gave me access to his diary.

18 NAI S6786; *Irish Press,* 25 December 1933, 22 March 1934.

19 *Irish Times,* 28 May 1935.

20 *Irish Independent,* 29/30/31 October 1933; *Southern Star,* 6 January 1934.

21 *Southern Star,* 20 January 1934.

22 NAI 2006/132/123

23 NAI 2008/117/867

24 This was an alias – his name was in fact Thomas Morgan from Jonesboro, County Armagh. The cattle were kept for a time on a farm in Ravensdale, County Louth and later disposed of by smuggling them across the border at Dromad, with the full knowledge of local gardaí. The cattle were quietly sold in Northern Ireland while an official 'blind eye' was turned owing to the difficulty of selling the cattle in the state. [NAI 2008/117/796]

25 NAI 2008/117/867

26 *Cork Examiner,* 16 August 1934; NAI 2008/117/867.

27 *Anglo Celt,* 1 September 1934.

28 *Irish Press*, *Irish Times*, 18 October 1934; *Sunday Independent*, 21 October 1934.

29 Owen Moore was from Meigh, Co Armagh, born in 1899; John Kennedy was born in Co Down in 1895 and John Rogers was born in Belfast, Co Antrim in 1909. All joined as 'Harriers' in 1933.

30 *Irish Independent*, 2 March 1937.

31 *Irish Press*, 31 July 1937.

32 *Irish Independent*, 10 May 1935.

33 NAI 2008/117/501

34 John R Cruise, Garda No. 8247, a 'Harrier', born Dublin 1902, joined 1933.

35 NAI 2008/117/908

36 *Irish Independent*, 8 October 1943.

37 *Cork Examiner*, 4 May 1935.

38 *Irish Press*, 6 June 1935.

39 *Irish Times* 21 December 1935; NAI 2008/117/945.

40 NAI 2008/117/945

41 *Irish Times*, 21 December 1935 & NAI 2008/117/945.

42 Manning, *The Blueshirts*, p. 242.

43 NAI 2008/117/872

44 *Ibid.*

45 *Ibid.*

46 Joseph Lalor, (8469), a native of Trim, Co Meath – a Harrier.

47 Dáil Reports 25 April 1934, Vol. 51 No. 17; *Irish Press*, 26 April 1934

48 *Anglo Celt*, 18 August 1934; Dáil Reports, 10 August 1934, Vol. 53 No. 20

49 Born in Yorkshire, England in 1897, joined the 'Harriers' in 1933, dismissed in 193.7

50 *Irish Press*, 9/10/11 March 1937; NAI 2008/117/88.0

51 *Ibid.*

52 *Ibid.*

53 NAI 2008/117/880

54 NAI 2008/117/888

55 *Ibid.*

56 *Ibid.*

57 *Irish Press* & *Irish Independent*, 19 June 1937.

58 *Irish Press*, 30 June 1937.

59 *Irish Press*, 1 July 1937.

60 It is likely that this was a revolver seized from the RIC during the War of Independence.

61 Keeping guns as souvenirs from the War of Independence period was not that unusual at the time. A former Special Branch man Daniel J. Walker of Sorrento Road, Dalkey, was sentenced to the Probation Act in Dun Laoghaire District Court on 22 September 1938 for having a revolver and ammunition that 'was not an official issue but a souvenir of the troubled times' [*Irish Press*, 23 September 1938].

62 *Irish Press*, 23 July 1938; NAI 2008/117/888.

63 *Irish Independent*, 15 & 21 July; *Irish Press*, 21/22 July 1938.

64 http://mspcsearch.militaryarchives.ie/docs/files//PDF_Pensions/R7/MSP34REF8945%20Margaret%20

Hewitt/MSP34REF8945%20 Margaret%20Hewitt.pdf (p. 32).

65 The Harriers retained their reputation as formidable gunmen with many of them still serving up to the 1960s. In 1954, a young garda Bill Herlihy was on duty at the ferry port in the North Wall where trucks were bringing cattle from the RDS Spring Show for transport to the UK. A bull broke loose and ran amok causing panic and those present looked to the young officer to do something. Garda Herlihy, armed only with a humble baton, telephoned Store Street for assistance and in about twenty minutes a car with two detectives (Harriers) wearing suits and hats arrived on the scene. Hats were a *de rigueur* item of dress for detectives at the time. The detectives got out and after briefly surveying the scene one of them calmly went to the boot and took out a .303 rifle. Tipping his hat back slightly he dropped to one knee, adjusted the sight and at about 100 yards range fired a single shot dropping the bull dead on the spot. He then calmly got up and put the rifle back in the boot. Before departing the driver, Detective Garda Henry Payne (8261) remarked, 'Thank God for the Broy Harriers.' The name of the marksman is unknown. When the bull was later skinned by a butcher, they saw that he had been shot dead centre between the eyes. [As related to author by retired chief superintendent Bill Herlihy on 13 April 2012]

66 Brady, *Guardians of the Peace,* p. 204.

Chapter 7

1 Lyons, F.S.L. – *Ireland since the Famine* (London: Collins Fontana, Revised Edition, 1973), pp. 531-532.

2 Coogan, Tim Pat - *The IRA*, 2nd Edition (London: Pall Mall Press, 1970), p.118.

3 *Ibid.*

4 Lyons, p.532.

5 NAI 2008/117/385

6 *Ibid.*

7 *Ibid.*

8 NAI 2008/117/385; *Irish Independent,* 19 July 1935.

9 NAI 2008/117/389

10 *Irish Press,* 4 May 1934; *Southern Star,* 5 May 1934.

11 *Ibid.*

12 NAI 2008/117/191

13 *Southern Star,* 11 May 1935.

14 *Irish Press,* 25 April, 3 July 1935, *Irish Independent,* 26/27 April 1935; O'Bradaigh, *Dílseacht,* pp. 21/22; NAI 2008/117/679.

15 *Irish Press,* 2 April 1935; NAI Jus 8/212.

16 John Reynolds and two others were killed when their own bomb exploded in a cottage in Castlefin, County Donegal on 28 November 1939. NAI 2008/117/991; *Irish Independent,* 1 December 1939.

17 *Irish Independent, Irish Times,* 13 July 1935.

18 *Irish Times,* 11 December 1935; NAI Jus 8/211

19 *Irish Times,* 16 December 1935.

20 NAI 2008/117/488

21 Probably Thomas Sinnott (8339) from County Wexford, a 'Harrier'.

22 Thomas Lindsay (8491) from Mayo, a 'Harrier', who joined in 1933.

23 John Preston, (8514), native of County. Tipperary, born 1892, a 'Harrier'.

24 NAI Jus 8/195

25 NAI Jus 8/386

26 MacEoin, Uinseann, *The IRA in the Twilight Years,* p. 327/8.

27 *Sunday Independent*, 24 March & *Irish Press*, 25 March 1935.

28 NAI 2008/117/612, *Irish Press*, 28 March 1935.

29 McCullagh, *De Valera RULE*, p. 69.

30 *Irish Times*, 1 April 1935; NAI S7494

31 NAI 2008/117/672

32 O'Coillte to Justice 29 September 1934 in NAI 2008/117/740.

33 *Irish Press*, 28 March 1935.

34 *Irish Press,* 27 & 30 April 1935.

35 *Harry White,* p. 158.

36 *Irish Press* & *Irish Times*, 25 April 1935 & *Anglo Celt*, 27 April 1935; NAI Jus 8/194.

37 *Irish Press* & *Irish Independent*, 13 May 1935; NAI 2008/117/793.

38 *Irish Press*, 8 June 1935.

39 *Irish Independent,* 5 May 1938.

40 *Irish Independent*, 8 June & *Irish Press*, 12 June 1935.

41 NAI 2008/117/793; O'Brien, *An Garda Síochána and the Scott Medal*, p. 49.

42 Garda report in NAI Jus 8/1053.

43 Reg. No. 3693, born in Derry 1898, joined the force in 1923.

44 *Harry White,* pp 46/47; *Ulster Herald*, 20 July 1935.

45 Harry White is not named among the prisoners listed in the papers of that period. He states in his biography that he gave the name John Brown, which is listed. However, his ruse was rumbled somehow as he discovered that the RUC called to his mother in Belfast to inform her he was in custody [*Harry White,* p. 48].

46 *Irish Press*, 16 & 31 July 1935.

47 NAI 2008/117/765 & 2008/117/776

48 NAI 2008/117/765

49 *Irish Press*, 30 September 1936.

50 NAI 2011/25/121

51 *Irish Press* 15 September 1936.

52 *Irish Press*, 23 September 1936; NAI Jus 8/249.

53 Garda report in NAI 2008/117/676.

54 NAI S9155

55 Garda report in NAI 2008/117/676.

Chapter 8

1 NAI S8986

2 NAI S11564A

3 *Irish Independent*, 26 March; *Irish Press*, 28 March 1936; NAI 2008/117/866.

4 NAI 2008/117/866

5 Coogan, *De Valera,* p. 480.

6 NAI 2008/117/866, *Irish Press & The Liberator (Tralee),* 7 September 1933.

7 Colonel Warren Peacock was shot and killed at his home by two armed and masked men on 31 May 1921. An ex officer of the Grenadier Guards and the Iniskilling Fusiliers, 32-year-old Peacock served with distinction in WW1. He was awarded the DSO and Bar and the *Croix de Guerre*.

8 Report from Superintendent Joseph Ward dated 17 April 1936 in NAI 2008/117/866.

9 NAI 2007/117/937

10 NAI Jus 8/802

11 Egan was not a police agent per se but when interrogated about IRA activities had admitted his involvement and named others who were involved with him. Report from Chief Supt. E. O'Dubthaigh (Duffy) of Waterford to Commissioner 'A' on 8 July 1936. [NAI S8980]

12 *Irish Independent*, 28 April 1936; NAI S8980.

13 NAI 2002/15/174; 2008/117/924

14 NAI 2008/117/938

15 *Irish Press*, 1 May 1936.

16 NAI 2002/15/174 & 2008/117/924

17 NAI 2002/15/174, *Irish Press*, 22 June 1936.

18 *Irish Independent*, 6 May 1938.

19 NAI S8980

20 *Irish Press*, 30 July 1940.

21 Coogan, *IRA*, p. 225.

22 Michael Cunningham, (8502) born in Dublin 1902; John J. O'Sullivan (8327), born in Dublin 1909, both of whom joined the force in 1933, and Thomas McDermott (8793), born in Dublin 1909 who joined the force in 1935. All three were 'Broy Harriers.'

23 *Irish Independent*, 22 May 1936.

24 Ferriter, *Judging Dev*, p. 187.

25 *Irish Press*, 20 June 1936.

26 NAI S9088

27 NAI 2011/25/138

28 NAI 2008/117/721

29 NAI 2008/117/970

30 NAI 2008/117/844

31 *Irish Times*, 13 May 1937.

32 NAI 2008/117/885, *Cork Examiner*, 26 & 27 July 1937.

33 NAI 2008/117/844

34 NAI 2008/117/887

35 *Ibid.*

36 Memo by Commissioner Broy to Dept. of Justice 26 October 1937 in NAI 2008/117/887.

37 NAI 2008/117/995

38 In December 1892 a bomb planted in Exchange Court by the Fenians had killed Detective Constable Patrick Sinnott of the G Division of the DMP. McCracken, Donal P. *Inspector Mallon*, p. 169.

39 NAI 2008/117/984; *Evening Herald*, 29 October; *Sunday Independent*, 30 October; *Cork Examiner*, 31 October 1938.

40 *Irish Press*, 12 January 1939.

41 NAI 2008/117/984

42 Report from Supt. E. O'Riordan, Blarney Station dated 31 October 1938 in NAI 2008/117/984; Jus 8/255; *Cork Examiner*, 12 January 1939.

43 *Irish Independent*, 20 October 1939.

44 NAI 2011/25/637

45 *Harry White*, p. 84.

46 *Harry White*, p. 90; NAI 2011/25/637

47 NAI 2011/25/637

Chapter 9

1 IRA chief of staff Seán Russell did, in fact, visit Berlin in May 1940 and was treated as a diplomat and given the status of a representative of the 'Irish Republic'. He urged the Nazi regime to use the IRA for attacks in Northern Ireland when an invasion of Britain was being actively considered by the Germans [Maguire, J. *IRA Internments*, p. 25]. Russell later died while on a German U-boat travelling from Lisbon to Ireland around April 1941. He probably died from a perforated ulcer though there were also rumours that he could have been poisoned. [NAI DFA/A20/4]

2 Gantly was promoted to chief superintendent on 1 Oct 1941 [*Irish Press*, 1 October 1941]. On 21 January 1948 he was accidentally shot and killed by one of his own men during an exchange of fire with two escaped prisoners in the Lower Mount St area of Dublin. *Irish Independent*, 22 January 1948.

3 O'Bradaigh, *Dílseacht*, p.37.

4 A reference to the execution of four republican prisoners without trial on 8 December 1922 (See chapter 2.).

5 Reproduced in O'Bradaigh, *Dílseacht*, pp. 62/63.

6 *Meath Chronicle*, 21 January 1939.

7 NAI Jus 8/802

8 From an Article in *The Bell* magazine in 1951 by Stephen Hayes in NAI Jus 8/998

9 Maguire, *IRA Internments*, p. 3.

10 Michael Mansfield (8319), born in Waterford 1897, joined the force as a 'Harrier' in 1933.

11 *Irish Press*, 22 September 1939; *Irish Independent*, 24 October 1939; *Harry White*, p. 66.

12 *Irish Press*, 12 September & 24 & 30 October 1939, *Ulster Herald*, 16 September 1939, *Southern Star*, 22 September 1939.

13 *Irish Press*, 24 October & 8 December 1939; NAI DT S11506

14 *Irish Press*, 30 October 1939.

15 *Irish Press*, 29 November 1939.

16 *Harry White*, p. 66.

17 *Irish Press*, 12 January 1940.

18 NAI 2011/25/41

19 NAI 2011/25/36

20 *Irish Press*, 27 July 1940.

21 *Irish Press*, 4 January & 2 February 1940.

22 *Irish Independent*, 2 February 1940.

23 Report from Chief Superintendent J. Hannigan of Cork to Commissioner Crime & Security on 18 November 1937 in NAI S8923

24 NAI 2008/117/946

25 NAI 2011/25/377 & 2011/25/382

26 *Irish Press*, 12 June; Irish Independent, 13 June 1940.

27 *Irish Press*, 14 June 1940.

28 *Irish Press*, 11 July 1940; MacBride, *That Day's Struggle*, p. 129.

29 Article by John-Paul McCarthy, 'Amnesties can create greater problems than they solve' in *Sunday Independent*, 24 November 2013.

30 In interview with Pat Butler of RTE – Dan Keating, Little Big Man - see https://www.youtube.com/watch?v=tdjeoNrsFWM

31 Fanning, Ronan, *Eamon De Valera: A Will to Power*, p. 22.

32 Article in *Irish Times*, 15 October 1968.

33 O'Brien, *The Garda Síochána and the Scott Medal*, pp. 56/57.

34 NAI 2011/25/78; *Irish Press*, 20 February, 16 March 1940.

35 NAI S11564A & S11403

36 Report from Inspector E. Lambert, (2100), McCurtain Street, dated 15 April 1940 in NAI S11403

37 NAI S11403

38 Report by Inspector J. F. Carroll (1180) dated 29 June 1940 in NAI 2011/25/61

39 MacEoin, *The IRA in the Twilight Years*, p. 813.

40 *Irish Press*, 26 April 1940; *Connaught Tribune*, 27 April 1940; Bowyer Bell, *The Secret Army*, p. 185.

41 MacEoin, *The IRA in the Twilight Years*, p. 535.

42 *Irish Press*, 13 March, 1941; NAI S12365

43 Bowyer Bell, *The Secret Army*, p. 193.

44 MacEoin, *The IRA in the Twilight Years*, p. 535.

45 NAI 2011/25/629

46 MacEoin, *The IRA in the Twilight Years*, p. 889.

47 *Irish Press*, 9 May 1940.

48 *Irish Independent*, 8/9 May & 20 July 1940; NAI DT S11758A

49 *Irish Press*, 20 July 1940.

50 O'Brien, *An Garda Síochána and the Scott Medal*, p. 56.

51 *Irish Press*, 8 May 1940; O'Brien, *An Garda Síochána and the Scott Medal*, pp. 55/56.

52 *Westmeath Examiner*, 1 June 1940.

53 *Irish Independent*, 3 July 1940; NAI 2011/25/120.

54 NAI S13301

55 O'Donovan, *The Devil's Deal*, p. 216.

56 *Irish Press*, 6 May 1947.

57 *Irish Press*, 24 May 1947.

58 *Sunday Independent*, 22 October 1961.

59 *Irish Times*, 18 October 1968.

60 *Irish Independent*, 15 December 1945.

61 *Irish Independent*, 5 August 1940.

62 *Irish Press*, 20 August 1940.

63 *Irish Press*, 3 October 1940; NAI S12136 & S12137

64 *Irish Press*, 5/18/31 September 1940.

65 *Irish Independent*, 17 October 1941; NAI S12138.

66 Patrick McKeown, born 1901, was from Clea, Co Armagh.

67 Richard Hyland was born in Mayo in 1903; Michael Brady was born in Dublin in 1907; Robert Mullally was

born in Dublin in 1904; and Richard Wilmot was born in Limerick in 1898. All joined as 'Broy Harriers' in 1933.

68 From statement of Detective Garda Brady in NAI S12048.A

69 McGrath had been released from custody without charge the previous October after he became seriously ill following a hunger strike.

70 *Irish Press*, 17 & 21 August 1940; NAI S12048A.

71 *Irish Press*, 19 August 1940.

72 NAI S12048A

73 Copy in NAI Jus 8/1053.

74 NAI 2011/25/8

75 MacEvilly, *A SPLENDID RESISTANCE*, p. 261.

76 *Irish Independent*, 17th August 1940, p. 7.

77 *Garda Review*, Vol. 5, No. 3 March 1977, pp.13-14; Hyland was the first in the door indicating that he was the lead detective on the raid. D/Sgt McKeown had been recently assigned to the unit.

78 Letter from Eamon de Valera to widow of Detective Garda Hyland 21 August 1940.

79 O'Brien, *An Garda Síochána and the Scott Medal*, pp. 57/58.

80 *Irish Times*, 26 August 2021.

81 NAI 2011/25/397; TG4 documentary *Ceart agus Cóir*, 11 February 2010.

82 *Irish Press*, 10/11/12/19 December 1941; 2/7 January & 13/14 February 1942.

83 NAI S11564A

84 NAI S12682

85 NAI Jus 8/891

86 *Irish Press*, 15/17/18/19 February 1942; NAI 2011/25/397.

87 NAI S12682 & Jus 8/891

88 *Irish Press*, 24 Feb 1942; NAI S12682

89 *Irish Press*, 20/21/24/25/26 February, 6 March 1942.

90 NAI S12540

91 IRA man Paddy Murphy confirmed that Richard Goss and Joe Callaghan were on these raids along with himself, Willie Gaughan, Paddy Dermody and Willie Stewart. MacEoin – *The IRA in the Twilight Years*, pp. 528-529.

92 *Ibid.*

93 *Irish Independent*, 19 July, 3 October 1941; *Irish Press*, 24/30/31 July, 1/11 August, 10 October 1941; NAI S12127

94 Related to author by Garda Kelleher in the 1970s. Daniel Kelleher, Reg No. 8989, a native of County Kerry who joined the force in 1939.

95 *Harry White*, p. 96.

96 Account of Liam Burke one of Hayes' minders in MacEoin, *The IRA in the Twilight Years*, p. 446.

97 From Stephen Hayes article in *The Bell* magazine in 1951, copy in NAI Jus 8/998.

98 *Harry White*, pp. 166/7.

99 NAI 12590

100 *Irish Press*, 18 & 26 September 1941, 9 April 1942, 11 May 1946; NAI S11136

101 Eamon de Valera – Dáil Eireann Debates, 9/7/1943 – Vol.91, No.5

102 *Irish Independent*, 4 & 20 June 1942

103 NAI S12620

104 Behan, *Confessions*, p. 30/31.

105 *Ibid.*, p. 32

106 Behan, *Confessions*, p. 44.

107 *Ibid.*, p. 47.

108 O'Connor, *Brendan Behan*, pp. 66/67.

109 Behan, *Confessions*, p. 52.

110 NAI S12815

111 NAI S12814

112 *Irish Press*, 25 April 1942 & 19 December 1946; *Irish Times*, 18 June 1960; NAI S12813

113 *Irish Press*, 4 October 1944.

114 NAI S11564A

115 NAI 2011/25/83

116 The O'Brien murder took place exactly one week after the execution of IRA man Thomas Williams in Belfast for the murder of a Catholic RUC man named Patrick Murphy. As will be seen, the Dublin government was determined that whoever was convicted of the O'Brien murder would also pay the ultimate penalty.

117 *Irish Press*, 10 October 1942.

118 NAI S13075

119 The three ladies' perjured evidence saved Quill from almost certain execution and they were later rewarded for their services by the IRA in Belfast who bought them three new reversible coats costing about six pounds each – apparently all the rage at the time. *Harry White*, p. 129.

120 *Irish Press*, 5/13/14/15/16/19/21 January 1943.

121 *Irish Press*, 4 October 1944.

122 *Irish Press*, 4 September & 3 October 1944.

123 *Irish Press*, 3/4/10 October 1944; *Irish Independent*, 10 October 1944; NAI DT S13567, S13567/1, S13567/1A

124 *Sunday Press*, 6 October 1985, *The O'Higgins Mystery Solved* - copy in NAI S5478B

125 *Harry White*, p. 105.

126 Griffith's grandfather was RIC Sergeant John Griffith, born in 1844 in Skibbereen, Co Cork. He was stationed in the village of Annestown, near Tramore, Co Waterford. [https://comeheretome.com/2022/02/06/the-life-and-death-of-ira-volunteer-jackie-griffith-1921-1943/]

127 Edward Fergus, born 9 April 1898 in Dooleague, Islandeady, Co Mayo. He joined the force on 20 March 1925 and moved to S Branch on 20 November 1930. He was promoted to sergeant on 26 April 1940.

128 Peter Byrne, Reg No. 4324, born 1902 in Carrickmacross, Co Monaghan. He joined the force on 5 May 1923, transferred to S Branch on 10 October 1939 and retired on 14 January 1961.

129 NAI 2011/25/888; *Irish Press*, 14 March 1942, 5 & 7 July 1943; *Harry White*, p. 98.

130 NAI 2006/132/197; article by historian Ryle Dwyer, *Irish Independent*, 10 September 2017.

131 The Tuites had seven children, one of whom was Gerard Tuite, who escaped from Brixton Prison in December 1980 while awaiting trial for firearms and explosives offences. He was later arrested in Ireland and in July 1982 was sentenced to ten years imprisonment for the offences under The Criminal Law (Jurisdiction) Act 1976.

132 NAI 2011/25/708 & 2011/25/366

133 *Harry White*, pp. 111-113.

134 *Ibid.*, p. 113.

135 *Irish Press*, 30 November 1942; *Anglo Celt*, 5 December 1942; *Harry White*, pp. 113-115; NAI 2011/25/708.

136 Mordaunt was a native of Ballycanew, Gorey, County Wexford. He was a member of the Dublin Brigade of the IRA during the War of Independence and joined the National Army after the Truce. He joined the force in 1925.

137 *Irish Press*, 30 October, 1 November 1946.

138 *Irish Independent*, 4 November 1942.

139 *Irish Independent*, 5 November 1942.

140 *Irish Independent*, 6 November 1942.

141 *Irish Press*, 13 November 1942; NAI S12996 & S13004.

142 *Irish Press*, 22/25/30 October, & 12 November 1946; *Harry White* p. 155.

143 *Irish Press*, 30 October 1946.

144 *Irish Independent*, 1 November 1946.

145 *Irish Press*, 30 November & 19 December 1946.

146 *Irish Press*, 4/5/6/7/10 December 1946.

147 *Sunday Independent*, 8 December 1946; *Irish Press*, 10/11 December 1946.

148 *Irish Independent* & *Irish Press*, 12/13 December 1946 & 7 February 1947; NAI S13975.

149 *Irish Press*, 8 October 1985.

150 NAI Jus 8/944; S11564A

151 NAI S13706A & S11552B

152 McCullagh, *De Valera, RULE*, p. 224.

153 NAI S5478A; Dáil Debates, 14 March 1929.

154 Dáil Debates, 30 June 1948.

BIBLIOGRAPHY

Abbot, Richard, *Police Casualties in Ireland 1919-1922* (Cork: Mercier Press, 2000).
Allen, Gregory, *The Garda Síochána*, (Dublin: Gill & McMillan, 1999).
Andrews, C.S., *Dublin Made Me* (Dublin: The Lilliput Press, 2001).
Andrews, C.S., *Man of No Property* (Dublin: The Lilliput Press, 2001).
Behan, Brendan, *Confessions of an Irish Rebel* (London: Arrow Books, 1991).
Bowyer Bell, J. *The Secret Army – The IRA 1916-1979* (Poolbeg Press: Dublin, 1983.
Brady, Conor, *Guardians of the Peace,* Prendiville Publishing Ltd, 2000
Coogan, Tim Pat, *De Valera, Long Fellow, Long Shadow* (London: Hutchinson, 1993).
Coogan, Tim Pat - *The IRA*, 2nd Edition (London: Pall Mall Press Ltd, 1970).
Coogan, Tim Pat. *The IRA* (Harper Collins, 2000).
De Vere White, Terence. *Kevin O'Higgins* (London: Methuen & Co., 1948).
Dorney, John, *The Civil War in Dublin* (Dublin: Merrion Press, 2017).
Durney, James, *The Civil War in Kildare* (Cork: Mercier Press, 2011).
English, Richard. *Armed Struggle. The History of the IRA* (Pan Books, 2012).
Evans, Bryce. *Sean Lemass, Democratic Dictator* (Cork: The Collins Press, 2011).
Fanning, Ronan. *Eamon De Valera, a Will to Power* (London: Faber & Faber, 2015).
Ferriter, Diarmaid. *Judging DEV* (Dublin: Royal Irish Academy, 2007).
Fitzpatrick, David. *Terror in Ireland 1916-1923* (Dublin: Lilliput Press, 2012).
Hanley, Brian. *The IRA, a Documentary History 1916-2005* (Dublin: Gill & Macmillan, 2010).
Hennigan, Hal, *The World of Constable John Hennigan* (Leicester: Troubador Publishing Ltd., 2018).
Herlihy, Jim. *The Dublin Metropolitan Police, A Short History and Genealogical Guide* (Dublin: Four Courts Press, 2001).

Herlihy, Jim, *The Dublin Metropolitan Police, A Complete Alphabetical List of Officers and Men, 1836-1925* (Dublin: Four Courts Press, 2001).
Hopkinson, Michael, *Green Against Green* (Dublin: Gill & McMillan, 2004).
Jefferies, John, *Death on the Pier* (Cork: Lettertec Publishing, 2017).
Jordan, Anthony J, *W.T. Cosgrave 1880-1965, Founder of Modern Ireland* (Dublin: Westport Books, 2006).
Jordan, Anthony J. *John A. Costello, 1891-1976 Compromise Taoiseach* (Dublin: Westport Books, 2007).
Keane, Elizabeth. *Sean MacBride, A Life* (Dublin: Gill & Macmillan, 2007).
Lyons, F.S.L. – *Ireland since the Famine* (London: Collins Fontana, Revised Edition 1973).
MacBride, Sean, *That Day's Struggle* (Dublin: Currach Press, 2005).
MacEoin, Uinseann. *SURVIVORS* (Dublin: Argenta Publications, 1980).
MacEoin, Uinseann. *The IRA in the Twilight Years, 1923-1948* (Dublin: Argenta Publications, 1997).
MacEvilly, Michael, *A SPLENDID RESISTANCE, The Life of IRA Chief of Staff Dr. Andy Cooney* (Edmund Burke Publisher, 2011).
Maguire, John, *IRA Internments and the Irish Government, Subversives and the State 1939-1962* (Dublin: Irish Academic Press, 2008).
Malcolm, Elizabeth, *The Irish Policeman, 1822-1922: a life* (Dublin:Four Courts Press, 2006).
Manning, Maurice, *The Blueshirt* (Dublin: Gill & MacMillan, 2006).
Matthews, Ann. *Dissidents, Irish Republican Women 1923-1941* (Cork: Mercier Press, 2012).
McCarthy, Brian. *The Civic Guard Mutiny* (Cork: Mercier Press, 2012).
McCarthy, John P. *Kevin O'Higgins: Builder of the Irish State* (Dublin: Irish Academic Press, 2006).
McCracken, Donal P. *Inspector Mallon – Buying Irish patriotism for a five-pound note* (Dublin: Irish Academic Press, 2009).
McCullagh, David. *De Valera, RULE* (Dublin: Gill Books, 2018).
McEniffe, Liam. *A History of the Garda Síochána* (Dublin: Wolfhound Press, 1997).
McGarry, Fearghal. *Eoin O'Duffy, A Self-Made Hero* (Oxford: Oxford University Press, 2007).
Mulcahy, Risteárd, *Richard Mulcahy (1886-1971) A Family Memoir* (Dublin: Aurelian Press, 1999).
Neligan, David. *The Spy in the Castle*, Prendiville Publishing Limited, 1999.
O'Bradaigh, Ruairí. *Dílseacht, The Story of Comdt. General Tom Maguire and the Second (All-Ireland) Dáil* (Irish Freedom Press, 1997).
O'Brien, Brendan, *The Long War, The IRA & Sinn Fein* (Dublin: The O'Brien Press, Dublin, 1999).

O'Brien, Gerard, *An Garda Síochána and the Scott Medal* (Dublin: Four Courts Press, 2008).
O'Connor, Ulick. *Brendan Behan* (London: Hamish Hamilton, 1970).
O'Donovan, David, *The Devil's Deal. The IRA, Nazi Germany and the Double Life of Jim O'Donovan* (Dublin: New Island, 2010).
O'Halpin, Eunan, Defending Ireland, *The Irish State and its Enemies since 1922* (Oxford: Oxford University Press, 1999).
O'Higgins-O'Malley, Una. *From Pardon and Protest – Memoirs From the Margins* (Dublin: Arlen House, 2001).
O'Malley, Ernie, *The Singing Flame* (Anvil Books, 1979).
Patterson, Henry. *The Politics of Illusion* (London: Hutchinson Radius, 1989).
Redican, Noel, *Shadows of Doubt* (Cork: Mercier Press, 2008).
Regan, John M. *The Irish Counter-Revolution, 1921-1936* (Dublin: Gill & Macmillan, 1999).
White, Harry. *The Story of Harry White as related to Uinseann MacEoin* (Dublin: Argenta Publications, 1986).
White, Robert W. *Ruairí Ó Brádaigh, The Life and Politics of an Irish Revolutionary* (Bloomington: Indiana University Press, 2006).

NEWSPAPERS

An Phoblacht
Anglo Celt
Connaught Telegraph
Connaught Tribune
Cork Examiner (now the Irish Examiner)
Daily Sketch
Donegal Democrat
Donegal News
Freemans Journal
Irish Independent,
Irish News
Irish Press,
Irish Times
Kerryman

Leitrim Observer
Limerick Leader
Meath Chronicle
Southern Star
Sunday Independent
Sunday Press
Ulster Herald
Westmeath Examiner

NATIONAL ARCHIVES OF IRELAND (NA)

Numerous files as quoted in endnotes.

POLICE CASUALTLIES (26-COUNTY AREA) 1922–1947

RANK	NAME	REG NO	DATE	LOCATION	KILLER(S)
Det. Officer	John J Murray*	Oriel House	25 Aug 1922	Deansgrange, Dublin	IRA
Det. Officer	Anthony Deane*	Oriel House	17 Sep 1922	Oriel House	IRA
Asst Inspector	Matt Daly*	Oriel House	22 Dec 1922	Ellis Quay, Dublin	IRA
Det. Officer	Thomas Fitzgerald*	Oriel House	19 Oct 1923	Finglas, Dublin	Criminals
Garda	Henry Phelan	1347	14 Nov 1922	Mullinahone, Co Tipperary	IRA
Sergeant	James Woods	2358	3 Dec 1923	Scartaglen, Co Kerry	Criminals
Garda	Patrick O'Halloran	651	29 Jan 1924	Baltinglass, Co Wicklow	Criminals
Det. Garda	Arthur Nolan	11993 (DMP)	29 Feb 1924	Pearse St Garda Stn, Dublin	Deranged man
Sergeant	Thomas Griffin	814	7 May 1924	Carrick-on-Suir, Co Tipperary	IRA
Garda	John Murrin	3919	19 Oct 1924	Carrick-on-Suir, Co Tipperary	IRA
Garda	Thomas Dowling	5708	28 Dec 1925	Fanore, Co Clare	Poteen makers
Sergeant	James Fitzsimons	2566	14 Nov 1926	St Luke's, Cork	IRA
Garda	Hugh Ward	5663	16 Nov 1926	Hollyford, Co Tipperary	IRA
Det. Garda	Timothy O'Sullivan**	6670	11 Jun 1929	Tullycrine, Co Clare	IRA
Superintendent	John D Curtin	783	21 Mar 1931	Tipperary Town	IRA
Det. Garda	Patrick McGeehan**	7794	14 Feb 1932	Ballinamore	Deranged man
Det. Garda	John Roche**	4905	4 Jan 1940	Patrick St, Cork	IRA
Det. Garda	Richard Hyland**	8333	16 Aug 1940	Rathgar, Dublin	IRA
Det. Sergeant	Patrick McKeown**	11919 DMP	17 Aug 1940	Rathgar, Dublin	IRA
Det. Sergeant	Denis O'Brien**	8288	9 Sep 1942	Ballyboden, Dublin	IRA
Det. Garda	Michael Walsh**	6658	1 Oct 1942	Ballyjamesduff, Co Cavan	IRA
Det. Garda	George Mordaunt**	6712	24 Oct 1942	Donnycarney, Dublin	IRA

* = Oriel House ** = Special Branch

Killed by IRA: 16 (*incl. 7 Special Branch men, 3 Oriel House men & 6 uniformed Gardaí*)

Killed by others: 6

TOTAL: 22

Printed in Great Britain
by Amazon

86183550R00162